# Critical Pluralism, Democratic Performance, and Community Power

STUDIES IN GOVERNMENT
AND PUBLIC POLICY

# Critical Pluralism, Democratic Performance, and Community Power

Paul Schumaker

 University Press of Kansas

Published by the University Press of Kansas (Lawrence, Kansas 66045), which was
organized by the Kansas Board of Regents and is operated and funded by Emporia
State University, Fort Hays State University, Kansas State University, Pittsburg State
University, the University of Kansas, and Wichita State University.

Library of Congress Cataloging-in-Publication Data

Schumaker, Paul.
    Critical pluralism, democratic performance, and community power   /
    Paul Schumaker.
        p.      cm.   —   (Studies in government and public policy)
    Includes bibliographical references (p.    ) and index.
    ISBN 0-7006-0439-1
    1. Lawrence (Kan.) — Politics and government — Decision making — Case
studies.   2. Municipal government — United States — Case studies.
3. Community power — Case studies.   4. Pluralism (Social sciences) —
United States — Case studies.   5. Representative government and
representation — United States — Case studies.      I. Title.
II. Series.
JS992.L8S38      1991
320.8'09781'65 — dc20                                                90–12621
                                                                        CIP

British Library Cataloguing in Publication Data is available.

Printed in the United States of America
10 9 8 7 6 5 4 3 2 1

To Jean, Jesse, and Scott,
who remind me that democratic ideals
apply to the family as well as the city

# Contents

# Tables and Figures

*Figures*

# Acronyms

| | |
|---|---|
| CBD | central business district |
| CDBG | community development block grant |
| CENA | Crescent-Engel Neighborhood Association |
| DCEIC | Douglas County Environmental Improvement Council |
| DLA | Downtown Lawrence Association |
| ELIA | East Lawrence Improvement Association |
| FAA | Federal Aviation Agency |
| IRB | industrial revenue bond |
| JVJ | Jacobs Visconsi Jacobs |
| LAPSAC | Lawrence Association of Parents and Professionals for Safe Alternatives in Childbirth |
| LCC | Lawrence Chamber of Commerce |
| *LJW* | *Lawrence Journal-World* |
| LMH | Lawrence Memorial Hospital |
| LWV | League of Women Voters |
| MSA | metropolitan statistical area |
| OB/GYN | obstetrics and gynecology |
| ONA | Oread Neighborhood Association |
| OWL | Old West Lawrence |

RD          resident-dormitory

RM-2        resident-multifamily, second most restrictive requirements

SES         socioeconomic status

TIF         tax-increment financing

UDAG        Urban Development Action Grant

# Preface

For the discipline of political science, theories about community power have been very important, because they have focused on questions about the democratic performance of (local) governments. Do elected representatives exercise more political power than do the private elites, governmental bureaucrats, or special-interest groups in the policymaking process while remaining responsive to citizen preferences? Are there legitimate explanations for the dominance of certain interests (e.g., "the Growth Machine," people from upper-income neighborhoods, and whites) over their counterparts (e.g., "Preservationists," people from lower-income neighborhoods, and minorities)? Are the general policy directions of local governments consistent with dominant values within local political cultures? Orthodox pluralism, which constituted the theoretical mainstream of political science for many years and which is exemplified by Robert Dahl's *Who Governs?* has suggested that these questions usually have affirmative answers and that American cities are governed democratically.

Orthodox pluralism has, however, come under severe attack. Private elites, governmental bureaucrats, or special-interest groups are said to be the main power wielders in community politics, and citizens are said to be too distracted by private concerns to play a role in the resolution of community issues. The Growth Machine is believed to dominate opponents of rapid economic development because of "systematic bias" in local decision making, and the poor and minorities are alleged to be victims of pervasive discrimination in some communities. Policy decisions in important issue areas are thought to be determined by economic imperatives rather than by dominant cultural values. Because of these challenges to orthodox pluralism, a wide variety of theoretical perspectives has emerged as alternatives to pluralism, and pluralism is undergoing revisions that recognize deficiencies in democratic performance by local governments.

My intention in writing this book is to contribute to the revision of pluralism in ways that incorporate some of the main concepts and methods developed by critics of pluralist orthodoxy. If pluralism is to remain a viable theoretical perspective for studying local government, it should enable community power analysts to provide continual vigilance against failures of democratic performance. Thus, my main objective is to develop a conceptual framework and methodology for analyzing both the successes and the failures that communities experience in achieving three normative ideals of pluralist democracy. One ideal is that of responsible representation: The power to resolve public policy issues should reside primarily with elected representatives and secondarily with the voting public, and the power of private elites, bureaucrats, and special-interests should be limited. A second ideal is that of complex equality of political influence among various segments of the community: inequalities in the success of competing segments over a wide range of issues must have reasonable explanations. A third ideal is principle-policy congruence: public policies should reflect the dominant principles (or the general policy goals) of citizens within local political cultures.

In the empirical portion of this analysis I focus on the extent to which these three goals have been achieved on twenty-nine issues that have arisen and been resolved in Lawrence, Kansas, between 1977 and 1987. I have developed a "comparative-issues" methodology that is based primarily on Dahl's decisional method but that incorporates aspects of competing methodologies for studying community power. Structured interviews were conducted with most participants in this sample of issues, providing a rich data base measuring the abstract principles, policy preferences, and participation of representatives, bureaucrats, notables, group leaders, and individual activists. Biannual public opinion surveys were conducted to provide data about the principles and preferences of citizens. Although such data are subject to the obvious limitations associated with their collection in one community, they facilitate a detailed analysis of central political questions in that community.

This study should be of primary interest to urban theorists who are concerned with local democracy, but it may also be of interest to other political scientists who are interested in broader theoretical and methodological issues within the discipline. David Ricci has argued that *The Tragedy of Political Science* is the incompatibility of the discipline's normative attachment to democratic ideals and its professional commitment to the scientific study of political life. According to Ricci, this problem has arisen because positivists within political science have maintained that normative prescriptions and scientific analysis are incompatible in two different ways. Some positivists have argued that scientific research undermines the underlying premise of democratic life; for example, survey research showing that most citizens are ill informed and apathetic about politics vitiates normative democratic theories about the importance of an active and informed citizenry. Other positivists have argued that there is simply an unbridgeable gap between normative and empirical analyses; in this view, normative or philosophical studies make arguments about democratic ideals, while scientific studies must remain silent about normative ideals and concern themselves solely with actual political practices. For many years "postbehavioralists" have urged political scientists to reject positivism and wed normative and empirical analyses, but few studies demonstrate how this might be done. *Critical Pluralism* presents one approach to the postbehavioral enterprise by suggesting that an evaluative political science requires the specification of political ideals, the measurement of the extent to which these ideals are realized in practice, and the development of theories stating the conditions of higher levels of political performance.

Although this study is intended primarily for professional political scientists, democratic theorists may be especially obligated to make their work as accessible as possible to the broader public. Toward this end, I have tried to minimize the jargon that plagues social science research, to use the simplest adequate statistical procedures, and to relegate many disciplinary, theoretical, and methodological details to the notes.

The book is organized as follows. In Chapter 1 I introduce the main question that is addressed in this study: To what extent (and under what conditions) are local policy issues resolved democratically? Discussion focuses on the answers to this question provided by four major theoretical perspectives on community power: elite theory, orthodox pluralism, the economistic paradigm, and regime theory. In Chapter 2 I clarify the ideals of responsible representation, complex equality, and principle-policy congruence and outline the analyses that must be conducted to determine the extent to which pluralist democracies achieve these ideals in practice. In Chapter 3 I describe the study of Lawrence, focusing on the comparative-issues methodology that facilitates the analysis of the democratic performance of local governments. In Chapter 4 I discuss nine pairs of contrasting principles and the distribution of support for these principles within Lawrence's political culture.

The next six chapters describe the twenty-nine concrete issues that are the central units of analysis of this study. Readers interested in more general theoretical conclusions might focus on the discussion (at the beginning of Chapter 5 and in the Appendix) of the methodology for discerning these principles that are relevant to these concrete issues, and then proceed directly to those chapters addressing policy areas of greatest interest to them.

The next three chapters summarize and analyze the achievement of democratic ideals in Lawrence. Chapter 11 discusses principle-policy congruence or the concern that policy outcomes should reflect the principles that are most dominant in local political cultures. Chapter 12 discusses responsible representation or the concern that direct power in resolving community issues should reside with representatives and (to a lesser extent) citizens. Chapter 13 discusses complex equality or the concern that there should be legitimate explanations for unequal policy responsiveness to the preferences of members of different classes, races, sexes, and other social groupings. A concluding chapter then summarizes the analysis in terms of its implications for the "rules of the game" in pluralist politics.

Although most of the costs of conducting this research have come out of my own pocket, partial support has been provided by grants from the University of Kansas General Research fund and by allocations for supplies and computer time from the Department of Political Science. The secretarial staff in the department — especially Ginny Shipley, Kit Pittier, Joanne Sedricks, and Virginia Postoak — have also helped with such tasks as keypunching and preparation of tables.

Other people have contributed to this study and to the preparation of the manuscript. I would first like to thank the 239 participants in the Lawrence issues who provided interviews and the more than 2,000 citizens who answered survey questions during the course of the project. I would also like to thank the students enrolled in my course on "Power in American Communities" at the University of Kansas who participated in the surveys of citizens. Since over fifty students contributed to the completion of the surveys, they cannot all be named here, but I would like to acknowledge Bill Romstedt and Jerry Mitchell, who interviewed some of the participants and served as capable research assistants.

I would also like to thank Jeff Henig, Bryan Jones, and an anonymous reviewer for their many helpful comments and suggestions on earlier versions of this manuscript. Special thanks must also be given to Russell Getter, John Bolland, and Nancy Burns, who helped nurture this project at various stages in its development. My initial interests in the themes covered here were sparked by earlier collaborations with Getter on the "policy responsiveness" and "responsiveness bias" of local governments. Bolland provided me with the results of his 1983 and 1985 reputational studies of elites in Lawrence and is the coauthor of the section on community notables in Chapter 12. Burns contributed to my understanding of "complex equality" through our collaborative work on gender conflicts and the unequal treatment of women and also provided comments on earlier versions of the manuscript.

I am most appreciative, however, of the contributions of my wife, Jean, who provided encouragement through the many years invested in this study and made many valuable suggestions through her careful editing of the manuscript.

# 1

# Evaluating Democratic Performance in Community Policymaking

The governing bodies of American cities are besieged by various types of participants representing different interests and articulating alternative principles about the proper resolution of community issues. What principles ought to be reflected, and what principles are reflected in policy decisions? Who should have power, and who does have power when making policy decision on such issues? Although democratic theory is concerned with providing concepts and generalizations that answer these questions, it has been plagued by as much conflict as have concrete community issues. In short, there are several theories providing alternative descriptions, explanations, and evaluations of the democratic performance of city governments.

## THREE POLICY ISSUES IN LAWRENCE

This book provides a new conceptual framework and methodology for analyzing democratic performance in American communities and applies this framework to twenty-nine recent policy issues that have been raised and resolved in Lawrence, Kansas. To place this study within the context of the theoretical debate about the democratic performance of city governments, a brief introduction to three of these issues is useful.

### Replacing a Toy Factory with a Parking Lot

In September 1979 the five-member Lawrence City Commission voted unanimously to approve a resolution to build a small parking lot at 600 Massachusetts Street, a location adjacent to the newly built City Hall and to the offices of the *Lawrence Journal-World*, the city's only daily newspaper. City Manager Buford Watson had urged this project not only to serve City Hall's

1

parking needs but also as a means of stimulating downtown redevelopment. At that time, the issue generated little controversy, and two months later the commission authorized $310,000 in parking revenue bonds to finance the project. Part of this cost was to permit acquisition of the property, which included an old toy factory owned by Bryan Anderson. Anderson, however, refused an offer of $115,000 for the building and began to mobilize opposition to the parking lot. Arguments were advanced that the parking lot was not needed (as nearby lots were underused), expensive (each space would cost $7,763), premature (future needs were projected without benefit of a comprehensive downtown plan), and unsafe (the entrance and exits of the lot might not be sufficiently visible to oncoming traffic). City commissioners responded that the bonds had already been issued and were not callable and that Anderson was simply raising the issue in hopes of "turning a handsome profit" on the building.[1]

Discontent mounted as activists who had long opposed the dominance of "pro-growth" and "good government" forces in Lawrence were joined by people concerned with the direction of downtown development. A public opinion survey showed that 58 percent of those citizens having informed and unambiguous preferences opposed the parking lot, but neither such opposition nor 500 signatures on a petition protesting the project swayed the "city fathers." Only Marci Francisco, the sole woman commissioner, opposed the parking lot. With the quiet support of the Downtown Lawrence Association (DLA) the commissioners voted to demolish the toy factory, Anderson was awarded $185,000 for his building in a court settlement, and the parking lot was built.

The resolution of this issue was generally applauded by the administrative staff of the city, downtown businesspeople, the *Journal-World*, and other supporters of economic development. In contrast, Commissioner Francisco, neighborhood activists, and left-leaning opponents of "the Growth Machine"[2] viewed the outcome as an example of the unresponsiveness of Lawrence government to citizen protest and participation. The commission's handling of the parking-lot issue was much discussed during the next local election, and the voters responded by putting into office candidates who were generally critical of the prevailing orientations in Lawrence government.

*Controversy over the City Manager*

In February 1982 Buford Watson, who had served as city manager of Lawrence since 1970 and who had consistently been a strong supporter of economic growth, received a letter from newly elected City Commissioner Tom Gleason requesting his resignation. Watson refused to resign, setting the stage for a highly controversial battle over whether he ought to be retained or fired. There were few specific accusations of wrongdoing by Watson; rather the objections to him were based on broader philosophical concerns of equity and responsiveness. He was charged with favoring the well-to-do and business interests and ignoring minorities and neighborhood organizations. His administrative style was also questioned as opposition activists viewed him as "the boss of the Growth Machine," and dissident commissioners argued that he advocated staff proposals too strongly and failed to provide policy alternatives and information relevant to both sides of an issue. Watson's fate was widely discussed — in the *Journal-World*, in community organizations, and among the public generally. Surveys showed that 75 percent of the public was aware of the issue, with 70 percent of these aware citizens supporting Watson's retention. The Chamber of Commerce, most community leaders, and most activists on the issue rallied to Watson's defense, and a committee was formed to gather petitions to recall Gleason.

Watson served at the pleasure of the commission. It took only three votes to fire him, and the composition of the commission was such that firing Watson was a distinct possibility. In addition to Gleason, voters had elected Nancy Shonz, a long-time observer of local government who frequently spoke out for neighborhood and environmental concerns against the interests of the Growth Machine; it was clear that Shontz had little affection for Watson. The third possible vote against Watson seemed to be that of Mayor Marci Francisco, who was elected in 1979 by a neighborhood-based constituency. Francisco had acquired a reputation for independence and unpredictability because she frequently dissented from the policy decisions of her fellow commissioners during the 1979–81 period and because of her "alternative lifestyle," which included adopting a bicycle as her sole means of transportation. After three weeks of controversy, the commission met in executive session to decide Watson's fate. But instead of voting to fire or retain Watson, they adopted a set of review procedures. Mayor Francisco, upholding her reputation for unpredictability, was credited with "disarming the charged and emotional atmosphere" surrounding the issue. Although she voted against Watson three months later when the issue was on the agenda, the crisis had passed, and Watson was subsequently retained.

Watson, who was later (in 1986) elected president of the International City Management Association, was not the only winner on the issue. His support was especially strong among the reputed leaders of the community, the Chamber of Commerce, people living in more affluent neighborhoods, men, conservatives, and Republicans. These people were victorious on the issue, as they expected Watson's retention to result in the continuance of policies embodying their concerns about Lawrence government — that it should promote economic growth, protect property rights, keep taxes low, and generally run City Hall like a business. Neighborhood activists, the lower class, women, liberals, and Democrats were among those participants who tended to oppose Watson. For these people, Watson's retention was a setback, as it diminished the possibility of new policy directions involving slower growth, more neighborhood protection against disruptive development, more governmental services and welfare, and a greater infusion of "political" concerns about openness and fairness into the policymaking process.

### East Lawrence Downzoning

Shortly after Watson was retained, a local developer, Dick Edmondson, built two houses on a lot in East Lawrence zoned for multiple-family dwellings. Neighborhood residents—the majority of whom were women—took the matter to the East Lawrence Improvement Association (ELIA) and expressed concern for maintaining the single-family character of their neighborhood against an increasing number of multifamily, retail, and business developments. Since large portions of East Lawrence were zoned to accommodate such developments, the ELIA sought a "massive downzoning" that would provide more restrictive zoning designations for 700 lots in the neighborhood. Their contention was that such downzoning would bring these lots into conformity with existing uses or, if the lots were vacant, with the character of the neighborhood. They hoped to stabilize the neighborhood, protecting it from speculative construction by developers. Of course, developers and real estate interests who owned some of these lots objected to such new restrictions on their property rights. While receiving widespread attention in the press, interest in this issue was mostly restricted to the neighborhood involved. Surveys showed that 70 percent of the citizens of Lawrence were unaware of the controversy, and they had no clear preference regarding its outcome. Shontz, Gleason, and Francisco were predictably sympathetic, and by a 3–2 vote, much of East Lawrence was downzoned.

This decision of the commission emphasized neighborhood protection principles over property rights principles. Those persons asserting neighborhood protection principles—predominantly women, the lower class, and liberals—wielded more power on the issue than men, the upper class, and more conservative actors who asserted the right to develop their property as they saw fit.

## THEORIES ABOUT COMMUNITY POWER

These three cases are too few to permit confident conclusions about democratic performance, but they can help to illustrate the conflicting perspectives that scholars typically employ when analyzing community power. In the remainder of this chapter, the evaluations and interpretations that might be provided by the proponents of four theoretical perspectives—elite theory, pluralism, the economistic paradigm, and regime theory—are considered. Later, the pool of cases will be expanded to allow for more systematic analysis.

*Elite Theory*

Elite theorists maintain that, despite the trappings of formal democracy, political power within American communities is concentrated in the hands of a small number of people—mostly like-minded upper-class businessmen who eschew public office and rule indirectly and perhaps covertly without being accountable to the public through electoral processes. Such elite domination, it is argued, has three results. First, public policies are unresponsive to the wishes and needs of the broader public. Second, those interests within the community (such as the lower class, minorities, and neighborhood organizations) who might oppose the elite agenda repeatedly fail to obtain their objectives. Third, the elite goal of economic development is given unquestioned priority over other community goals such as protecting neighborhoods from the disruptive effects of development, providing social services, and facilitating citizen participation in the policymaking process.

From the perspective of elite theory, the outcomes of the parking lot, city manager, and downzoning controversies suggest that democratic ideals are seldom realized, at least on important issues. According to elite theorists, the parking lot issue illustrates a typical pattern of elite domination. Despite widespread grassroots opposition and adverse public opinion, city commissioners built the parking lot because it served elite interests in promoting growth. On this issue, elites (the wealthiest and most socially prominent members of the community) remained behind the scenes, avoiding extensive participation or the application of overt pressure, because city commissioners could be counted on to act as agents for elite interests. In the city manager issue, elite theorists might suggest another pattern of elite domination. The removal of Watson threatened elite interests in having a businesslike regime committed to economic growth and low taxes. Thus, community elites rallied to Watson's support, mobilizing community organizations, shaping public opinion, and pressuring city commissioners. On the Watson issue, elite domination required extensive involvement, but the great social and economic resources available to elites ensured the success of that involvement. On the East Lawrence downzoning issue, elite theorists might hold that the realtors and developers who opposed downzoning did not command elite resources;[3] because elites were not involved in the issue, it could be resolved in a fairly democratic fashion. From the perspective of elite theory, this case better illustrates the maximum capacities of democratic political institutions than it does the possibility of the regular attainment of democratic ideals.[4]

Elite theorists provide several interpretations and explanations for these failures of democratic performance. First, elite domination may be due to "fear, pessimism, and silence" among those in the community who oppose elite initiatives and policies, but whose participation is retarded by their resulting political alienation.[5] This interpretation is illustrated by the claims of some opponents of Watson that Mayor Francisco's swing vote on the issue would have been initially cast against Watson if she had heard the complaints of other disgruntled citizens who remained silent during the controversy because they feared harassment by the city staff and community elite.

Elite domination may also occur because of elite capacities to define the policy agenda and to suppress issues that threaten elite interests.[6] To illustrate this interpretation, elite theorists might point to the fact that the issue of firing Watson has not resurfaced. By threatening to recall Tom Gleason — the commissioner who initially sought Watson's removal — elites have created a context in which liberal commissioners who might prefer new blood in the city manager's office refrain from raising the issue.

Elite domination may also arise from the ability of elites to create a political culture and shape public attitudes in ways that ensure acquiescence to their goals.[7] From this perspective, widespread support for Watson and his businesslike regime was not due to most citizens' independently concluding that his regime served their interests but rather to elites' successfully selling citizens on the value of Watson's priorities and style.

Finally, elite domination may be due to the incentives that predispose public officials to be systematically biased toward those who control capital, who lead community organizations, and who have high social status — in short, to the elite of the community.[8] In order to provide more services without raising taxes, officials are encouraged to attract and retain businesses and citizens who add to the tax base of the community. Because organizations facilitate collective actions on behalf of public goals (as when the Chamber of Commerce recruits new businesses to town) and can influence electoral support, officials are inclined to defer to the wishes of organizational leaders. Officials are also inclined to respond to the preferences of citizens with high status because of their reputed competence, civic-mindedness, and other admirable qualities. In short, when those with abundant resources confront those without such resources, officials are biased toward elites. This explanation would seem to explain fully the outcomes of the three Lawrence issues. The parking lot and Watson issues pitted those with resources against those without them, and the systematic biases of officials were evident in the resolution of these issues. Since no elite resources were brought to bear on the East Lawrence downzoning issue, commissioners were able to respond to grassroots concerns.

## Pluralism

Compared with elite theorists, orthodox pluralists would maintain that the three Lawrence issues were resolved quite democratically. First, pluralists would not disregard the East Lawrence downzoning issue simply because elites showed no interest in it. Indeed, pluralists might regard the downzoning controversy as a "key issue" because it imposed extensive regulations affecting the property values and quality of life of many residents.[9] Most importantly, pluralists would argue that the issue was resolved in a way that furthered democratic ideals by providing a victory for grassroots organizations. Second, pluralists would note that the decision to retain Watson was responsive to the preferences of most citizens (as revealed by public opinion polls), in accordance with democratic ideals. Third, pluralists would question the assumption that commissioners simply acted as puppets of elites (or bureaucrats) when they built the parking lot. Instead, pluralists would suggest that the commissioners reached independent judgments that the parking lot served the public interest. These judgments proved to be unpopular, and voters had the opportunity to express their dissatisfaction by subsequently electing new commissioners who might better represent their preferences. For pluralists, democratic ideals do not require that representatives always respond to grassroots concerns or to popular majorities. For pluralists, democracy simply requires that voters be permitted to cast an overall retrospective judgment on the decisions of representatives at the next election.

Thus, pluralists tend to provide positive evaluations of the democratic performance of local governments in resolving community issues. They deny that power is concentrated among unrepresentative elites and claim that it is widely dispersed; various citizens — even those lacking substantial economic and social resources — can enter the policy arena, mobilize supporters, get a fair hearing, and perhaps achieve success in affecting policy outcomes. Pluralists refute the critical evaluations of elite theorists in several ways. First, they argue that elected officials (rather than private elites) are the most influential people in the resolution of community issues and that the voting public retains substantial "indirect influence."[10] Second, pluralists point out that there are many interests (i.e., groupings of people on the basis of common policy preferences) who participate in community politics. Though these interests may not have equal power, most legitimate interests are at least partially accommodated through pluralist bargaining processes.[11] Third, pluralists deny that the elite goal of economic development constitutes a policymaking imperative; instead, they maintain that community policies are "muddled through" as competing goals are compromised and as particular goals are first emphasized and then de-emphasized in response to diverse community pressures.[12]

Pluralists provide several interpretations and explanations for the achievement of democratic ideals. In response to the argument that elites are dominant because of the silence of potential adversaries, pluralists argue that elite interests are increasingly challenged. Pluralists maintain that social and economic modernization lead to political diversification, with the emergence of many interests and organizations that compete with traditional elite ones.[13] From the pluralist perspective, each Lawrence issue was highly politicized; each involved open and intense conflict among different interests and organizations. Such contemporary conflict and politicization contrasts with earlier periods of political development in which citizens simply deferred to rule by patricians[14] or bureaucrats.[15]

Second, pluralists question the ability of elites to restrict and control the policy agenda; they point instead to the vast and fragmented policy arenas that arise within communities. Dominance by a unified elite is thwarted by the numerous and diverse issues raised and suppressed, by the large number of governing bodies that exist in each community, and by the delegation of authority to administrative agencies, public task forces, and private organizations.[16] Thus, pluralists would notice that — except for the recurrent involvement of the city commissioners and the city manager — different participants representing different interests raised, participated in, and influenced the outcomes of the three Lawrence issues.

Third, pluralists would deny the existence of a monolithic and repressive political culture that stifles opposition to elite goals. Instead, pluralists would point to the existence of distinct subcultures within the nation and within communities.[17] They would argue that only the most abstract democratic principles are consensually embraced and that this consensus quickly dissolves when these cultural values are at stake in concrete policy issues.[18] For example, most participants in the East Lawrence downzoning issue may have affirmed the abstract idea of "property rights," and elites may have been instrumental in shaping cultural support for property rights. Nevertheless, such an acceptance of elite ideals did not prevent different interpretations of the practical implications of property-right norms. On the one hand, opponents of downzoning interpreted property rights to mean permitting property owners to develop their land as they pleased. On the other hand, proponents of downzoning interpreted property rights to mean that the value of their property should be protected from intrusive developments that threatened their neighborhoods. In short, pluralists argue that local political cultures embrace many competing values and goals. Cultural consensus on certain abstract ideals facilitates peaceful and civil resolution of issues but does not suppress the expression of policy differences.[19]

Perhaps the most common pluralist interpretation of why communities achieve high levels of democratic performance is that the policymaking process is open and fair — not biased, as elite theorists maintain.[20] In this interpretation, pluralists view issues as arising when opposing interests contest a policy outcome, and the role of public officials is to act as referees between contending forces. Few pluralists would assert that the public officials who adjudicate these issues are entirely neutral in the sense that their decisions are guided by an objectively defined public interest. Instead, pluralists believe that democratic accountability provides officials with incentives to tilt their policies in favor of those interests that should be favored according to the democratic rules of the game. Perhaps the parking lot issue should have been resolved in favor of its pro-growth proponents because most of the commissioners who refereed that controversy campaigned on pro-growth platforms and were presumably given a public mandate to further growth. Perhaps the city manager issue should have been resolved in favor of Watson's supporters because cultural values favored Watson's "good government" regime and because public opinion supported Watson personally. And perhaps the decision to downzone much of East Lawrence was an appropriate response to the intensity of homeowner preferences and the extensiveness of ELIA participation on the issue. In short, pluralists suggest that — on the basis of normative democratic principles — policymakers should resolve issues in ways consistent with their campaign promises, with dominant cultural values, with public opinion, and/or with the distribution of political participation. Empirically, pluralists suggest that electoral considerations prompt officials to favor the side of an issue having the greatest number of active supporters, the most public support, and the most congruence with dominant cultural values.

## Beyond the Elitist-Pluralist Debate

Between 1950 and 1975, elite theorists and pluralists debated the democratic performance of local governments. Table 1.1 summarizes some of the main questions addressed in this debate and the answers to these questions provided by each camp.

Different normative standards regarding democratic performance seem to have accompanied this debate. Seeking a further democratization of political life, elite theorists argued that pluralists too quickly concluded that power was already democratically distributed, and they rejected the concepts, methods, and findings provided by pluralists.[21] Seeking "realistic democracy" and hoping to prevent various "democratic distempers,"[22] pluralists rejected approaches and findings provided by elite theorists.[23] Partisans in the debate argued primarily about the adequacy of alternative methodologies.[24] As these arguments became both more polemical and more obscure, most political scientists concluded that the field was hopelessly ideological and that a scientific theory of community power was unachievable.

Several more recent developments have, nevertheless, reduced tensions between elite theorists and pluralists and stimulated the resurgence of scientific analysis about democratic life in American cities. First, there is increasing tolerance of diverse approaches to the analysis of community power, as scholars ask, "What can this approach tell us?" rather than "What are the shortcomings of this approach?"[25] For example, the reputational approach — a favorite methodology of elite theorists involving informants' judgments about the most powerful people in a community — may provide little information about the influence of the least powerful members of a community, but it is useful for identifying some of the most powerful people in a community

Table 1.1   The Debate between Elite Theorists and Pluralists: A Summary

| The Issues | The Views of Elite Theorisits | The Views of Orthodox Pluralists |
|---|---|---|
| What indicates that a person has power? | Reputation for power and/or control of power resources, especially large economic organizations. | Active and effective participation in the policy process. |
| How many people exercise significant amounts of power? | Very few. Real power is reserved for "the people at the top." | While only a few exercise extensive power, opportunities exist for many persons to exercise some influence. |
| What types of people are most powerful? | Private elites, especially owners and managers of large corporations. | Elected governmental representatives. |
| Are there significant limits on the influence of the most powerful actors? | Very few. Influence flows downward from unified elites, through subordinates and voluntary associations. Ordinary citizens are subjects, not influential participants. | Private elites are accountable to public officials, and public officials are responsive and accountable to voters. There is significant upward flow of influence from citizens. |
| How much coordination or fragmentation is there across policy arenas? | Elite interlocking provides cohesiveness among various policymaking bodies. | Policymaking is specialized. People powerful in one arena are not likely to be powerful in other arenas. |
| How well are the views of various interests represented in defining policy issues? | Poorly. Issues reflecting the interests of "the relatively powerless" are suppressed. | Reasonably well. All legitimate interests get a fair hearing. |
| How well are the views of various interests represented in the resolution on policy issues? | Poorly. Like-minded elites dominate the policy process, coopting the opposition and making only token concessions to other interests. | Very well. Issues tend to be resolved by compromise. |
| How difficult is it for average citizens to get involved in policymaking? | There are numerous obstacles to effective citizen mobilization and involvement. | Citizens can effectively mobilize their slack political resources and participate when their primary interests are involved in specific policy issues. |

Table 1.1   The Debate between Elite Theorists and Pluralists: A Summary (continued)

| The Issues | The Views of Elite Theorisits | The Views of Orthodox Pluralists |
|---|---|---|
| Do all citizens have access to important political resources? | No. The most important political resources—control of capital, organizational leadership, and status—are concentrated among few people. | Yes. Power resources are unequally but noncumulatively distributed. Most people have some useful political resources. |
| How open is the power structure to change? | Elites perpetuate a strong class structure. Access to upper levels of power is restricted. Meaningful policy changes to improve the life chances of the lower class are resisted. | Class structure is weak and fluid. Access to upper levels of power is open to those with merit. While rapid change is difficult to achieve, incremental changes in policies have furthered the interests of the disadvantaged. |

and some of the resources they possess.[26] The decisional method—a favorite methodology of pluralists, which involves the identification of the participants in specific community issues—may fail to discern the power that people exercise in keeping certain issues from being considered by city officials.[27] However, such a method can describe who succeeds and who fails in resolving issues.[28] Increasingly community power analysts recognize each of these methods as providing information that is a "piece of the puzzle" in the study of community power.

Second, both elite theorists and pluralists now seem to accept the idea that communities differ in democratic performance. Reputational, decisional, and other methods have been used to measure differences in the distribution of power across large samples of cities.[29] Comparative analyses suggest that communities having more social and economic diversity and "unreformed" political institutions and processes that allow for greater representation of such diversity tend to have more dispersed (pluralistic) power structures that are more responsive to citizen preferences and achieve more equality in responding to diverse interests.[30]

Third, community power analysts have moved away from the juxtaposition of the simple portraits of community power provided by the orthodox elite and pluralist models portrayed in Table 1.1. Some authors have argued, for example, that elite theory has gradually been absorbed into a broader "managerial perspective," which emphasizes the organizational and bureaucratic bases of political power.[31] This perspective suggests that power is undemocratically concentrated not only among owners and managers of large corporate organizations but also among governmental bureaucrats and managers who strive to achieve their own goals (e.g., the growth of their agencies) and values (e.g., professionalism) at the expense of democratic goals.

Meanwhile, several pluralist models have emerged, and these alternatives to orthodox pluralism have often pointed out failures in democratic performance, even when policymaking processes are basically pluralistic. For example, proponents of the "hyperpluralist model" suggest that power is sometimes widely dispersed among many active, demand-making groups within the community and that governmental officials lack the "means or the will to resist any of the many competing demands that barrage it."[32] Hyperpluralist politics are viewed as both ineffective (because policy processes are paralyzed into inaction) and undemocratic (because electoral victory fails to endow representatives with sufficient power to resist the parochial demands of special-interest groups). "Privatized pluralism" has been presented as another perverted form of pluralism that occurs when policymaking devolves to many policy arenas (e.g., education, mass transportation, housing, and so forth), and where bargaining is restricted to a few participants in each arena.[33] For example, the land-use policy arena may be restricted to professional planners, local developers, and other members of the Growth Machine. If other groups and the broader public are shut out of land-use policy formulation, the emergent policies predictably favor the private interests of those involved rather than the broader public interest.

More generally, some scholars argue that a new generation of pluralist theory has supplemented the orthodox pluralist model.[34] Still retaining the basic pluralist contention that power is widely distributed, proponents of this new pluralist model recognize a variety of obstacles to the full realization of democratic ideals. For example, though orthodox pluralists suggest that normally inactive citizens can be readily mobilized to defend their interests, proponents of the newer versions of pluralism recognize "the collective action problem." According to Mancur Olson, mobilization is unlikely even when all members of a group could reap policy benefits through a collective effort; potential members of the group may decide to be free riders and hope that others will bear the costs of mobilization while they reap the (indivisible) benefits.[35] As a result, many important interests are likely to be unrepresented in the bargaining processes of pluralism. Furthermore, some who support the newer versions of pluralism recognize that while many groups share in power, business groups occupy a privileged position in community decision making.[36]

During the late 1970s and early 1980s, both elite theorists and pluralists increasingly accepted—at least in part—central ideas from the other camp. Elite theorists lost their obsession "to ferret out an elite composed of business leaders"[37] and usually accepted the pluralist contention that political officials are indeed key actors in the game of community politics.[38] Pluralists acknowledged the existence of persistent inequalities, such as that some interests (especially business interests) seem more successful than other interests in the community. In effect, elite theorists conceded that community politics were more democratic than they had portrayed them earlier, and pluralists conceded that such politics were less democratic than they had portrayed them earlier. They also agreed that the extent to which democratic ideals were realized varied across communities and policy areas.

## The Economistic Paradigm

In the early 1980s a new perspective emerged — the economistic paradigm most forcefully developed by Paul Peterson — which seemed to transcend the elitist-pluralist debate by suggesting that what was important in the study of community power was not the evaluation of policy outcomes in terms of democratic criteria but rather the explanation of these outcomes in terms of economic incentives.[39] According to Peterson, both elite theory and pluralism provide a partially correct view of local politics; allocational policies are best explained by pluralism, and developmental policies are best explained by elite theory.

Allocational policies involve the delivery of basic housekeeping public services (such as garbage collection) to a small segment of the community (such as particular neighborhoods). Such policies neither contribute nor detract from the economic well-being of the community; although some citizens may derive benefits, and other citizens may be burdened, allocational policies have neutral economic consequences for the community as a whole. As a result, elites have no great interest in allocational policies. When issues regarding allocational policies arise, other interests in the community (e.g., public employees, neighborhoods, ethnic and minority groups) confront each other and issues are resolved pluralistically. Thus, because the East Lawrence downzoning issue was such an allocational issue, pluralist concepts are helpful in analyzing it.

Developmental policies involve attempts to attract industry to the community or to enhance the physical infrastructure of the city (with roads, sewer systems, and so forth) in order to sustain growth. According to Peterson, developmental policies have positive economic consequences for the community because they attract new resources such as capital, skilled labor, and jobs. Business leaders often become involved in developmental policymaking because their firms prosper in a healthy economic climate, because they have expertise in achieving growth, and because they can attain a "halo effect" as civic-minded "pillars of the community" by contributing to projects that benefit the city.[40] Such businesspeople often become members of the community elite who dominate "closed and consensual" decision-making processes[41] that ignore political concerns about equity and responsiveness to public preferences. In short, proponents of the economistic paradigm suggest that the "unitary" economic interest of the city is a much more important concern in formulating developmental policies than are political concerns about democracy.[42] Because building the parking lot contributed to downtown redevelopment, it was a developmental issue best explained by concepts from elite theory.[43]

The economistic paradigm is intended to be explanatory rather than evaluative, but its application results in uncritical endorsement of community decision-making processes. Even when developmental policies harm particular citizens, they are justified in Peterson's perspective because they promote the overall "city interest." Elite dominance of developmental policy is justified because it facilitates economic growth. Citizen participation is discounted because it can disrupt a "quiet arena of decision making where political leaders can give reasoned attention to the longer range interests of the city."[44] Inattention to welfare issues is justified because "the competition among local communities all but precludes a concern for redistribution."[45] And—from the economistic perspective—it is rational for concerns about equality to yield to concerns about economic efficiency at the local level.[46] Such normative implications of the economistic paradigm have made Peterson bashing a major cottage industry in political science[47] and have resulted in efforts to create yet another theoretical perspective on community power.

## The Regime Paradigm

Formulated principally by Clarence Stone and Stephen Elkin, two urban political theorists at the University of Maryland, the regime paradigm directly challenges the economistic paradigm by calling for explicit evaluations about the character of governing coalitions in cities—otherwise known as "urban regimes"—in terms of political, as well as economic, criteria. Regime theorists recognize that those who govern cities have strong incentives to promote economic growth (as Peterson had shown), but they argue that such policies as providing tax exemptions or service inducements for businesses often fail to enhance economic prosperity and may have unacceptable political costs. The extent to which the policies of urban regimes have positive economic and political consequences depends on the character of governing coalitions, which vary across communities and within particular communities over time. According to Stone and Elkin, urban regimes are generally dominated by an alliance of public officials and local businesspeople, but these arrangements can be relatively open (or pluralistic) when electoral forces enhance the representativeness of public officials, or they can be relatively closed (or elitist) if various community interests are ignored.[48]

Regime theorists specify several criteria for evaluating the effectiveness of urban regimes. Most generally, regime theorists argue that the policies of governing coalitions should serve the public interest rather than the private aims of the governing elite. The "problem of oligarchy" arises when governing arrangements permit elites to protect their position and secure special privileges.[49] Although regime theorists imply that policies should be evaluated on a scale of the extent to which they serve the public interest, they recognize that providing objective measures on such a scale is difficult, if not impossible. Was the outcome of the parking lot issue inconsistent with the public interest because some private interests reaped a disproportionate reward? Was the outcome of the Watson issue inconsistent with the public interest because some people alleged that Watson sometimes sought to protect his position? Clear departures from the public interest can occasionally be documented,[50] but on most policy issues the public interest cannot be positively identified either in theory[51] or in practice. Elkin recognizes that "the commercial public interest" — a summary evaluative standard encompassing the economic, social, and political consequences of policies — is a highly subjective concept; indeed, he understands politics to be a "struggle and debate" over the definition of the commercial public interest in specific circumstances.[52] Thus, while regime theorists remind us of the importance of the public interest as an evaluative standard, they do not provide an objective operational definition for it in specific cases.

According to regime theorists, another criterion for evaluating urban regimes is their effectiveness in coping with problems that arise within the community.[53] According to Elkin and Stone, effective problem solving does not entail finding the one best solution known only to some experts. Instead, an effective problem-solving process is "very much one of trial-and-error."[54] From this perspective, the process of finding desirable solutions (or promoting "social intelligence") is impeded by governing arrangements that tend to "reject new ideas and policies, even though social conditions are changing and new problems are emerging"[55] and that provide inadequate feedback "capacity to detect error" from initial policy proposals.[56] While effective problem solving is certainly an important normative goal of urban governance, it is difficult to specify the degree of effectiveness of any particular policy. Was the parking lot an effective solution to redevelopment at the north end of downtown Lawrence? Though the case can be made that the parking lot proved to be an effective step in cleaning up the blight in that area, the case can also be made that an alternative use of that land could have sparked even more desirable developments in the area at less cost. The effectiveness of a policy can be measured only against the effectiveness of alternative (and often untried) solutions to the underlying problem. Policies that seem effective in solving particular urban problems may be undesirable because they contribute to other problems. Regime theorists recognize that there are no objective standards for evaluating the effectiveness of public policies.

A third criterion for evaluating urban regimes, suggested by Stone and Elkin, is justice or fairness, defined as the absence of "systematic bias" or the absence of "the problem of factionalism." Factionalism occurs when there are "permanently subordinate group[s]"[57] because "public officials are disposed to favor some actors and some kinds of policies over others and some political actors are substantially better placed than others to realize their purposes."[58] When applying their concerns about systematic bias to the Lawrence issues, regime theorists would probably applaud the downzoning decision because it provided a victory for normally subordinate interests. They would probably also question the outcomes of the parking lot and Watson issues because they provided additional losses for these subordinate interests. However, regime theorists have not argued that justice requires strict political equality — that a policy victory for the rich should be balanced by an equally important policy victory for the poor. And, by recognizing that certain interests are better positioned than others to contribute to effective policymaking, regime theorists recognize that some inequalities in power are legitimate.[59]

A final criterion for evaluating urban regimes, according to Stone and Elkin, is the extent to which they contribute to an active, informed, and public-spirited citizenry. When the population is large, fragmented, and preoccupied with private life, and when urban regimes are closed to citizen involvement, "the problem of mass vulnerability" arises.[60] For Elkin, the most important goal associated with the political institutions of the city is to facilitate the transformation of economic (private) men and women into (public) citizens. "The goal is to make citizens more intelligent about public life . . . to help form a citizenry capable of governing itself in conformance with its liberal [i.e., commercial] aspirations."[61] Thus regime theorists remind us that citizens should be capable of intelligently pursuing policies that reflect *their* broader political and economic goals. Such a goal is important because regime theorists believe that the development of such a citizenry will reduce systematic bias and improve social intelligence.

## SUMMARY AND CONCLUSIONS

All communities continuously confront a variety of policy issues such as the parking lot, city manager, and downzoning controversies. Community power theorists are in the business of applying democratic theory to the analysis of such issues. Nevertheless, the present state of development of this important subfield of political science[62] is such that community power theorists cannot offer objective assessments of the democratic performance of communities nor scientifically informed prescriptions for communities to improve their democratic performance.

The elitist-pluralist debate was important for the analysis of community power because each theoretical perspective addressed democratic ideals. Elite theorists and pluralists provide many case studies describing the realization of, and departures from, these goals, and they develop theories that seek to explain the successes and failures of democratic performance.[63] Nevertheless, various disputes between elite theorists and pluralists impede the development of scientific consensus about the extent to which policymakers achieve democratic ideals and the determinants of more democratic regimes.

Proponents of the economistic paradigm have sought to resolve the elitist-pluralist debate by specifying the policy arenas where elite theorists and pluralists provide generally correct interpretations of community decision making, but — at least implicitly — economistic theorists suggest that the aggregate economic interest of the city is the *only* appropriate criterion for evaluating the resolution of community issues. Thus, this paradigm turns community power analysts away from the study of democratic ideals.

In contrast, regime theorists have approached the study of urban governance in a promising way. They have placed explicit normative concerns at the center of analysis and have suggested appropriate criteria for assessing democratic performance, but they have yet to develop objective measures of the extensiveness of the problems of oligarchy, ineffectiveness, factionalism, and mass vulnerability. Regime theory "directs us toward an investigation of the conditions under which elite tendencies are checked,"[64] but such investigations are only beginning.

A suitable paradigm for the analysis of community politics requires the specification of democratic ideals, the measurement of the extent to which these ideas are realized in practice, and the development of theories specifying the conditions of higher levels of democratic performance. The purpose of this book is to contribute to these aspirations of community power theorists by drawing on the strengths of previous paradigms of community power in order to develop a conceptual framework and methodology for addressing, in a scientific manner, three main questions about the democratic performance of American communities:

1. What principles (or general policy directions) guide the resolution of community issues, and do these principles usually reflect the dominant values of citizens within local communities (as Elkin suggests they should) or do they generally reflect economic imperatives (as Peterson suggests they must)?

2. To what extent are political communities dominated by the private elite (as argued by elite theorists), by governmental bureaucrats (as suggested by the managerial perspective), or by special-interest groups (as suggested by the hyperpluralist model), and under what conditions are community issues resolved through democratic processes that instead empower citizens and elected representatives (as claimed by orthodox pluralists)?

3. To what extent do political communities exhibit systematic biases that result in the political subordination of such people as the lower class, minorities, and women (as suggested by regime theorists), and do the inequalities in power that are observed in the resolution of community issues have legitimate explanations (as implied by orthodox pluralists)?

# 2

# Three Ideals
# of Pluralist Democracy

It is easy to criticize local governments for failing to realize such goals as popular rule or equality, but these goals are beyond the ideals of pluralist democracy and are not widely embraced by most Americans.[1] To facilitate an internal critique of local government — to determine the extent to which governments live up to the goals that they (and their citizens) set — identification of the fundamental and widely accepted ideals of pluralist democracy becomes necessary. Identification of such ideals is complicated, however, because pluralist democracies permit — and indeed encourage — debate about about the ideals of good government. Although any attempt to specify central and consensual goals is thus bound to be problematic, most scholars and citizens committed to pluralist democracy agree that the following three ideals should normally be realized:

1. Principle-policy congruence. Policy decisions should reflect the principles (or general social, economic, and political goals) that are dominant in local political cultures;
2. Responsible representation. Policymaking processes should empower (primarily) elected representatives and (secondarily) the voting public but should also be responsive to the persuasive participation of public administrators, community notables, group leaders, and individual activists;
3. Complex equality. Inequalities in the power of various "interests" within communities (e.g., the lower class and the upper class) should have reasonable explanations.

These ideals have been chosen for analysis for several reasons. First, they reflect the broad themes discussed in the various theoretical perspectives on community power, and they address central concerns of democratic theorists. Second, they span the ideals of people with different ideological orientations

18

within pluralist politics. Third, they can be clearly spelled out both conceptually and operationally, and thus lend themselves to scientific analysis.

The focus of this chapter is on the concepts of principle-policy congruence,
responsible representation, and complex equality, placing them within democratic theory, with an emphasis on their appeal to the ideological "friends"
of pluralism — conservatives, liberals, and democratic socialists.[2] Methodological considerations about measuring the attainment of these hypotheses about
their attainment are also introduced.[3]

If "normative pluralism" is the label given to efforts to justify pluralist
ideals,[4] and if "orthodox pluralism" is the label applied to those empirical
studies that describe governments achieving pluralist goals,[5] then "critical
pluralism" might be the label assigned to analyses that measure and explain
variances in the extent to which governments approach pluralist ideals. In
this book I develop a conceptual framework and methodology for determining the extent to which communities achieve principle-policy congruence,
responsible representation, and complex equality. I apply critical pluralism
to the analysis of twenty-nine issues resolved in Lawrence between 1977 and
1987.

## PRINCIPLE-POLICY CONGRUENCE

In monistic communities, public policies reflect absolute principles set forth
by some authoritative source (for example, Karl Marx or the Qur'an), but
in pluralist communities public policies should reflect the principles most
widely accepted within local political cultures. Political principles specify
general social, economic, and political goals for the community; the ideas
that government ought to promote economic development and that government should regulate and slow growth illustrate competing political principles. According to pluralists, abstract theoretical or philosophical reasoning cannot determine which of these principles should guide public policy;
what matters is which of these principles is most widely accepted within the
political culture. If the importance of economic growth is widely recognized
among Lawrence citizens and if such growth is facilitated by a parking lot
at 600 Massachusetts Street, then the ideal of principle-policy congruence
will (at least partially) justify the demolition of Bryan Anderson's toy factory. If slow-growth principles are dominant in Lawrence's political culture,
however, the rejection of the parking lot would further the ideal of principle-
policy congruence.

Principle-policy congruence is important because the policies of pluralist
democracies are "intended to reflect the long-term values and policy objectives embodied in the political culture."[6] Because a central tenet of conservatism is that governmental actions should reflect the traditional principles

about the aims of government held by most citizens, conservatives are committed to principle-policy congruence.[7] Additionally, democratic theorists more to the center and left of the ideological spectrum also suggest the importance of this ideal. For liberal democrats and democratic socialists, responding to dominant principles within a culture enhances the authority of the public because such principles provide general guidelines to policymakers about the public's desired destinations for the political community.[8] By responding to dominant principles, public input transcends unstable, more easily manipulable policy-specific preferences.[9] By responding to dominant principles, officials can also transcend the narrow and immediate interests of those having the most social and economic resources in the community.

Several kinds of information must be available to determine whether principle-policy congruence is achieved in the resolution of specific community issues. First, dominant cultural principles must be known. Second, the relevance of particular principles to specific community issues must be demonstrated. Third, policy outcomes must be related to those principles that are dominant in a local culture and relevant to an issue.

## Determining Dominant Principles within Political Cultures

Despite conservative aspirations for cultural consensus about traditional values, there is often extensive disagreement within pluralist communities about political principles. In pluralist communities, some citizens want their government to promote economic growth, but others do not. Some citizens believe in unrestricted property rights (enabling property owners to use their land as they see fit), but others believe more strongly in "neighborhood rights" (involving restrictions on those uses of property that harm neighbors or the community as a whole).[10] Citizens can also disagree on the importance of many other political principles, and different principles may be dominant in different cultures.

Given this diversity, the question arises, which principles predominate in local political cultures? Although informed observers can provide insightful judgments about local political cultures,[11] survey research is a more precise instrument for measuring the distributions of support for alternative policy principles that exist within a particular community. Such research shows that pro-growth principles predominate in Lawrence, but neighborhood-protection principles are more widely accepted in the community than are property-rights principles.

## Determining the Relevance
## of Principles to Specific Issues

More difficult than determining the distribution of support for various political principles is the task of determining the dominant principles within a culture that are relevant to a specific issue. The art of politics largely involves persuading people that particular popular principles are at stake on concrete issues.[12] For example, opponents of downzoning argued that extensive restrictions on their property rights would curtail the widely sought goal of economic growth, and proponents of downzoning argued that such restrictions were necessary to achieve neighborhood protection, another widely accepted principle.

Was either or were both of these claims correct? Clearly, a principle is not necessarily at stake on an issue simply because someone has claimed that a particular policy outcome will further a widely accepted goal. However, there is compelling evidence that certain principles are at stake on an issue if support for these principles is systematically distributed among supporters and opponents of a particular policy outcome. On the one hand, if most proponents of downzoning held neighborhood-protection principles and most opponents of downzoning held contrasting property-rights principles, these principles would seem to have been at stake. On the other hand, if pro-growth and slow-growth principles were randomly distributed among proponents and opponents of downzoning—if there was no general relationship between principles and preferences regarding the issue—there would be little basis for concluding that principles regarding growth were at stake. A method for determining the principles relevant to issues is presented in detail in the Appendix.

## Assessing Policy Outcomes

The outcomes of community issues are often ambiguous because participants and observers can have different interpretations of the goals sought (e.g., Did Bryan Anderson really want to keep his toy factory, or did he simply want a higher price for his property?), of the decision (e.g., Was the policy of subjecting City Manager Watson to more frequent reviews a genuine compromise, or was it a token concession to his opponents?), and of the ultimate impacts of the decision (e.g., Would the downzoning ordinance really halt intrusive developments in East Lawrence?). Such ambiguities ensure that the interpretations of outcomes of community issues are necessarily subjective. This difficulty, however, does not preclude attaining high levels of intersubjective agreement in measuring outcomes and using these measures for evaluating principle-policy congruence.

To obtain comparable measures of policy outcomes in disparate issue areas, a procedure has been designed that incorporates the judgments of the people involved and produces policy outcome scores ranging from zero (when issue outcomes uphold the status quo) to 100 (when outcomes result in changes in previous policies and laws and in new programs and developments).[13] For example, the parking lot issue was assigned an outcome score of 100, reflecting the unanimous judgments of participants that the demolition of the toy factory and the building of the parking lot constituted a victory for the proponents of change. The city manager issue was assigned an outcome score of 7.5, which reflects some judgments that the status quo was slightly altered (by the provision to review Watson's performance more closely) even though Watson was retained. The East Lawrence downzoning issue had an outcome score of 90, which reflects widespread judgments that the new downzoning ordinance contained most of the policy changes sought by neighborhood-protection forces while providing some concessions to those who sought to maintain existing policies that permitted higher-density land uses.

Once one knows what dominant community principles are relevant to an issue and the perceived policy outcome, the question of whether principle-policy congruence has been achieved would seem straightforward. If dominant pro-growth principles were relevant to the parking lot issue and if the outcome of the issue was a clear victory for those citizens who wanted economic growth, principle-policy congruence appears to have been achieved. However, pluralist politics are complex, and initial appearances can be deceptive. Building the parking lot may have been congruent with the dominant and relevant principle of promoting growth, but it may have been incongruent with other dominant and relevant community principles, such as responding to citizen participation. In short, several dominant, competing cultural principles may be relevant to an issue, providing conflicting guidance.

### Hypotheses about Principle-Policy Congruence

The most important hypotheses about the determinants of principle-policy congruence would seem to address the question, Which dominant principles relevant to an issue are most likely to be reflected in policy outcomes? In this study, three hypotheses are considered.

First, policy outcomes may reflect those dominant cultural principles most relevant to specific issues. For example, neighborhood-protection principles may have been more relevant than economic-growth principles to the East Lawrence downzoning issue. The downzoning decision may simply have reflected the urgency or centrality of protectionist values and the questionable relevance of growth principles to the issue.

Second, policy outcomes may reflect the principles most widely supported by citizens and participants within a political culture. For example, both economic-growth and citizen-participation principles may be dominant within Lawrence, but there may be more disagreement about the value of citizen participation than about growth. Thus, the parking lot issue may have been resolved in a way consistent with economic-growth principles and inconsistent with citizen-participation principles because there is more consensus about economic-growth principles in the local culture than about citizen participation.

Third, the extent to which policy outcomes reflect principles may depend on whether these principles promote the economic interests of the city — regardless of the distribution of support for these principles within the political culture. For example, Buford Watson may have been retained as city manager because he supported pro-growth principles but rejected redistributive public-welfare principles that, while dominant in the culture of Lawrence, undermine economic imperatives.[14]

In summary, principle-policy congruence is important for pluralist democracies because its attainment ensures that policymakers have respected the broad concerns that prevail among the public. However, principle-policy congruence may be difficult to achieve because a variety of conflicting dominant cultural values may be relevant to an issue. Policymakers may respond to this difficulty by enacting policies that embody the principles most widely held in the community or most relevant to specific issues, or they may simply ignore dominant cultural principles and decide issues on the basis of economic imperatives.

## RESPONSIBLE REPRESENTATION

Authoritarian governments maintain that legitimate governmental power resides in the hands of absolute rulers, but pluralist communities prefer representative government. A major contribution of liberalism to the ideals of pluralist democracy has been the insistence that predominant power reside with elected representatives. Representatives normally exercise their independent judgment when resolving community issues, but remaining accountable to voters, they are open to the persuasive participation of others. Although conservatives often seek institutions that maximize the independence of representatives, and though socialists often seek institutions that maximize the direct power of citizens, conservatives and socialists normally accept representative democracy.[15]

Democratic elections of representatives have, of course, reduced the danger of authoritarian rule in pluralist societies, but responsible representation can still be thwarted if elected representatives fail to use their authority. Maladies of elite rule and bureaucratic rule can occur if representatives simply rubber-stamp the policies of community notables and public administrators. Responsible representation can also be thwarted if elected officials defer to the demands of interest group leaders or individual activists. In order for local communities to achieve responsible representation in the resolution of policy issues, power must be appropriately distributed among representatives, citizens, community notables (elites), governmental bureaucrats, interest group leaders, and individual activists. Table 2.1 provides a scale of responsible representation based on whether the dominant preferences of these various participants are reflected in policy outcomes.

## Evaluating the Extent of Responsible Representation

To assess the level of responsible representation that occurs on specific issues, the preferences of various kinds of people (listed across the top of Table 2.1) must be mapped and related to policy outcomes. More specifically, representatives must be interviewed to determine their preferences (understood as independent judgments) about issues and their perceptions of citizen preferences. Public opinion surveys must be conducted to measure actual citizen preferences. Participants (other than representatives) who have sought to influence the outcome of each issue must be identified and categorized as notables, bureaucrats, group leaders (mobilizers), and/or individual activists, and their preferences must be ascertained. The procedures used to map these preferences are described in more detail in Chapter 3, but this brief discussion should be sufficient to indicate that the preferences of each type of actor must be determined through a variety of surveying and interviewing procedures.

In pluralist societies, unanimity among representatives, citizens, and other types of actors is unlikely. Because democratic theorists have emphasized the idea of majority rule as the procedure for resolving disagreement, policy outcomes should be congruent with dominant preferences. In practice, policy outcomes may be congruent (shown by plus signs in Table 2.1) or incongruent (shown by minus signs) with the dominant preferences of the various types of people.[16] The patterns of congruence and incongruence specified in Table 2.1 indicate the level of responsible representation achieved on specific issues.

Responsible representation is low (ranging from Level 1 to Level 4) if a policy outcome is inconsistent with the preferences of the majority of representatives involved in the resolution of an issue. Election to public office has "elevated" representatives to a "superior position" relative to citizens at large and other types of participants.[17] Except for those issues that legally require public referenda, representatives are empowered to use their independent judgments in deciding issues. In this context, the "independent judgments" of representatives are the outcomes that, after full consideration of the merits of policy proposals, representatives believe are appropriate for the community. Roll-call votes are not always indicative of the preferences of individual representatives; representatives are sometimes "pressured" by others and sometimes defer to them. Policy outcomes are not always indicative of the preferences of representatives as a whole; the majority of representatives may fail to hold independent judgments congruent with policy decisions. Thus, responsible representation is relatively low when most representatives indicate (as in in-

Table 2.1 Variations in Responsible Representation on Issues: Relationships between the Dominant Preferences of Various Actors and Policy Outcomes*

| Levels of Responsible Representation | Elected Representatives | Citizens | | Notables | Bureaucrats | Mobilizers | Individual Activists |
|---|---|---|---|---|---|---|---|
| | | Actual | Perceived | | | | |
| 1. External domination | – | – | – | – | – | – | – |
| 2. Elite or bureaucratic dominance | – | – | – | + or | + | – | – |
| 3. Minority dominance (and misrepresentation) | – | – | NR or + | NR | NR | + | + |
| 4. Representatives act as instructed delegates | – | + | + | NR | NR | NR | NR |
| 5. Unsupported control by formal authorities | | | | | | | |
|   A. Voters act through referendum | – | + | NR | NR | NR | NR | NR |
|   B. Representatives act as trustees | + | – | – | – | – | – | – |
| 6. Elite or bureaucratic persuasiveness | + | – | NR | + | + | – | – |
| 7. Minority persuasiveness | + | – | NR | NR | NR | + or | + |
| 8. Majority will | + | + | + | NR | NR | – or | – |
| 9. Mass will | + | + | + | – or | – | + | + |
| 10. Consensus | + | + | + | + | + | + | + |

+ : Outcome congruent with dominant preferences.

– : Outcome incongruent with dominant preferences.

NR : Not relevant to determination of responsible representation; dominant preference can be either congruent or incongruent with policy outcomes.

terviews conducted for this study) that they believe that a policy outcome is unfortunate or inappropriate but that political (or some other type of) constraints prompted them to defer to the preferences of others. Responsible representation is relatively high when most representatives indicate that a policy outcome is desirable and appropriate. Although democratic performance depends on whether policy outcomes reflect the dominant independent judgments of representatives, a more refined scale of responsible representation must take into account the preferences of other kinds of actors.

Responsible representation is lowest (Level 1 in Table 2.1) when policy outcomes are inconsistent with the dominant preferences of each of the various types of local citizens involved in the resolution of community issues. For example, in Boston, the majority of representatives, citizens, bureaucrats, notables, mobilizers (group leaders), and (individual) activists appear to have opposed a court-ordered busing policy as a means of integrating public schools in the mid-1970s.[18] An "external" participant—in this case Federal District Court Judge Arthur Garrity—dominated the resolution of the issue. In the Boston busing controversy, responsible representation was thwarted by the limited authority of representatives in controlling policies involving legal and constitutional issues. This case serves as a reminder that responsible representation may not lead to progressive social policies and thus is not an absolute ideal that ought to be achieved in the resolution of all policy issues.

If policy outcomes reflect the preferences of bureaucrats and/or notables but are inconsistent with the dominant preferences of representatives, citizens, mobilizers, and activists, the relatively undemocratic conditions of bureaucratic or elite dominance (Level 2) have been attained. Because policy outcomes reflect the preferences of some local participants (bureaucrats and/or notables), democratic performance is higher than when external actors make policies that are at odds with the dominant preferences of all local actors. However, as shown in Table 2.1, bureaucratic and/or elite dominance is a situation in which representatives remain unconvinced by bureaucratic or notable arguments but abandon their independent judgments about the policies that best serve the community. In such a situation, the conclusion that representatives have illegitimately deferred to the professional credentials of bureaucrats or to the economic or social resources of notables is easily derived.[19] Community power literature alleges numerous instances of bureaucratic or elite dominance, but because these studies fail to consider the preferences of other actors in any systematic way, it is unclear whether these are cases of elite and/or bureaucratic domination as defined here.[20]

If policy outcomes are consistent with the dominant preferences of mobilizers (group leaders)[21] and/or individual activists but inconsistent with the dominant preferences of representatives and citizens, Level 3 of responsible representation—minority dominance—occurs. In such a situation, representatives have not been convinced that the dominant demands of group leaders or activists serve the community, but they respond to such demands for several reasons. For example, they may be concerned about the intensity of preferences; if policy proposals impose severe burdens on affected groups and individuals, elected representatives may find justification in bowing to these intense and active interests. Representatives may also capitulate to the dominant demands of mobilizers and activists for pragmatic reasons (e.g., in order to prevent community conflict and electoral retaliation).

Responsible representation may also be at Level 3 because misrepresentation has occurred; this possibility is indicated in Table 2.1 by decisions congruent with dominant citizen preferences as perceived by representatives but incongruent with actual citizen preferences. In the absence of information about the actual preferences of citizens, representatives may perceive dominant group and activist preferences as reflecting dominant citizen preferences. In this situation, officials may believe that they are acting on instructions from citizens, and their errors of perception about the preferences of all citizens may reduce democratic performance. Nevertheless, minority dominance, based on nonelite participation, is considered more democratic than bureaucratic or elite dominance. Professional credentials, wealth, and status should not enhance political power; participation and representation of other citizens should be the controlling factors.

Level 4 of responsible representation, instructed delegation, occurs when the majority of representatives support a policy, when they perceive accurately that most citizens oppose their position, and when they consequently abandon their independent judgments and act as agents of the public. When policies reflect the preferences of all citizens, a higher level of democracy is attained than when policies reflect the preferences of only the active elements within the citizenry. Unfortunately, responsible representation is limited because representatives do not concur with dominant citizen preferences and because representatives have relinquished their authority to voters in situations where voters have (implicitly) consented to having representatives act as their trustees. Nevertheless, responsible representation is not seriously impaired when representatives act as instructed delegates who defer to public opinion. After all, elections make representatives accountable to voters.

If the majority of representatives and citizens have conflicting policy preferences, democratic performance is enhanced (to Level 5) when the proper formal authorities are empowered. State constitutions, statutes, and municipal charters are prior agreements that specify the appropriate powers of representatives and citizens. For the most part, constitutions delegate policymaking authority to elected representatives. Such agreements also specify when and how final authority reverts back to voters by providing for referenda on certain kinds of issues when appropriate petitions are submitted.

If there is a provision for a referendum and citizens invoke a referendum, the voters have authority. Responsible representation is at Level 5A when voters override the judgments of representatives and impose dominant citizen preferences through referenda. Both levels 4 and 5A concern instances in which policies reflect citizen preferences but not representative preferences. However, when issues are resolved through a legal referendum, more responsible representation (Level 5A) is achieved than when representatives defer to public opinion (Level 4).

If there are no provisions for a referendum, representatives have authority, and responsible representation is higher when representatives act as trustees (at Level 5B) than when they act as instructed delegates (at Level 4). Representatives are trustees of the overall welfare of the community, which may be more visible to them than to citizens; in comparison with voters, representatives are more involved in issues and (potentially) achieve a greater understanding of the merits of policy proposals. Rather than acting as passive agents of the public and capitulating to citizens' wishes (which may be ill-informed and based on unrealistic expectations or short-term considerations), representatives may be obligated to try to persuade the public to support their views. In Level 5B situations, representatives appropriately use their authority and make decisions on the basis of their own judgments, even though citizens and other participants disagree. Higher levels of responsible representation require that other participants support these judgments.

Levels 6 and 7 of responsible representation deal with situations in which the preferences of representatives and citizens are at odds, representatives use their authority to resolve issues, and their decisions are supported by other actors. At Level 6, notables and/or bureaucrats agree with the judgments of representatives. This situation is different from elite or bureaucratic dominance (Level 2) because at Level 6 the majority of representatives have independent judgments that coincide with notable or bureaucratic views. Representatives have not deferred to these actors but have been persuaded by them. When the power of bureaucrats and notables is rooted in their persuasiveness, those individuals contribute to responsible representation.

Though representatives are persuaded by bureaucrats and notables at Level 6, they are persuaded by mobilizers or activists at Level 7. Policy outcomes are more democratic when representatives attend to such citizen-based concerns than when representatives are persuaded by bureaucrats or elites.

Levels 8, 9, and 10 of responsible representation deal with situations in which the dominant preferences of representatives and citizens coincide, and their views are reflected in policy outcomes. Although each of these situations is relatively democratic, other types of participants disagree with the result. At Level 8, policy outcomes and representative judgments reflect the "majority will" (or dominant citizen preferences), but most mobilizers and/or activists hold conflicting preferences. At Level 9, policy outcomes and representative judgments reflect dominant citizen, group, and activist preferences, but either bureaucrats or elites dissent. Finally, at Level 10, policy outcomes reflect the dominant preferences of representatives, citizens, notables, bureaucrats, mobilizers, and activists. This level of responsible representation is labeled "consensus" because of the overall pattern of broad support for the outcome, not because the community is without dissent on the issue. Indeed, a policy would not become an issue if there were no dissent.

According to this conception of responsible representation and based on data to be presented in Chapter 12, the parking lot, city manager, and down-zoning issues were resolved in ways that avoided such maladies of democratic performance as elite rule, bureaucratic rule, and domination by special interests. Assuming that most thought that the community was best served by retaining Watson and subjecting him to more frequent reviews, Level 10 of responsible representation was achieved on the city manager issue, as this outcome was responsive to the predominant views among citizens and various types of participants. Responsible representation was somewhat lower (Level 8) on the East Lawrence downzoning issue. Although the resolution of this issue was consistent with the independent judgments of commissioners, the judgments were not supported by most bureaucrats, notables, or individual activists. Finally, responsible representation was lowest (at Level 6) on the parking lot issue. Despite the judgments of representatives that the city was best served by proceeding with the parking lot, the issue was resolved in a way that most activists and citizens opposed. While none of these decisions violated the norms of representative democracy, they illustrate that there can be different levels of responsible representation within pluralist communities.

*Hypotheses about Responsible Representation*

A wide variety of conditions surrounding the policymaking process may thwart or facilitate higher levels of responsible representation. For example, characteristics of the policymaking body may affect responsible representation. Elected commissions and boards are perhaps more responsive than are appointed governing bodies,[22] and those commissions dominated by representatives associated with mass-based organizations (e.g., neighborhood groups) may be more responsible than commissions dominated by representatives associated with elite interests (e.g., those supported by the Chamber of Commerce). The extensiveness of citizen participation may also affect responsible representation; for example, high voter turnouts may contribute to responsible representation, even though extensive issue-specific participation may retard democratic performance.[23] The characteristics of citizens may also affect responsible representation; for example, an aware and informed public may encourage democratic policy outcomes. Finally, responsible representation may suffer because of tensions between capitalism and democracy; for example, democratic outcomes may be difficult to achieve on issues in which the economic interests of the city are at stake—where economic needs rather than the preferences of people determine outcomes.[24]

In summary, the extent to which the ideal of responsible representation is achieved varies across issues and across communities, depending on whether representatives exercise their political authority in ways that are responsive to their constituents and other participants. Representatives should be open to persuasion by the expertise of bureaucrats, but they should not simply defer to bureaucratic recommendations. Representatives should be open to the arguments of private elites about the economic and social needs of the community, but they must not be pressured by the economic and social resources that elites command. Representatives should be open to the demands of group leaders while not becoming captives of the organizational resources of special interests. Representatives need to listen to the intense preferences of issue-specific activists, though such concerns must be balanced against the public interest. On most occasions, representatives need to be responsive to public opinion, but responsible representation involves making independent assessments about the effectiveness and fairness of policies and not acting as delegates who make policy merely on the basis of public opinion.[25] Responsible representatives provide community notables, governmental administrators, group leaders, and activists with opportunities to participate and to persuade other citizens of the legitimacy of their preferences. However, responsible representation is impaired if such participants prevail in the resolution of issues without being persuasive.[26]

## COMPLEX EQUALITY

Tyrannies permit the strong to dominate the weak. In racist societies, Caucasians normally dominate Africans and Asians. In sexist societies, men normally dominate women. There are many forms of tyranny, but they share a common feature. One segment of society has extensive political power, which it employs to ensure that issues are resolved in ways that uphold its interests and world view. The counterparts of the dominant interest are the victims because their interests and aspirations are continuously ignored.

Socialists have been concerned about political inequalities, and they often advocate "simple equality."[27] Simple equality would occur if political power were equally distributed between the upper and lower classes, whites and minorities, men and women, and so forth.[28] To achieve simple equality on a specific issue, the policy outcome would have to be equally responsive to the preferences of different segments of the community. To achieve simple equality over a broad range of issues and over time, the victories of the upper class, whites, or men on certain issues would be offset by the victories of the lower class, nonwhites, or women on other issues of comparable importance.

Because simple equality would, by definition, end tyranny, it is an attractive ideal, but pluralists have never fully embraced this ideal. Many issues have outcomes that are inherently dichotomous (as was the decision either to build or not to build the parking lot), and they cannot be compromised in ways that are equally responsive to all interests. Equal political power among competing interests will remain an impossibility. If power could be magically distributed equally today, it would become unequally distributed tomorrow, when the next issue is resolved in ways more responsive to one interest than to another. Most importantly, it is not clear that different interests *should* be equally powerful.[29] Perhaps the inequalities that occur can be explained, and perhaps these explanations justify the inequalities.

Consider the inequalities in power between classes in Lawrence. The lower class seemed to lose on the parking lot and the city manager issues, but it succeeded in having East Lawrence downzoned. Suppose that this pattern of power became even more pronounced on other issues, with the lower class almost always being defeated by the middle and upper classes. This pattern illustrates a condition of simple inequality, and members of the lower class would probably view themselves as the victims of the upper class. Nevertheless, merely describing such inequality is inadequate. In order to evaluate whether these inequalities are justified and to prescribe ways of achieving more equality, discovering the causes of inequality becomes important.

Perhaps upper-class domination of the lower class is due to the underrepresentation of the lower class among elected officials. In pluralist policymaking processes, representatives are supposed to be the most powerful participants, and their judgments are likely to be colored by their class backgrounds. The failure of the lower class to elect commissioners who represent their interests can explain the lack of policy responsiveness to the preferences of the lower class.

Perhaps upper-class domination of the lower class is due to the greater participation of the upper class in the resolution of issues. In pluralist processes, representatives are supposed to listen to the arguments of participants, and they are sometimes persuaded by these arguments. The failure of the lower class to participate in these roles can explain their lack of power.

Perhaps upper-class domination is due to support of positions relatively popular with the public. In pluralist processes, representatives should be sensitive to public opinion. If the positions of the lower class are unpopular, they are not likely to be successful in the resolution of community issues.

Finally, perhaps upper-class domination is due to their holding political principles that are more dominant in local political cultures than are the principles held by the lower class. In pluralist processes, policy decisions should reflect dominant community principles. If members of the lower class support policies that undermine dominant community values, their lack of political power is understandable.

Simple inequalities can thus occur because of inequalities in representation, participation, public support for conflicting policy preferences, and cultural acceptance of competing political principles. However, these simple inequalities may not undermine the pluralist goal of complex equality. The ideal of complex equality occurs when there are no significant unexplained inequalities in the political power of competing interests.[30] Conservatives and some liberals who hold differentiating (i.e., inegalitarian) principles of justice[31] can thus accept the ideal of complex equality because it permits legitimate inequalities of power.

The criterion of complex equality is thus "reasonable." Pluralists do not label every political inequality tyrannical, but if there are no adequate reasons for significant political inequalities, a prima facie case exists that discrimination has entered into the policymaking process. If the relative powerlessness of the lower class cannot be explained by class differences in representation, participation, popular support, compatibility with the political culture, or other plausible and compelling reasons, it can be concluded that class biases exist. When complex equality is unattained, policymakers discriminate against the lower class—or other subordinant interests—simply because they are lower class. Similarly, when complex equality is unattained, policymakers respond to upper-class people simply because they have more money, more education, and more status. Such discriminations violate pluralist ideals because such matters as wealth, educational background, social status, race, and gender should be irrelevant to the legitimate possession of power.[32]

Though the criterion of complex equality is reasonable, it can also be "radical"; it invites investigation of the causes of inequality. Simply because an inequality can be explained does not mean that it can be justified. If the subordination of the lower class is due to its underrepresentation among elected officials, questions about the legitimacy of such underrepresentation can—and probably will—be raised by those with concerns about inequality. The underlying causes of underrepresentation may be traced to structural features of the electoral system; perhaps lower-class and minority underrepresentation is due to the absence of partisan labels and wards in many local communities.[33] If so, institutional changes can be prescribed and sought. If the subordination of the lower class is due to its holding principles that conflict with dominant cultural values, questions can be raised about the legitimacy of dominant cultural values. Socialists are likely to trace resistance to redistributive principles to the systemic power of capitalism and the ability of capitalists to create cultural values conducive to the needs of capitalism.[34] If so, a transformation of cultural values will be urged as a means of achieving more political equality.[35]

The criterion of complex equality facilitates explanation and evaluation of the inequalities of power between opposite interests defined by various political cleavages. Three phases of analysis must be conducted to determine if communities achieve complex equality.

In the first phase, a sample of issues must be scrutinized to determine the presence or absence of various types of cleavages. Cleavages are defined on the basis of the predominant characteristics — rather than the universal qualities — of the individuals who oppose each other on issues. If *most* members of the upper class wanted to retain Watson but *most* members of the lower class wanted to fire him, there would have been a class cleavage. More specifically, a cleavage occurs when the majority of people defined by some characteristic (e.g., the upper class) are on one side of the issue, the majority of people with the opposite characteristic (e.g., the lower class) are on the other side of the issue, and the differences are statistically significant.

Although the discussion of complex equality has focused on class cleavages, other kinds of cleavages may be widespread on community issues and may exhibit more extensive and less legitimate inequalities than do those that occur along class lines. Table 2.2 lists the types of cleavages investigated in the Lawrence study and the interests that may oppose each other when these cleavages occur.

If class, racial, ideological, or other types of cleavages are observed on community issues, the second phase of analysis — the question, Which interests tend to prevail? — must be answered. Just as the standings on the sports pages help fans keep track of the win-loss records of teams in baseball, basketball, and football, so can political standings help keep track of the success of various interests in community politics. Is the Lower Class in last place in the Class Division? Does the Growth Machine dominate Preservationists on economic development issues? Is there a tight race in the Gender Division suggesting parity between men and women? In Chapter 13, I describe a procedure that involves relating the preferences of various interests to policy outcomes to determine the win-loss records of the interests listed in Table 2.2 on the twenty-nine issues examined in this study. These standings indicate that there are extensive simple inequalities among various interests; as in sports, the "have-nots" — those interests that are poor in social and economic resources — are at or near the bottom of the standings in the game of community politics.

The third phase of analysis involves attempts to explain these inequalities. Because inequalities in the success of various interests may be explained by inequalities in representation, participation, popular support, and cultural values, measures of these variables must be attained and incorporated in multivariate models relating the preferences of competing interests to policy outcomes. If the preferences of competing interests are equally potent determinants of policy outcomes when the effects of such variables are controlled, the ideal of complex equality is achieved.

Table 2.2   Various Community Cleavages and the Interests That Oppose Each Other When Such Cleavages Arise

---

Class
   The Upper Class: those in the top quartile of a scale of socioeconomic status (SES)
   The Middle Class: those in the middle quartiles of SES scale
   The Lower Class: those in the bottom quartile of SES scale
Neighborhood
   Country Clubbers: those living in upper-income neighborhoods
   Split Levellers: those living in middle-income neighborhoods
   Cellar Dwellers: those living in lower-income neighborhoods
Racial
   Whites
   Minorities
Gender
   Men
   Women
Age
   Rookies: those less than 30 years old
   Veterans: those between 30 and 55 years old
   Seniors: those over 55 years old
Length of Residence in the Community
   Hometowners: those residing in the community more than 20 years
   Newcomers: community residents for 5 to 20 years
   Visitors: community residents less than 5 years
Sector of Employment
   Public: those who work for governmental agencies
   Private: those who work in the private sector
University-Community
   Gown: students and employees at the university
   Town: those unaffiliated with the university
Ideological
   Liberals: those who define themselves as liberals
   Conservatives: those who define themselves as conservatives
Partisan
   Republicans: those who define themselves as Republicans
   Democrats: those who define themselves as Democrats
Ethos
   Managerialists: those who think government should emphasize businesslike efficiency and other "good government" values
   Politicos: those who think government should emphasize such political values as openness and fairness
Other Attitudinal Divisions
   The Growth Machine: those who prefer rapid economic growth
   Preservationists: those who prefer no or slow growth

   Market Providers: those who prefer low taxes and limited public services
   Public Providers: those who prefer more extensive public services, even if taxes must be raised

---

## SUMMARY

Principle-policy congruence, responsible representation, and complex equality are ideals that can be used for evaluating the resolution of policy issues in pluralist communities. Orthodox pluralists seem to assume that the ideals of principle-policy congruence, responsible representation, and complex equality are usually achieved. Those who subscribe to critical pluralism would be less certain, and they would want to provide continual vigilance against failures in democratic performance. Toward this end, the development of a conceptual framework and measurement instruments for analyzing principle-policy congruence, responsible representation, and complex equality are critical. No doubt these ideals will be more fully realized in the resolution of some issues than others, and some communities will have policy processes that more fully achieve these ideals than will other communities. Investigations into the conditions that facilitate and hinder the achievement of these ideals may yield prescriptions for realizing more fully the normative aspirations of pluralist democracy.

# 3

# A Comparative Analysis
# of Twenty-nine Lawrence Issues

In order to conduct a critical pluralist analysis, I have systematically investigated twenty-nine issues that became part of the political agenda in Lawrence, Kansas, between 1977 and 1987. I have mapped and analyzed the preferences and participation of those representatives, bureaucrats, notables, group leaders, and issue-specific activists involved in the resolution of these issues and the attitudes of uninvolved citizens about these issues. Though it would be desirable to extend the empirical base to the investigation of representative samples of policy issues in a large and random sample of communities,[1] the findings presented here are drawn from a fairly typical American community and are based on an unusually large and diverse sample of issues. These findings thus approximate how policy issues are normally resolved in American communities.

## LAWRENCE, KANSAS

Although no community is representative of the diverse places where Americans live, Lawrence is in the mid-range of American communities on a number of important characteristics. Located forty miles west of Kansas City, Lawrence is near the geographical center of the United States. With a population of fifty-six thousand, Lawrence is a small metropolitan statistical area (MSA), and 76 percent of all Americans live in MSAs.[2] Between 1980 and 1984, Lawrence experienced a 4.5 percent growth rate, a rate equal to the national growth rate. Whites make up 86 percent of Lawrence's population and 78 percent of the U.S. population. Lawrence has relatively few blacks (5.3 percent) and Hispanics (2.7 percent), but more native Americans (3 percent) and Asians (1.8 percent) than the national averages. With a mean per capita income of $10,152, Lawrentians are slightly poorer than most Americans (whose per capita incomes average $11,923), but only 7.7 percent of its citizens live below the poverty line (in comparison with 9.6 percent of all Americans). Lawrence's adult population is somewhat better educated than are Americans elsewhere (85 percent have high school diplomas compared with a national average of 66 percent), and its citizens are relatively young (the median age is 23.6 years compared with a national average of 31.2 years). The relatively low incomes, high education, and youth of the citizens of Lawrence are no doubt due to the presence of the University of Kansas. Nevertheless, the results of this study suggest that the university and its students are not major participants in Lawrence politics, and there is little town-gown conflict; thus, Lawrence's being a university town should not greatly affect the findings.

Lawrence also has fairly typical local governmental institutions. It has a council-manager form of government (though it is mislabeled a commission-manager form). Its five-member council, elected at large on nonpartisan ballots, is also typical. The only atypical feature of Lawrence's governmental institutions is its failure to provide for the direct election of its weak, largely ceremonial, mayor.[3]

## A COMPARATIVE-ISSUES APPROACH

Orthodox pluralists argue that the democratic performance of American communities can best be analyzed by a decision-making methodology that determines the success of various kinds of participants on the "key issues" in local politics.[4] In this study, the decisional method has been modified and developed into a comparative-issues method. Like the decisional method, the comparative-issues method examines who participates and who succeeds on specific issues in order to make inferences about the distribution of the first face of power.[5] There are, however, several important differences between the decisional method and the comparative-issues approach. Analysts using a decisional approach examine a few key issues to describe how the participation and influence of various actors tend to be limited to a specific policy domain. The comparative-issues approach samples a broader range of issues to describe and explain variations in policy outcomes and democratic performance across issues. While the decisional method focuses on active participants on issues, the comparative-issues approach also considers inactive persons, including citizens at large and those elites who remain "behind the scenes." While the decisional method focuses on behavior, the comparative-issues approach also considers attitudes. The distributions of preferences regarding both specific policy proposals and the philosophical principles underlying them are important data in a comparative-issues approach. The decisional method attempts to make inferences about who has power on specific issues,[6] but the comparative-issues method assumes that it is impossible to reach valid inferences about whose principles, preferences, and participation affect specific outcomes, and that inferences about whose preferences *cause* policy outcomes can be reached only through multivariate analyses with large samples of issues as the primary units of analysis.[7]

## SAMPLING ISSUES

To describe and explain variations in the attainment of principle-policy congruence, responsible representation, and complex equality, a fairly large and representative sample of issues is necessary. Table 3.1 represents an effort to reach this goal by examining the issues. Ideally, a sample of issues would be much larger and drawn from a variety of communities, and it would be representative of some theoretically defined dimensions of public policy.

There is no universe of issues from which to draw a random sample.[8] The sample of twenty-nine issues was therefore developed on the basis of the availability of citizen policy preference data drawn from a series of public opinion surveys conducted between 1977 and 1986. When selecting issues for these surveys, efforts were made to obtain variation regarding the type of governing body charged with resolving various issues, the levels of controversy surrounding these issues, and the types of political principles they embodied. In short, efforts were made to select a diverse and unbiased sample. Although the resulting sample was not random, it contains no known systematic bias, such as issues having outcomes known to reflect, for example, citizen or elite preferences.[9]

Column 2 of Table 3.1 shows the governing body that resolved each issue in the sample. The sample is weighted toward issues resolved by the city commission. Because both the school board and the hospital board have limited jurisdictions and because the county commission focuses on issues outside the city limit (though these issues often impact on Lawrence and its growth), this emphasis on the city commission appears justified.

Controversial issues are more likely than noncontroversial issues to generate responsiveness to public concerns.[10] Some variability in the levels of controversy across issues was therefore sought and attained. For example, survey research revealed that more than 80 percent of Lawrence citizens were aware of some issues, but only 25 percent were aware of other issues. Some issues stimulated the active participation of over 100 citizens, but participation was limited to fewer than twenty citizens on other issues. Despite such variation, controversial issues are probably overrepresented in the sample.

Efforts were made to obtain variation in the types of issues included in the sample. The analyses in Chapters 5 through 10 suggest that the Lawrence sample contains more economic-growth, land-use, and public-service issues than public-welfare, tax-distribution, and social-liberty issues. Perhaps economic-growth, land-use, and public-service issues are relatively prominent and important in community politics generally, and perhaps samples should be weighted accordingly. However, there is no basis for asserting that the sample is representative of the various types of issues that arise in community politics.[11]

These limitations of the Lawrence sample do not vitiate the comparative-issues approach, as larger samples involving various kinds of issues can be studied. Such samples can facilitate the analysis of democratic performance by particular types of governing bodies, for certain types of issues, and in particular policy areas. For example, large samples of economic-development issues in randomly selected cities could be examined to describe and explain responsible representation on these issues; large samples of public-service (and other kinds of) issues could be similarly analyzed. By examining a broader array of issues and by understanding the characteristics of issues on the institutional agendas of communities, it should be possible to estimate more closely the underlying parameters concerning the attainment of the ideals of pluralist democracy.

## DATA COLLECTION

Interviews and survey research provided most of the data on the issues in the sample. In 1984, when all but one of the twenty-nine issues in the sample (TOWNCENTER) were resolved, thirty-six semistructured interviews were conducted with local governmental officials (eleven city commissioners, three county commissioners, seven school board members, five hospital board members, seven upper-echelon administrators in city government, and three upper-echelon administrators in the school district).[12] No public official in Lawrence refused to be interviewed.

Officials were asked whether they were involved in each issue. If they were involved as advocates and/or decision makers on an issue, they were asked structured questions about their preferences and participation, their assessments of public opinion, and their perceptions of the existence of various cleavages. In more open-ended questioning, officials were also asked to indicate their perceptions about who was most involved and influential on each issue and what factors played important roles in shaping both their own positions on each issue and the outcome of the issue. Officials were also asked fixed-format questions about their backgrounds, their political principles, and their organizational allegiances and involvements.

Personal and/or telephone interviews were also conducted with 203 people centrally involved in these issues in nonofficial capacities: as notables in the community, as leaders of groups involved in the issues, or as other activists. Initially contacted were: (a) the 100 persons ranked as most influential in the

Table 3.1  Summary Measures of Policy Outcomes and Actor Preferences

| Issues | Policy Resolved by | Year[a] | Policy Change | Percentage of Various Types of Actors Supporting Policy Changes | | | | | |
|---|---|---|---|---|---|---|---|---|---|
| | | | | Elected Representatives | Bureaucrats | Notables | Group Leaders | Other Activists | Citizens |
| WARDS | PR | 77 | 0.0 | 0 | 0 | 0 | 12 | 31 | 35 |
| MAYOR | LCC | 80–84 | 97.5 | 67 | 100 | 100 | 25 | 62 | 59 |
| MANAGER | LCC | 82 | 7.5 | 50 | 0 | 5 | 10 | 63 | 32 |
| AIRPORT | LCC | 75–86 | 85.0 | 71 | 100 | 100 | 80 | 66 | 61 |
| N2ST | LCC | 79–83 | 67.5 | 100 | 100 | 100 | 84 | 79 | 81 |
| RAIL | LCC-DG | 82–83 | 12.5 | 38 | 83 | 88 | 90 | 73 | 65 |
| RESEARCH | LCC | 82–87 | 97.5 | 89 | 100 | 88 | 100 | 88 | 82 |
| IRB | LCC | 79–87 | 62.5 | 36 | 83 | 50 | 78 | 42 | 63 |
| SIGNS | LCC | 79–87 | 60.0 | 78 | 67 | 100 | 88 | 56 | 73 |
| OREAD | LCC | 77–87 | 28.5 | 40 | 50 | 40 | 87 | 47 | 58 |
| EAST | LCC | 82–83 | 90.0 | 60 | 33 | 25 | 71 | 51 | 55 |
| BLUFFS | LCC | 79–86 | 52.5 | 50 | 67 | 83 | 30 | 47 | 37 |
| CATH | LCC | 83–85 | 80.0 | 80 | 67 | 67 | 50 | 56 | 57 |
| ENVIR | LCC | 79–87 | 77.5 | 81 | 100 | 80 | 50 | 46 | 81 |
| DRUG | LCC | 80 | 77.5 | 80 | 50 | 100 | — | 56 | 81 |
| TRIBES | SB | 81 | 70.0 | 71 | 0 | 0 | 100 | 53 | 46 |
| BIRTH | HB | 78–80 | 5.0 | 43 | 0 | 60 | 60 | 60 | 57 |
| STORM | LCC-PR | 80–82 | 0.0 | 64 | 75 | 38 | 60 | 42 | 33 |
| CLOSE | SB | 81–82 | 10.0 | 29 | 100 | 60 | 09 | 34 | 58 |
| LIFELINE | LCC | 82–83 | 0.0 | 40 | 25 | 17 | 62 | 42 | 45 |
| SOCIAL | LCC-DG | 80–87 | 55.0 | 45 | 25 | 77 | 56 | 77 | 48 |
| VIDEO | LCC | 82 | 0.0 | 0 | 0 | 33 | 0 | 46 | 51 |

| | | | | | | | | | |
|---|---|---|---|---|---|---|---|---|---|
| INTANGIBLES | PR | 79–80 | 100.0 | 75 | 0 | 75 | 100 | 68 | 73 |
| REAPPRAISE | KS | 77–86 | 95.0 | 100 | 75 | 67 | 100 | 75 | 38 |
| CORNFIELD | LCC | 78–79 | 7.5 | 0 | 0 | 12 | 14 | 35 | 34 |
| BUNKER | LCC | 79–80 | 12.5 | 80 | 50 | 67 | 38 | 29 | 20 |
| PARK | LCC | 79–80 | 100.0 | 68 | 100 | 83 | 85 | 24 | 43 |
| SIZELER | LCC | 81–83 | 7.5 | | 100 | 100 | 90 | 55 | 45 |
| TOWNCENTER | LCC-PR | 83–87 | 25.0 | 44 | 100 | 88 | 40 | 56 | 29 |

LCC = Lawrence City Commission
DG = Douglas County Commission
SB = District 497 School Board
HB = Hospital Board
PR = Public Referendum
KS = Kansas Legislature

[a] Years that the issues were on the institutional agendas of governing bodies in Lawrence

community, as indicated by a 1983 reputational study of Lawrence;[13] (b) leaders of all community groups that sometimes become involved in governmental issues; (c) people (other than elected and administrative officials) mentioned during the interviews with officials, in newspaper accounts, and in minutes of meetings as being active on an issue; and (d) people cited by at least two other previously interviewed participants as one of their main supporters or opponents. Only 45 percent of the community influentials and 15 percent of the group leaders who were contacted said they were directly involved in any of the twenty-nine issues. Only 5 percent of those activists contacted refused to provide interviews.

The interviews with nonofficial activists were also semistructured. Interviewees were first asked whether they were involved in each issue (the mean number of involvements reported by individuals with regard to the twenty-nine issues was 3.7). If they were involved on an issue, they were asked about the degree of that involvement and their preferences on the issue. Further questioning focused on those issues of greatest involvement; interviewees were asked to provide ordinal-scale answers to questions about the importance of each issue, the form and extent of their participation, and their satisfaction with each outcome. In more open-ended fashion, they were asked to name their most important supporters and opponents and the reasons behind their positions and involvements on each issue. Furthermore, they were asked whether they participated as individuals or as members of a group on each issue. If interviewees said they were members of a group, questions were asked about the group's size, permanency, social composition, leadership, cohesion, and involvement on the issues. Finally, as in the interviews with officials, activists were also asked about their backgrounds, their political principles, and their organizational involvement.

Citizen preferences on each issue were obtained from five citizen surveys. The approximate dates when these surveys were conducted and their sample sizes are: April 1977 (N=373); April 1980 (N=512); March and April 1982 (N=269); March and April 1984 (N=406); and March and April 1986 (N=611). Random selection was used in 1977, and random-digit dialing techniques were used in subsequent surveys. Respondents were first asked to indicate whether they were familiar with several recent and ongoing issues. Those who were familiar with an issue were then asked if they supported or opposed the proposed policy change, if they supported some other policy alternative, or if they had "mixed feelings." Respondents were also asked about some issues that had been resolved in recent years and to indicate their degree of satisfaction with the outcome. Standard questions about the background and organizational involvements of respondents were asked on all citizen surveys, and the questions about political principles posed to officials and activists were also asked of citizens in the 1984 and 1986 surveys.

Finally, this study draws upon two reputational studies of Lawrence elites.[14] Informants provided the names of 181 (in 1983) and 236 ( in 1985) Lawrence leaders to be evaluated for their place in the power structure of the community. In both studies, over 60 percent of the persons so listed were then interviewed and asked to indicate the frequency and direction of their contacts with others on the list, their assessments of the main contributors to the community, and their perceptions of the main political resources possessed by others. Attention was directed to those most frequently cited for the possession of social and economic resources. Citations from the 1983 and 1985 studies were combined to provide the ranking of the top thirty-five economic and social notables provided in Table 12.3,[15] and the preferences and participation of these notables regarding the twenty-nine issues were then determined from the previously discussed interviews with participants.

## MEASURES OF KEY CONCEPTS

In order to compare the democratic performance of policymakers over a sample of issues, comparable measures of the policy outcomes on each issue and the preferences of various actors and interests about these issues must be attained.[16] This section describes such measures.

### Policy Change

As shown in column 4 of Table 3.1, each issue in the sample had a policy outcome score ranging from 0 to 100, depending on the degree to which the issue was resolved in a manner that involved changes in previous policies, new ordinances, facilities, developments, or programs. These scores were derived as follows. Participants indicated their degree of satisfaction with the outcome on a five-point scale. Highly dissatisfied participants were scored as "0," moderately dissatisfied participants as "25," those with mixed feelings as "50," moderately satisfied participants as "75," and highly satisfied participants as "100." Mean satisfaction scores were then calculated for all unambiguous supporters and for all unambiguous opponents of policy change on each issue. The policy change scores for each issue were then calculated, using the following formula:

Policy Change = [100 + mean supporter satisfaction − mean opponent satisfaction] ÷ 2.

*Representative Preferences*

During the interviews, elected officials were asked to indicate their independent judgments about each issue — whether, in the final analysis, they personally supported or opposed each policy change. On several occasions, elected officials indicated that their ultimate judgments departed from their initial positions and from how they voted when the issue was resolved. Representative preferences on each issue are measured as a percentage of those representatives whose independent judgments supported policy change;[17] these measures are reported in column 5 of Table 3.1.

*Bureaucratic Preferences*

At least one public administrator made policy recommendations or otherwise advocated particular outcomes on each issue in the sample. Usually there was little disagreement among top-echelon administrators about their positions on the issues. Bureaucratic preferences on each policy issue are simply the percentages of administrators supporting change and are reported in column 6 of Table 3.1.

*Preferences of Notables*

The top thirty-five social and/or economic notables were identifed by the modified reputational method. At least one notable indicated his involvement in each issue or was attributed involvement by other participants on the issue (the average number of notables involved in each issue was 7.3).[18] The preferences of economic and social notables were first examined separately. Because the preferences of economic notables and social notables are highly correlated across issues (r = .77), economic and social notables have been combined. Notable preferences on each issue is simply the number of notables supporting change divided by the total number of notables involved in the issue with unambiguous preferences regarding its outcome. This percentage is reported in column 7 of Table 3.1.

*Preferences of Group Leaders*

The groups involved in specific issues were identified through the interviews with officials and nonofficial activists. Measuring group preferences by simply calculating the percentage of groups supporting each policy change is inadequate because such a procedure counts each group equally regardless of its leadership, membership, or other resources. To address this difficulty, a measure of mobilizer support has been developed that makes use of four additional pieces of information: the number of LEADERS who actively represented the group's position during the resolution of the issue, the number of other persons in each group that were ACTIVISTS on an issue, the number of persons who were formally MEMBERS of each group, and the degree of COHESION among members of each group on each issue. The position of each group on each issue was then weighted by the following index:

Group weight = LEADERS + ACTIVISTS + [MEMBERS × cohesion]

where LEADERS is the actual number of group leaders, ACTIVISTS and MEMBERS are measured on five-point ordinal scales, and COHESION is measured on a scale from 0 to 1 where 1 represents a unified group.[19] Net group leader (or mobilizer) support for each issue was then calculated by adding the resulting weights for each group supporting policy change and dividing by the weights of all involved groups. The resulting scores are reported in column 8 of Table 3.1 and used in Chapter 12 to determine the power of group leaders relative to the power of other participants in the resolution of community issues.[20]

*Preferences of Other Activists*

The interviews with participants also revealed the names of people active on issues but not public officials, notables, or group leaders. These activists remain potentially important participants, whose policy preferences have been calculated simply as the number of other activists supporting policy change divided by the total number of other activists involved in the issue. The percentage of other (issue-specific) activists supporting policy change on each issue is reported in column 9 of Table 3.1.

*Preferences of Citizens*

Three measures of citizen attitudes on the issue in the sample are employed: "actual" citizen preferences, perceived citizen preferences, and citizen satisfaction.

When an issue first arose, public-opinion survey questions were framed in ways that corresponded closely with the way the issue appeared on the institutional agenda. Actual citizen preferences for each issue are simply the percentage of persons preferring policy change among those persons surveyed who were aware of the issue and who had an unambiguous preference regarding its outcome. The survey conducted prior to major decisions was used in determining actual citizen preferences. If the issue was unresolved when more than one survey was conducted, citizen preferences were calculated by considering the valid responses from several surveys. Four issues (WARDS, STORM, INTANGIBLES, and TOWNCENTER) were ultimately subjects of referenda; in these cases, the referenda results have been used instead of the survey data.[21]

Those elected officials responsible for resolving each issue were asked to indicate their perceptions of the extent of citizen support for proposed policy changes using the following seven-point scale:

1. "consensual opposition" (0–20 percent support)
2. "predominant opposition" (20–35 percent support)
3. "more opposition than support" (35–45 percent support)
4. "equal opposition and support" (45–55 percent support)
5. "more support than opposition" (55–65 percent support)
6. "predominant support" (65–80 percent support)
7. "consensual support" (80–100 percent support)

The mid-points of each of those intervals selected by officials were averaged to measure perceived citizen support for each issue.

The Pearson correlation between official perceptions of citizen preferences and survey (actual) measures of citizen preferences was .69. Because surveyed citizen preferences and perceived citizen preferences can be considered to be "inputs" into the policy process, these measures have been averaged to yield a summary index of citizen preferences reported in the last column of Table 3.1 and used in the regression models reported in Chapters 12 and 13.

Citizen satisfaction with policy outcomes were ascertained for twenty issues in surveys conducted after these issues had been resolved. Respondents who recalled each issue were asked if they were dissatisfied, satisfied, or neutral about its outcome. The citizen satisfaction scores have been calculated by dividing the number of respondents who indicated satisfaction with the policy change by the number of respondents who were aware of the issue and had an unambiguous attitude about its outcome. The Pearson correlation between actual citizen preferences and citizen support was only .37.

The measures of the preferences of representatives, bureaucrats, notables, group leaders, other activists, and citizens presented in Table 3.1 are essential for investigating responsible representation within communities. These measures are also useful for estimating the direct power of these various types of actors, as will be shown in Chapter 12.

### Preferences of Competing Interests

In order to investigate complex equality among competing interests, the preferences of participants and citizens had to be broken down according to people's characteristics regarding various political cleavages (see Table 2.2). Sorting people by demographic and attitudinal characteristics was usually straightforward.

To determine the social class of participants and citizens, an index of socioeconomic status (SES) was developed based on seven- to ten-point ordinal-level scales of income, occupational status, and educational attainment.[22] These scales were then standardized and summed. The lower class is defined as those in the bottom quartile of the SES scale. The upper class is defined as those in the top quartile of the SES scale. The middle class is, of course, those between the twenty-fifth and seventy-fifth percentiles on the SES scale.

People were also sorted according to the average property values in their neighborhoods. Country Clubbers live in neighborhoods in which mean property values of residences exceed $85,000; Split Levellers are those living in neighborhoods having mean property values between $50,000 and $85,000; and Cellar Dwellers are those living in neighborhoods having mean property values of less than $50,000.[23]

Few minorities participated in Lawrence issues; thus persons were simply divided into white and nonwhite categories. People were asked their age and classified as Rookies (those less than thirty years old), Veterans (those between thirty and fifty-five years old), and Seniors (those over fifty-five years old). People were asked how long they had lived in Lawrence and classified as Hometowners (those residing in Lawrence for more than twenty years), Newcomers (those residing in Lawrence between five and twenty years), and Visitors (those residing in the community for less than five years). They were also asked where they worked and classified as Public (those working in the public sector) or Private (those in the private sector) and as Gown (those working or studying at the University of Kansas or Haskell Junior College) or Town (those unaffiliated with KU or Haskell).

People were also classified on the basis of various attitudinal variables. Their ideological self-characterizations were used to classify them as liberals or conservatives. They were also asked to indicate whether they normally voted for Democrats or Republicans or were independents; their self-characterizations in this regard were used in the analysis of partisan cleavages. Participants and citizens were also asked to indicate their priorities among various local governmental functions. Members of the Growth Machine were defined as those who said they gave highest priority to promoting economic growth. Preservationists were those who gave highest priority to "effective land-use regulations." Market Providers were those who gave highest priority to keeping taxes low, and Public Providers were those who gave highest priority to improving the quality and quantity of public services. Finally, Politicos were those who said they believed that the role of government is to resolve issues openly and fairly. Managerialists were those who said they believed that the role of government is to provide services effectively and economically.

After participants and citizens were sorted on the basis of these demographic and attitudinal variables, the percentages of various kinds of participants and citizens supporting and opposing policy changes were calculated. The resulting measures permitted identification of various kinds of cleavages on issues. For example, if most liberals favored one outcome on an issue and if most conservatives favored a different outcome — and if the difference in preferences between liberals and conservatives was statistically significant — an ideological cleavage was identified. These data also permitted identification of unequal responsiveness to different interests. For example, if policy outcomes were more closely related to the preferences of conservatives than to those of liberals, Lawrence policymakers would seem to be biased against liberals. The question that remained, in a critical pluralist analysis, is whether this unequal responsiveness had legitimate explanations.

## CONCLUSIONS

The comparative-issues approach facilitates the collection of data and the development of measures that can be used to evaluate the extent to which local governments achieve the ideals of principle-policy congruence, responsible representation, and complex equality. The "case study" of the resolution of twenty-nine issues in Lawrence provides a "plausibility probe"[24] of critical pluralist analysis using the comparative-issues method. Certain limitations of the Lawrence study preclude definitive judgments about the democratic performance of American communities generally. The greatest problem is the lack of a sample representative of the issues that arise in communities beyond Lawrence. More refined data collection techniques and measures can also be developed. Nevertheless, with further refinement, the comparative-issues approach offers the potential to achieve normal scientific progress in understanding the role of principles and the distribution of power in the resolution of community issues.

# 4

# Competing Principles
# and Urban Ideologies

In contrast to monistic communities, which insist that certain principles are correct, pluralist communities have political cultures in which various views are recognized and tolerated. Within pluralist communities, diverse principles are often organized by the competing ideologies of conservatism, liberalism, and democratic socialism.[1] Because of the weakness of socialist ideology in the United States,[2] conservatism and liberalism are the main competing ideologies that provide alternative principles for resolving issues.

Four major questions about political principles characterize political cultures and their effects on the resolution of policy issues in American communities:

1. What are the competing principles that divide conservatives and liberals?
2. Which principles are most widely held by various people within local communities?
3. How do particular principles become relevant to concrete issues?
4. What principles are most reflected in policy decisions?

By describing the differences in principles held by self-defined liberals and conservatives and the distribution of support for liberal and conservative principles in Lawrence in this chapter I describe the cultural values that should guide policy decisions in Lawrence if the ideal of principle-policy congruence is to be realized. In subsequent chapters I deal with the questions of the relevance of various principles to Lawrence issues and whether principle-policy congruence has been achieved on specific issues and in Lawrence generally.

## IDEOLOGICAL ORIENTATIONS AND SUPPORT
## FOR PRINCIPLES: AN OVERVIEW

Political principles are abstract beliefs about preferred policy directions and policymaking processes.[3] Such principles are sometimes thought of as absolute — as "the final court of appeals in practical reasoning" — but in pluralist societies people hold a variety of often competing principles.[4] As a result, few principles are regarded as absolute, conclusive guides for policymakers.

The diversity of principles that people hold prohibits their being fully specified and catalogued. To facilitate the systematic and empirical investigation of the role of principles in the resolution of community issues, however, it is useful to focus on certain principles. Contrasting principles regarding the desirability of economic growth, the appropriate levels of public services, welfare, and social control, the proper basis for taxation, the most important policymaking criteria, and the importance of citizen participation have been chosen for analysis because they are frequently discussed in the literature on community and urban politics[5] and because documentary evidence (such as minutes of meetings and newspaper accounts) and exploratory interviews suggest their relevance to a variety of issues.

Table 4.1 summarizes the distribution of support in Lawrence for liberalism and conservatism and for nine pairs of competing principles about the role of local government. These data were obtained from interviews with 239 participants involved in the Lawrence issues and from surveys with 1,017 citizens conducted in 1984 and 1986.

### Self-Defined Ideological Orientations

Participants — representatives, bureaucrats, notables, mobilizers, and individual activists — and citizens were asked to define their overall ideological orientation, and over 90 percent of each sample chose to define themselves in liberal, moderate, or conservative terms. Thirty-two percent of Lawrence citizens identified themselves as either very liberal or moderately liberal; 35 percent identified themselves as either very conservative or moderately conservative; 26 percent identified themselves as being in the middle of the road. Participants were modestly skewed toward liberal ideological orientations. For both participant and citizen samples, about 2 percent labelled themselves "radicals," about 3 percent provided other labels, and about 3 percent declined to respond.[6] As shown in the first section of Table 4.1, people were provided ideological scores ranging from very liberal ($-2$) to moderate (0) to very conservative ($+2$), to facilitate ascertaining relationships between self-defined ideological orientations and the political principles that they held.

*Alternative Political Principles*

In order to measure the distribution of support in Lawrence for alternative political principles, participants and citizens were asked about their views on nine abstract issues. Respondents were told to imagine a series of debates regarding general purposes and procedures of local governments. For each abstract issue, two viewpoints were presented, and respondents were asked to indicate their degree of agreement with these viewpoints. If a respondent agreed equally with both views or was neutral about them, a score of "0" was assigned. If a person agreed strongly or moderately with the (presumably) conservative position, a score of "2" or "1," respectively, was assigned. If a person agreed strongly or moderately with the (presumably) liberal position, a score of "−2" or "−1," respectively, was assigned.[7]

The graphics under Distribution of Views in Table 4.1 summarize the ideological orientations of participants and citizens and their support for the alternative principles on these nine abstract issues. The mean scores on each issue for participants and citizens are indicated by X's. Positive mean scores indicate tendencies toward conservative orientations and principles, and negative scores indicate tendencies toward liberal orientations and principles. The < > notation shows the 95 percent confidence intervals for the location of the population means.[8] Larger standard deviations — shown by the dashes — indicate greater diversity of viewpoints within samples.

The two right-hand columns in Table 4.1 concern the relationships of principles to self-defined ideological orientations. The Pearson correlation coefficients (r) indicate significant relationships between almost all principles and ideological orientations, with higher support for the presumed conservative principles among self-identified conservatives. In order to assess the core principles of liberal and conservative ideologies in the urban context (those principles having the greatest independent impact on ideological orientations), stepwise regression analysis was also conducted. The resulting standardized regression coefficients are shown in column B of Table 4.1. They suggest that principles concerning three abstract issues — those regarding the extent of public services, public welfare, and social control — form the core of urban liberal and conservative ideologies; they explain 42 percent of the ideological orientations of participants and 16 percent of the ideological orientations of citizens.[9] The nine abstract issues, their relationships to ideological orientations, and the distributions of support for the alternative principles on each issue are summarized below.

Table 4.1   The Political Culture of Lawrence: The Distribution of Support for Alternative Principles about the Role of Local Government among Various Types of Actors

| | Distribution of Views (-2, -1, 0, 1, 2) | Relationships with Conservatism r | B |
|---|---|---|---|
| **IDEOLOGY** | Liberal vs. Conservative | | |
| Participants (N=239) | ----------<-X->--------- | — | — |
| Representatives (N=21) | ------<----X---->------ | — | |
| Bureaucrats (N=10) | --<---X--->- | — | |
| Notables (N=21) | ------<----X---->------ | — | |
| Mobilizers (N=54) | ------<-X-->------ | — | |
| Other Activists (N=136) | ----------<-X->----------- | — | |
| Citizens (N=943) | ----------<X>----------- | — | — |
| | | | |
| **SUBSIDIZE GROWTH** (GROW) | Governmental Subsidies of Business: Oppose vs. Support | | |
| Participants | ------------<-X->-------- | .15* | .10 |
| Representatives | ------<-X---->------ | .00 | |
| Bureaucrats | -----<----X----->----- | .27 | |
| Notables | -------<-------X------> | .41* | |
| Mobilizers | -----------<----X---->------- | .24* | |
| Other Activists | -----------<--X-->----- | .15# | |
| Citizens | -----------<X>------------ | .06* | .01 |
| | | | |
| **LAND USE** (NEIGH) | Neighborhood Rights vs. Property Rights | | |
| Participants | ----------<-X->--------- | .37** | .07 |
| Representatives | -----<----X--->----- | .57** | |
| Bureaucrats | --<-------X------->----- | .17 | |
| Notables | ---<----X---->----- | .66** | |
| Mobilizers | ------<---X--->--------- | .39* | |
| Other Activists | ----------<--X-->------------ | .32** | |
| Citizens | -----------<X>----------- | .10** | .07* |
| | | | |
| **PUBLIC SERVICES** (SERV) | More vs. Less | | |
| Participants | ----------<-X->------------ | .52** | .18** |
| Representatives | ------<----X--->------ | .43* | |
| Bureaucrats | -<----X--->-- | .32 | |
| Notables | -------<----X---->----- | .37# | |
| Mobilizers | ---------<--X-->------- | .48** | |
| Other Activists | -----------<--X-->------------ | .55** | |
| Citizens | -----------<X>------------ | .23** | .14** |
| | | | |
| **PUBLIC WELFARE** (WELF) | Governmental Spending vs. Private Giving | | |
| Participants | ------------<-X->------------ | .62** | .39** |
| Representatives | ---<----X--->----- | .65** | |
| Bureaucrats | ---<----X--->---- | .31 | |
| Notables | -------<------X------>------- | .50* | |
| Mobilizers | -----------<---X-->----------- | .69** | |
| Other Activists | -------------<--X->------------ | .65** | |
| Citizens | -------------<X>------------ | .31** | .23** |

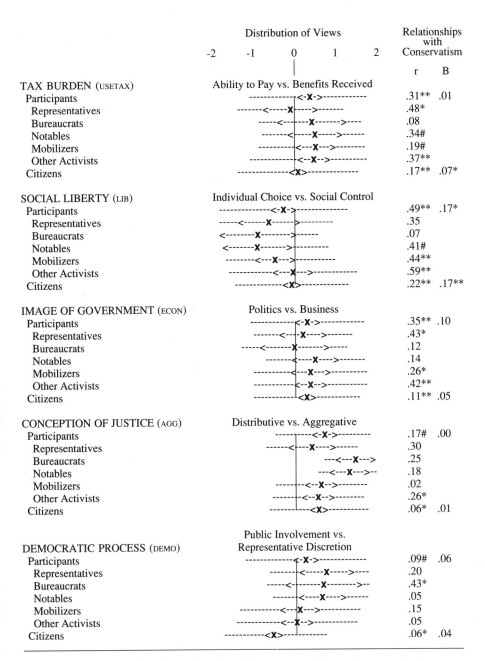

Distribution of Views — Relationships with Conservatism

| | Distribution of Views (–2 to 2) | r | B |
|---|---|---|---|
| **TAX BURDEN** (USETAX) — *Ability to Pay vs. Benefits Received* | | | |
| Participants | | .31** | .01 |
| Representatives | | .48* | |
| Bureaucrats | | .08 | |
| Notables | | .34# | |
| Mobilizers | | .19# | |
| Other Activists | | .37** | |
| Citizens | | .17** | .07* |
| **SOCIAL LIBERTY** (LIB) — *Individual Choice vs. Social Control* | | | |
| Participants | | .49** | .17* |
| Representatives | | .35 | |
| Bureaucrats | | .07 | |
| Notables | | .41# | |
| Mobilizers | | .44** | |
| Other Activists | | .59** | |
| Citizens | | .22** | .17** |
| **IMAGE OF GOVERNMENT** (ECON) — *Politics vs. Business* | | | |
| Participants | | .35** | .10 |
| Representatives | | .43* | |
| Bureaucrats | | .12 | |
| Notables | | .14 | |
| Mobilizers | | .26* | |
| Other Activists | | .42** | |
| Citizens | | .11** | .05 |
| **CONCEPTION OF JUSTICE** (AGG) — *Distributive vs. Aggregative* | | | |
| Participants | | .17# | .00 |
| Representatives | | .30 | |
| Bureaucrats | | .25 | |
| Notables | | .18 | |
| Mobilizers | | .02 | |
| Other Activists | | .26* | |
| Citizens | | .06* | .01 |
| **DEMOCRATIC PROCESS** (DEMO) — *Public Involvement vs. Representative Discretion* | | | |
| Participants | | .09# | .06 |
| Representatives | | .20 | |
| Bureaucrats | | .43* | |
| Notables | | .05 | |
| Mobilizers | | .15 | |
| Other Activists | | .05 | |
| Citizens | | .06* | .04 |

**x**: Mean scores on 5-point rating scales where "0" equals neutrality, positive scores indicate increasingly conservative orientations, and negative scores indicate increasingly liberal orientations.

< >: 95 percent confidence intervals for the location of population means.

---: Distances one standard deviation from the mean, as a measure of the degree of variation in principles among respondents within various types of actors.

#: p < .10 (significant at .10 level).

*: p < .05 (significant at .05 level).

**: p < .01 (significant at .01 level).

## LET'S GROW – PROVIDED OUR
## NEIGHBORHOODS ARE PROTECTED

Many concrete policy issues concern the growth of the community. At the level of national communities, the issue of growth is largely an issue of immigration policy,[10] but local politics is different from national politics.[11] Citizens of local communities in a federal system cannot deny newcomers membership in their communities; all U.S. citizens have rights of mobility limited only by their capacity to secure residences in an unrestricted market. Thus, at the local level, issues of growth revolve around economic-development policies rather than around immigration policies.

People may hold pro-growth principles because growth enhances the economic and human resources available in their community. When people hold pro-growth principles, they believe that local governments should promote the development of industries that export products to other communities and thus import wealth into the local economy. According to Peterson, "When a city is able to export its products, service industries prosper, labor is in greater demand, wages increase, promotional opportunities widen, land values rise, tax revenues increase, city services can be improved, donations to charitable organizations become more generous, and the social and cultural life of the city is enhanced."[12] Usually, economic development entails population growth.[13] If labor shortages exist, workers can command salaries and wages that make local products uncompetitive elsewhere. Thus, it is essential for economic growth that skilled labor and professional and managerial talent be available in the community.

Despite the attractions of pro-growth principles, citizens of local communities may also hold slow-growth principles, especially when they discover some of the problems that accompany the rapid and unregulated growth that often occurs in suburbs and boom towns.[14] Growth can erode the natural environment, resulting in health dangers. It can have aesthetic costs, as open vistas and historical structures are replaced by cramped and undistinguished developments. Local resources, such as water supplies, may be strained, and public services, such as schools, may become inadequate and overcrowded. As growth continues, diseconomies of scale may enhance the cost and reduce the quality of public services. Ultimately, citizens may acquire a sense of "lost community," and they may view growth as a phenomenon beyond local control promulgated on their community by outside developers.

A diversity of views about the desirability of growth exists both within and across communities. To measure the views that prevail in Lawrence, participants and citizens were asked whether they believed that "local governments should encourage economic growth by providing tax incentives, services, and other inducements to attract new industry and commerce to the community" or whether "the city should reduce its willingness to subsidize business and industry, as this often ends up costing tax dollars and giving an unfair competitive advantage to recipients of subsidies."[15] As shown in Table 4.1 under Subsidize Growth, pro-growth principles are widely held in Lawrence; most participants and citizens are willing to subsidize economic growth even when some of the costs of growth are presented. Although conservatives are somewhat more strongly committed to pro-growth principles than are liberals, the issue of subsidizing growth is not a major determinant of urban ideologies. Liberals, as well as conservatives, are generally inclined to view the pursuit of developmental policies as desirable. As Peterson argues, support for economic-growth principles is especially high among community notables but is also "broad and continuous" among the public as a whole.[16]

Such support can make the pursuit of specific economic-development projects highly consensual, but in pluralist communities such consensus can break down — not only because "groups may put their separate interests ahead of that of the community"[17] — but because of competing principles. Although those with slow-growth principles constitute a significant portion of the opposition to developmental policies, those who normally support growth can be persuaded to oppose projects that threaten other principles they hold.

Those who bear the burdens of economic development often assert neighborhood-protection principles: they agree that "City officials should be more sensitive to the rights of neighbors when developers want to build facilities that change the character of neighborhoods and adversely affect others in the community." If residents must be removed from their existing neighborhoods to permit new industries or businesses or if new developments abut existing neighborhoods — bringing traffic congestion, noise and air pollution, and reducing property values — governments are asked to restrict land use that harms others. Zoning regulations, site requirements, and building codes are common devices used for purposes of neighborhood protection. Of course, such regulations restrict the property rights of owners and developers to use their land as they wish; such people are likely to agree with the property-rights principle that "City officials should be more sensitive to the rights of property owners in the city, allowing them more latitude to use and develop their property as they see fit or in accordance with forces in the free-market."

As shown in Table 4.1 under "Land Use," neighborhood-protection principles are more prominent than property-rights principles in Lawrence. Although liberals are more committed to neighborhood protection than are conservatives, principles regarding land use are not a major determinant of ideological orientations. Neighborhood-protection principles are accepted by most conservatives as well as by most liberals.

In summary, the political culture of Lawrence is generally receptive to economic development. Most Lawrence participants and citizens recognize the desirability of economic growth and believe that their local governments should actively promote such growth. This does not mean, however, that economic-development proposals can expect a favorable reception in the community; opposition can emerge from those holding slow-growth and/or neighborhood-protection principles.[18] Thus, economic-development projects often become controversial political issues — especially when the downtown or neighborhoods are threatened. How such issues are resolved is the subject of Chapters 6, 7, and 10.

## MORE PUBLIC SERVICES — BUT EASY ON REDISTRIBUTION

According to Michael Walzer, there is a "sense in which every political community is a welfare state" as members of communities owe each other those "goods that are necessary to their common lives,"[19] and the communal provision of some such goods is an essential role of all local governments. When considering the communal provision of goods and services, it is useful to classify the services into two categories. First are public services, such as police and fire protection, roads, parks, libraries, schools, sewers, water supplies, and trash collection, which are available to all and which have patterns of consumption independent of the economic class of those using them. Second are welfare services, which may be available to all but which are consumed primarily by lower-income people. Because some people lack the ability to pay for essential needs, citizens of local communities may subsidize such welfare programs or social services as shelters for the homeless, group homes for the handicapped or mentally disabled, public health clinics, lunch programs, or minivan transportation systems for the elderly and poor.

Though some level of communal provision is an essential feature of all political communities, communities have different levels of public services. A "minimal state," where the government provides little beyond police protection, is a possibility,[20] but most communities — especially democratic ones — recognize a greater variety of social needs as "the people's sense of what they need encompasses not only life itself, but also the good life."[21] The level of public services provided is thus an open question, which is largely resolved by the internal politics of a community.[22]

To measure the political culture of Lawrence concerning the provision of public services, participants and citizens were asked whether they believed that "local governments should provide more and better services even if taxes must be raised proportionately" or whether "local governments should reduce spending on governmental services to keep taxes down, even if the quality of services is reduced proportionately." As shown under Public Services in Table 4.1, support for more extensive public services is strongly related to liberal ideological orientations, and both participants and citizens tend to support liberal spending and taxing principles. Such liberal communal provision principles are particularly strong among public employees, who benefit from the growth of their public bureaucracies.

The level of welfare services provided by local governments is also a political issue, but those who support more welfare are disadvantaged by the structural context of local politics. As Peterson argues, "The pursuit of the city's economic interest . . . makes no allowance for the care of the needy and unfortunate members of the society" because redistributive programs have negative economic effects; "while they supply benefits to those least needed by the local economy, they require taxation on those who are most needed."[23] Thus, when one community has more generous welfare policies than do other communities, it attracts persons who contribute little to the economy, and it repels individuals and businesses that contribute the most. Hence, there is usually less support for the communal provision of welfare services than of public services.

Despite this structural bias against public welfare at the local level, the political cultures of communities can provide significant support for the communal provision of welfare. Helping the needy and unfortunate makes "a plausible claim for public support"[24] — after all, people can hold conceptions of justice that prompt them to forgo some economic gains and make some economic sacrifices on behalf of "the least-advantaged" members of the communities.[25] Because the American national government — which has far greater welfare responsibilities than do local governments[26] — "maintains one of the shabbier systems of communal provision in the Western world,"[27] local communities may seek to surpass national welfare standards. Especially during periods of retrenchment of welfare programs at the national and state levels, citizens may want their local governments to increase welfare services.

When residents reject public-welfare principles, they do not necessarily reject making provisions for the needy; instead, they often adopt the principle of voluntary giving. They want private organizations such as the United Fund to seek voluntary contributions and disperse them to agencies helping the poor. But private giving to private organizations does not constitute communal provision. Public welfare, provided by public funds, is based on a shared understanding among members of a community about the goods that people need in order to sustain membership in the community. Once these needs are recognized and public-welfare programs are developed, individuals have welfare rights to those goods that are communally provided. When private charitable organizations provide for needs, such welfare rights are absent.

To measure the distribution of support for principles regarding public welfare in Lawrence, participants and citizens were asked whether "city government should allocate more funds to social service agencies — to provide more benefits and services to the needy — even if taxes must be raised," or whether "social services should be supported by private contributions, with local government reducing its allocations for social welfare purposes." Contrasting principles regarding the local provision of public welfare are the strongest predictors of urban ideological orientations among citizens and participants. As shown in Table 4.1 under Public Welfare, there is significantly more support in Lawrence for liberal public-welfare principles than for the conservative emphasis on providing for the needy through private charity. However, there is little consensus in Lawrence about public welfare; public-welfare principles are only slightly more prevalent than "private-giving" ones. Interestingly, community notables, who are perhaps most concerned about the adverse consequences of welfare for economic growth, expressed little enthusiasm for public welfare.

Of course, communal provisions of services and welfare must be paid for through taxation, and communities can vary in the types of tax principles that are widely supported. The most divisive tax principles in local politics seem to deal with the question of tax incidence: Who pays? Under the benefits-received principle—which is most closely approximated by user charges—residents are taxed in proportion to the services they consume. Thus, in Lawrence and in many other communities, "benefit districts" are created, and residents of these districts are taxed for the local streets and sewers that they use. The benefits-received tax principle is designed to make payment for public services conform as closely as possible to market principles. A strict application of the benefits-received principle would greatly limit the communal provision of welfare, since welfare is, of course, provided without payment. Under the ability-to-pay principle, residents are taxed progressively; higher-income residents pay higher percentages of their incomes in taxes than do lower-income people. Although national governments tend to respond to ability-to-pay principles and adopt some progressive tax policies, local governments rely more on the benefits-received principle. According to Peterson, local communities adopt regressive tax politics for the same reason that they avoid the provision of welfare services. The benefits-received principle is usually preferred because it is not redistributive and thus attracts those contributing most to the local economy.[28]

To estimate the distribution of support for alternative tax principles in Lawrence, respondents were asked whether they thought that "in local government, residents should be taxed mainly on the principle of ability-to-pay, as when higher-income persons pay proportionately higher taxes," or that "residents should be taxed mainly on the principle of equal taxes for equal services, as when residents are charged user fees for services they use." Progressive ability-to-pay tax principles are associated with urban liberalism, but views about appropriate distributions of tax burdens are not a major determinant of ideological orientations. The data in Table 4.1 under Tax Burden show that in Lawrence the conservative view that taxes should be based on benefits received is dominant over liberal ability-to-pay principles.

Thus, Lawrence's political culture provides little consensus about the communal provision of goods and services. Providing more public services and public welfare, and paying for these provisions through progressive tax measures are liberal principles. Although participants in Lawrence tend to see themselves as liberals, their liberalism is most evident in their espousal of the principle of providing more public services. Participants are more ambivalent about the provision of welfare, and they tend to reject progressive tax measures as a means of paying for communal goods and services. Among inactive citizens there is even less clarity about communal provision principles: support for liberal and conservative values is fairly evenly split among the public as a whole. How specific issues involving communal provision principles are resolved in such a context is the subject of Chapter 9.

## MINIMIZE THE LEGISLATION OF MORALITY

If all communities are, in principle, welfare states, they are also, in principle, agents of social control. When people join communities for the sake of communal provision, they also join for the sake of common lives. As conservatives have long argued, communities exist for the purpose of social bonding and seek to achieve common understandings about values, appropriate social conduct, and morality.[29] Civil libertarians may wish to deny the function of communities in exercising social control and in proscribing certain types of individual conduct; indeed, our liberal constitutional traditions prohibit social control in certain areas. However, communities without some common understanding about appropriate social conduct and morality are unlikely to be "communities of character,"[30] and the residents of such communities are unlikely to share a social bond.

The issue of social control within a community is not, then, whether there is to be social control, but instead how much social control there should be?[31] On this question the political cultures of communities can differ. Some communities may celebrate social diversity, granting individuals great latitude to adopt their chosen life-styles, behaviors, and moral codes. In contrast, the citizens of other communities may prefer clear codes of conduct and seek public policies that enforce these moral and behavioral codes.

In general, social-control policies are more extensive at the local than national level. National communities are highly pluralistic in that they encompass many diverse life-styles and moral values. Thus, at the national level, it is difficult for factions to impose their moral values on others. The turmoil accompanying the prohibition era suggests that extensive social controls are best left to local communities.

The residents of local communities are, of course, bound by the social-control policies of central governments, but they can impose on themselves greater control if they wish. In smaller, more homogeneous, more parochial communities, social-control principles may be particularly prominent. In contrast, larger, more heterogeneous, more cosmopolitan communities take on the social pluralism of the nation. In such communities, there is likely to be little consensus about what constitutes public morality, and there is greater tolerance for diverse life-styles.

To measure attitudes about social control in Lawrence, political participants and citizens were asked to choose between John Stuart Mill's classic liberal formulation ("local government should not legislate individual behaviors that don't harm others") and the more conservative position, "local government should enact and enforce laws upholding the moral standards of the majority in the community". As shown in Table 4.1 under Social Liberty, liberals are particularly supportive of individual choice, and conservatives tend to support the regulation of morality. These contrasting principles are key determinants of urban ideology. Moreover, there is significantly more support for the liberal principle of maximizing individual choice in Lawrence than for regulating morality.

Citizens tend to support individual-choice principles, but social-control principles are more widely held by citizens than by elites. Public officials and notables are especially skeptical of legislating morality; they may view extensive social controls as costly ventures that divert community resources away from economic-growth projects and public services. Not only does it cost money to police "victimless crimes," but the local economy can suffer as firms shy away from locating in parochial communities that have more extensive social controls.

Although liberal individual-choice principles predominate in Lawrence, an open question remains as to whether specific issues embodying such principles will be resolved in a way that is consistent with individual-choice principles. While such principles help frame the debate of specific regulatory issues, they may not determine the outcome, as suggested in Chapter 8.

## RUN THE CITY LIKE A BUSINESS

Policy outcomes concerning community growth, the provision of communal goods, and social control are affected by the criteria employed by policymakers when resolving issues. Should local governments stress "political" or "economic" concerns when they resolve issues?

When governments resolve issues, they exercise sovereignty and are by definition engaged in "politics," for a critical aspect of politics is the making of authoritative decisions on issues that affect broad publics within a community. Aristotle understood this aspect of politics to be an ennobling activity, as the exercise of political power helps those involved in community decision making to develop their moral capacities. Through politics, members of the community make decisions about their common goals and seek fair ways of resolving conflict and allocating the benefits and burdens of community life.

In contemporary American communities, however, politics is not always understood in this way. Many citizens equate politics with favoritism, corruption, empty promises, the abandonment of principle, and so forth. Indeed, the corrupt nature of local politics in the era of political machines spawned the widespread view that city governments ought to be businesslike rather than political organizations. From this point of view, state governments incorporate local governments to provide certain goods and services to local communities, just as state governments incorporate businesses to produce and market private goods. In providing such communal goods as police and fire protection, roads, and education, local governments should adopt good business practices—they should be effective, economical, and efficient. The assumption that there exists within the community a broad consensus about the goals or purposes of local government makes this view plausible. For example, if there is agreement that local governments are to promote economic growth, then the job of government is to achieve such growth as effectively and efficiently as possible. If there is agreement that local governments are to maintain existing services, then the job of government is to provide such services as economically as possible.

Nevertheless, the absence of consensus about community goals and purposes encourages the view that local governments are inevitably political. Disagreements about the desirability of projects designed to enhance economic growth, the need to provide more communal goods, or the requirements of social control lead some people to recognize that local governments cannot escape their political functions. Recognizing the inevitability of local political conflict leads some people to believe that local governments should maximize such political values as providing open forums for the expression of all viewpoints and satisfying as many interests as possible when making policy decisions.

In local communities generally, support for the priority of economic criteria should be especially strong. Since the turn of the century, the progressive ideology that local governments are like businesses has become deeply entrenched, especially in smaller cities. Nevertheless, during the past twenty years, an era of "postreformism" has emerged, enhancing support for such political values as openness in decision making and citizen involvement.[32] Since many cities have become battlegrounds on social and economic issues, participants and citizens may increasingly recognize the political character of local governments.

To measure the distribution of views in Lawrence about these competing principles, people were asked to choose between two contrasting images of local government and the central decision-making criterion associated with each image of government. According to the more liberal image, local government is concerned with politics. Conflict between different groups is inevitable whenever community projects are proposed. The role of government is to resolve differences of opinion openly and fairly. According to the more conservative image, local government is like a business; it should provide good services such as schools, roads, and fire protection as inexpensively and efficiently as possible. As shown in Table 4.1 under Image of Government, conservatives tend to favor economic criteria, and liberals political ones. Furthermore, local government is generally seen as a business activity rather than as a political activity, especially by community notables.[33]

## GIVE THE PUBLIC INTEREST PRIORITY OVER JUSTICE

Another abstract issue that arises in resolving political decisions involves different conceptions of " the public interest" and/or "justice." Aggregative concerns about "the public interest" are foremost in the minds of some participants who want issues to be resolved in ways that benefit the community as a whole. To employ a common image, they want the pie of human values to increase in size. Utilitarians provided a somewhat more precise conception of this decision-making principle when they suggested that public policies were good when they provided maximum pleasure and minimal pain for the sum of all individuals in a community. Policy analysts often invoke this sort of criterion through cost-benefit analysis; policies that provide maximum benefit for minimal cost are the desired solutions to political issues. Of course, it is often difficult to be certain about the full range of benefits and burdens that flow from policy decisions, thus making utilitarian and cost-benefit analysis problematic. Nevertheless, the ideal that policy choices should conform to the aggregate good — understood loosely as the "greater good for the greater number" — still commands the allegiance of many participants in community politics and is a powerful argument employed on behalf of many policy proposals.

Aggregative concerns, however, are not universally seen as the most important criteria in policymaking; distributive concerns about "justice" are sometimes of greater importance to various participants. In short, some people are more concerned about how the pie of human values is sliced than they are about its total size. In his seminal book, *A Theory of Justice,* John Rawls provides a critique and alternative to utilitarianism.[34] The problem is that utilitarianism is indifferent to the distribution of benefits and burdens that emerge from policy decisions. When only utilitarian principles are employed, great burdens on some individuals can be justified if they are outweighed by the greater benefits that accrue to others. For example, a policy proposal for a new expressway may satisfy utilitarian criteria by providing more benefits than costs for most individuals in a community, but the expressway may impose extreme hardships on residents of neighborhoods in the path of the new road. According to Rawls, communities committed to justice as their highest principle will "take seriously the plurality and distinctness of individuals,"[35] for people would not voluntarily consent to be members of communities where their interests were sacrificed for the greater good of others.

As an alternative to utilitarian principles, Rawls developed a specific distributive alternative; he argued that "the least-advantaged" individuals in the community—defined as those having relatively few economic resources—should be given special consideration in the political process. For Rawls, the criterion to be used in resolving issues is "What does an outcome do for the poor?" rather than "What does an outcome do for the community as a whole?" While Rawls provides a compelling argument for this distributive criterion, it is not the only distributive criterion that can be posed as an alternative to the aggregative concerns of utilitarianism. For example, some have argued for "equity" as a distributive principle: policymakers should distribute policy benefits and burdens in accordance to the (tax) contributions that people make to the community.[36] Others have suggested "unpatterned inequalities" as a distributive principle.[37] Because policy decisions inevitably benefit and burden some more than others, justice may entail that these distributions not be cumulative so that some people usually benefit and others usually suffer. Where inequalities are "unpatterned" or "unbiased," benefits and burdens get evened out over various policy areas and over time.

Although communities can differ in the distributive principles that dominate their culture, the more general question that can be asked is whether the citizens of a community believe *any* distributive principle is more important than aggregative concerns. In local communities, aggregative principles are likely to be more widespread than are distributive ones, especially among bureaucrats and notables. Public administrators may believe that it is their job to serve the community as a whole and that the overall good of the community must take priority over the concerns of smaller groups of individuals. Notables may believe in pursuing those projects that contribute most to the economic and social life of the community, and they are likely to have a low opinion of the special interests that impede such projects. Community pride and a desire to win the competition with other cities for economic and cultural resources means giving priority to utilitarian concerns for most citizens. In such a context, distributive principles may seem unimportant.

To measure the distribution of views in Lawrence regarding this political concept, people were asked to choose between utilitarian principles ("If a project is generally beneficial for the community as a whole or for most citizens in the community, officials should approve and promote that project even if a few individuals are hurt by it") and a highly general distributive principle ("If a project poses *significant* burdens on specific individuals in the community, it should be abandoned even if most citizens would benefit from it").[38] In Lawrence, the utilitarian conception of justice is very strong. As seen in Table 4.1 under Conception of Justice, the principle that policy decisions should benefit the community as a whole is more strongly held, especially by bureaucrats and notables, than is the principle that policy decisions should not harm specific individuals. Because this notion is widely held by both self-defined liberals and conservatives, it is not significantly associated with urban ideological orientations.[39]


## LET THE VOTERS DECIDE

A final abstract issue to be analyzed as it impinges on the resolution of concrete issues concerns the openness of the decision-making process to citizen participation. The formal players in the game of community politics are elected officials and voters. Constitutions provide for voters to elect representatives and decide certain issues by referenda, but elected representatives are empowered to decide most issues. Despite these formal provisions, the behavioral relationship between voters and elected representatives is a matter of great controversy because people hold diverse principles about the nature of this relationship.

For modern Jeffersonians, elected representatives are agents of citizens. This view begins with the assertion that representatives should listen to the views of their constituents and be persuaded by their most convincing arguments. Stronger conceptions of citizenship in democratic societies include the notion that representatives should be "instructed delegates" acting as if "constituents were acting themselves"[40]; indeed, on important issues, representatives are asked to relinquish their policymaking power and permit voters to decide directly, through referenda.

For modern Hamiltonians or Burkeans, however, the relationship between elected officials and voters is much more tilted in favor of representatives, who are expected to use their independent judgment. From this perspective, elected officials who have the courage of their convictions and withstand the pressures of popular opinion are hailed as statesmen, a bit more noble than the mere politicians who cower when confronted by aroused constituents.

One might think that Jeffersonian principles are strong in local government. When the scale of communities is small and City Hall is nearby, residents can still be citizens, as there are opportunities for involvement and influence. Despite such opportunities, however, most "citizens are too distracted by nonpolitical matters" to have much interest in local government;[41] prompting them to hold Hamiltonian principles, which assert that their elected officials should make important decisions.

Nevertheless, communities can vary in their allegiance to citizen-participation principles. In communities with moralistic cultures, such as Lawrence, politics is "a matter of concern for every citizen" and it is "the duty of every citizen to participate in political affairs."[42] While citizens in such communities may have little interest in routine matters, they may be reluctant to delegate their authority to representatives on major community issues. However, even in moralistic cultures, participants may be less likely than citizens to hold Jeffersonian principles. Elected officials may believe that their election authorizes them to make key decisions. Bureaucrats and notables may think that their proposals will receive a more favorable hearing from elected officials with whom they have continuing access than from the unpredictable public.

To assess the political culture of Lawrence regarding the desirability of widespread citizen participation in the resolution of policy issues, political participants and citizens were asked whether they believed that "In local government, it is usually best to let decisions on major community issues be made by voters" or that "It is generally best to let decisions on major community projects be made by elected officials." As shown in the last section of Table 4.1, support for voter participation is only weakly linked to ideological orientations. Most citizens — regardless of ideology — believe that voters should be empowered to decide major issues. Most participants — particularly representatives, bueaucrats, and notables — believe that elected officials should exercise decision-making authority.

Thus, participants and citizens have significantly different dominant principles on the issue of the desirability of voter participation. On all the other issues, their dominant principles were the same. This raises the important question of whether the principles of participants or citizens should prevail with regard to this issue. Because the political culture of a community refers to the attitudes widely held throughout the community (rather than to the views of participants only), public opinion calling for more participation is adopted here as the benchmark for assessing whether concrete issues are resolved in ways that correspond to dominant principles in the community. When principles about the democratic process and the balance of power between representatives and voters are at stake in concrete issues, Lawrence's political culture suggests that such issues should be resolved in ways congruent with citizens' concerns for more public involvement.

## LOCAL POLITICAL CULTURES

Perhaps the most important reason for analyzing the political cultures of communities is to determine the principles widely held within particular communities and thus to permit examination of whether policy decisions reflect dominant principles. Because of the diversity of views within pluralist communities, the number of principles within a culture that are relevant to policy decisions doubtless exceeds those under consideration here.[43] However, the conceptions of political culture that dominate the social-science literature typically consider only a few dominant principles.[44] For example, Clark and Ferguson considered two abstract issues — whether a community pursues extensive public services and whether it pursues extensive social control — to create a typology defining four types of political culture.[45] If one wanted to consider an additional abstract evaluative issue, the number of cultures in the typology would, of course, double. Assuming some principle dominates its competing principle on each of the nine issues considered here, there are 512 possible combinations of dominant principles, yielding 512 distinguishable political cultures. Thus, more parsimonious conceptions of political culture that account for a variety of political principles are obviously required.

The terms "liberal" and "conservative" can be usefully employed to define two types of political culture. The core principles that comprise a conservative local culture declare that there should be minimal public services and welfare and that morality should be legislated. To the extent that citizens believe that taxes should be based on the benefits-received principle, property rights should be protected, and policy decisions should stress economic criteria, the political culture can also be defined as relatively conservative.

The core principles that comprise a liberal political culture declare that there should be more extensive public services and welfare and that social control should be minimized. To the extent that citizens believe that taxes should be based on the ability-to-pay principle, land use should be regulated, and policy decisions should stress political criteria, the political culture can be defined as relatively liberal.

Perhaps cultures that adhere to dominant pro-growth principles, stress aggregative conceptions of justice, and de-emphasize citizen participation can be defined as relatively conservative. Perhaps cultures having dominant principles that de-emphasize economic growth, stress distributive conceptions of justice, and emphasize citizen participation are relatively liberal.[46] However, most liberals support economic growth and aggregative conceptions of justice, and most conservative citizens support citizen participation — at least in Lawrence. Thus, economic-growth principles seem to transcend conservative and liberal urban ideologies. The ideas that justice requires giving special consideration to those most harmed by public policies and that democracy requires public referenda on major issues may be called protest principles, and both liberals and conservatives may emphasize these principles.

Most American communities are probably characterized by the dominance of economic-growth principles and some mixture of liberal, conservative, and protest principles. The political culture of Lawrence is liberal in its support of more public services and welfare, individual choice, and neighborhood protection, but it is conservative in its allegiance to benefits-received tax principles and the importance of economic criteria. In Lawrence, the protest principle of citizen participation is dominant, but distributive concerns about justice are not. Perhaps most significantly, there is widespread support for economic-growth principles. If policies reflect these dominant principles when they are relevant to concrete issues, principle-policy congruence is achieved.

## SUMMARY: THE PLURALITY OF PRINCIPLES

The resolution of community issues cannot be understood or evaluated through the application of one set of political principles. As Walzer says, "The principles of justice are themselves pluralistic in form."[47] In pluralist communities, citizens and participants have competing principles about the desirability of certain kinds of public policies and policymaking processes. Though no principle may command universal support, certain principles may be dominant in a particular community. Such dominant principles should be reflected in the resolution of concrete issues.

Different principles may be dominant among different types of people in communities. For example, public-involvement principles may be strongly held by citizens, and representative-discretion principles may be dominant among participants. In democratic communities, we can make a strong case for issues to be resolved in ways that reflect the principles of citizens, rather than those of participants, but the inattention of the public to local issues and the ambiguity of public support for some principles suggest that the principles of various types of participants will dominate certain policy decisions. For example, the pro-growth principles of notables may dominate the resolution of developmental issues, and the respresentative-discretion principles of elected officials may dominate issues of organization and leadership. If, on the one hand, citizens and participants share the pro-growth principles of notables, it is the principles and not the notables that dominate economic-development policy. On the other hand, if citizens reject the representative-discretion principles of participants, citizens may believe that they are being dominated, not by political principles with which they disagree, but by the participants holding these principles.

Concrete issues may embody several principles. Some people will argue that a concrete issue really concerns certain principles, but other people will argue that the issue concerns other principles. The art of politics involves persuading other persons to define concrete issues in terms of popular principles.[48] For example, proponents of the parking lot might argue that the proposal was an economic-growth issue, because most citizens in Lawrence approve of economic growth in principle. In contrast, opponents of the parking lot might argue that the proposal was a citizen-participation issue, because most citizens approve in principle of more effective participation by citizens. If the principle of citizen participation is seen as more relevant than the principle of economic growth, the issue may be resolved in ways sought by parking lot opponents.

The dominant principles relevant to concrete issues often provide crosscutting criteria and thus inconclusive guidance to policymakers concerning the resolution of issues. On the parking lot issue, should policymakers ignore concerns about citizen participation and respond to the dominant desire to promote economic growth? Or should they give greater weight to cultural values concerning citizen participation than to those concerning economic growth? The crosscutting nature of dominant relevant principles makes particular principles indeterminant as criteria for resolving concrete issues. Nevertheless, the political culture is not thereby irrelevant to the resolution of issues. In well-functioning pluralist communities, policies should perhaps be most congruent with principles that are most relevant to issues and most consensually held in the community.

These notions about the plurality of principles are illustrated and developed in the following six chapters that describe the twenty-nine issues in the Lawrence study. To facilitate this discussion, the issues are grouped according to principles that most strongly underlie them. Three issues (WARDS, MAYOR, and MANAGER) dealing centrally with democratic-process principles are considered first in Chapter 5, as discussion of these issues helps to characterize the political setting affecting the resolution of other issues. Then, six relatively pure economic-growth issues (AIRPORT, N2ST, RAIL, RESEARCH, IRB and SIGNS) are considered in Chapter 6. The community's dominant economic-growth and neighborhood-protection principles seem to have collided on four issues in the sample; these issues (OREAD, EAST, BLUFFS, and CATH) are discussed in Chapter 7. Four issues (ENVIR, DRUG, TRIBES, and BIRTH) seemed to embody, at least in part, concerns about individual-choice and social-control principles; they are discussed in Chapter 8. Chapter nine discusses four issues (STORM, CLOSE, LIFELINE, and SOCIAL) that illustrate the application of principles dealing with the communal provision of services and welfare, and three issues (VIDEO, INTANGIBLES, and REAPPRAISE) that involve tax-distribution principles. The most visible and controversial issues in the community during the period of this study have concerned downtown redevelopment and a cluster of principles dealing with economic growth, protection of the existing downtown, and governmental spending to facilitate building an enclosed mall downtown; these issues (CORNFIELD, BUNKER, PARK, SIZELER, and TOWNCENTER) are discussed in Chapter 10. Finally, Chapter 11 summarizes the contribution that political principles make to the policy process.

# 5

# Challenging Existing
# Institutions and Leadership

As a legacy of the Progressive movement during the first half of this century, most American communities (except large central cities) have adopted major features of "reformed" governmental institutions that centralize executive leadership in the office of professional city managers who are accountable to city council members who are, in turn, accountable to voters through nonpartisan, at-large elections. Lawrence adopted a council-manager plan in 1950; since then, legislative power in Lawrence has resided among five city commissioners[1] who are elected at large, by nonpartisan ballots. Executive power has been vested in a city manager who holds office at the pleasure of the city commission and controls the administrative personnel of the city, formulates the budget, and makes policy recommendations.

In Lawrence, reformed institutions were directly challenged in 1977, when a referendum was held on a proposal to abolish the council-manager plan,[2] and in 1982, when an effort was mounted to fire the city manager. The method of choosing a mayor to head the city commission was an issue between 1980 and 1985, when attempts were made to strengthen the mayoral position as well as to provide more control over who presides as mayor. The descriptions of these three issues in this chapter indicate some of the cleavages that emerged on each issue (to facilitate analyses of complex equality), the distribution of support among various types of actors for each policy outcome (to facilitate analysis of responsible representation), and the principles that are relevant to each issue (to facilitate analysis of principle-policy congruence).

Because of the methodological complexity of determining principle-policy congruence, particular emphasis is devoted to describing the principles that are at stake in each issue. Three types of information must be marshalled to assess principle-policy congruence on such concrete issues. First, the dominant principles within the political culture must be determined—a task that was accomplished in Chapter 4. Second, the principles relevant to concrete issues must be ascertained. Third, policy outcomes must be related to those principles that are dominant in a local culture and are relevant to concrete issues. Before turning to a discussion of the wards, mayor, and manager issues, we must discusss these second and third methodological tasks further.

## ASSESSING PRINCIPLE-POLICY CONGRUENCE

To determine the principles that are relevant to particular concrete issues, I have analyzed two kinds of information. First I examine the arguments that participants presented either publicly or in interviews on behalf of their positions. As I discuss the twenty-nine issues in the sample, I present some of the more principled arguments.[3] Second, and more importantly, I assess the relevance of particular principles to specific issues by examining (1) the relationships between the principles of *participants* and their positions on issues and (2) the relationships between the principles of *citizens* and their positions on issues. A pair of contrasting principles is considered relevant to an issue if there is a significant standardized regression coefficient between principles and preferences on an issue for either participants or citizens. (See the Appendix for details about this procedure, and see Table A for the relevant statistics relating political principles to preferences for each of the twenty-nine issues in this study.)

If a pair of contrasting principles is found to be relevant to an issue, the question then arises as to whether the issue was resolved in a way that is consistent with the relevant principles that are dominant in the community. Principle-policy congruence occurs when a policy outcome is more responsive to the preferences of those participants (or citizens) whose relevant principles are dominant in the local culture (as revealed in Table 4.1) than to the preferences of those participants (or citizens) whose relevant principles are subordinate in the culture. Principle-policy incongruence occurs when a policy outcome reflects the preferences of those actors whose principles are subordinate in the culture to the alternative principles of their opponents.

Table 5.1 summarizes principle-policy congruence for the three issues (WARDS, MAYOR, MANAGER) described in this chapter. The first column indicates the concrete issues under consideration. The next nine columns indicate whether the outcomes of these concrete issues were consistent with the nine dominant principles described in Table 4.1. Thus, the data in the GROW column indicate if outcomes on specific issues were consistent with dominant pro-growth principles; the data in the NEIGH column indicate if outcomes on issues were consistent with dominant neighborhood-protection principles, and so forth. Instances of principle-policy congruence are signified by a "+" in the appropriate cell; instances of principle-policy incongruence are signified by a "−." Brackets indicate instances where participants presented different

Table 5.1    Principle-Policy Congruence on Three Issues of Structure and Leadership

| Issues | Principles | | | | | | | | |
|---|---|---|---|---|---|---|---|---|---|
| | GROW | NEIGH | SERV | WELF | USETAX | LIB | ECON | AGG | DEM |
| Create WARDS and strengthen the mayor | [+] | [−] | NR | NR | NR | NR | + | [+] | − |
| Open commission elections of the MAYOR | [+] | NR | NR | NR | NR | NR | NR | NR | − |
| Fire the city MANAGER | + | [−] | − | − | NR | NR | [+] | + | − |

NR : Alternative principles not relevant to issue.
 + : Outcome consistent with dominant principle, as specified in heading.
 − : Outcome inconsistent with dominant principle.
 [ ] : Alternative principles were articulated in interviews, but such principles were not significantly an directly related to the policy preferences of participants or citizens.

principles on issues but where both participants and citizens failed to relate significantly these principles to their policy positions, thus reducing the relevancy of these principles to the concrete issue under investigation. If there are no significant regression coefficients between principles and preferences, but competing principles were articulated, a "[+]" is used to indicate that the outcome was consistent with the positions of those participants who articulated dominant cultural principles, and a "[−]" is used to indicate that the outcome was instead consistent with the position of those participants who articulated principles subordinate in the local culture. If there are no significant standardized regression coefficients between principles and preferences on an issue for either participants or citizens, and if these principles were not articulated, an "NR" is placed in the cell to indicate the irrelevancy of such principles.

## MAINTAINING THE RULES OF REFORMISM: THE REFERENDUM TO CREATE WARDS AND STRENGTHEN THE MAYOR

In early 1977, neighborhood and student activists collected enough signatures on a petition to place a referendum question regarding the form of government on the ballot for the April 1977 election. Their petition called for (a) a full-time mayor having extensive formal powers (such as the ability to veto ordinances) to be directly elected by the voters, and (b) an eight-member city council composed of two representatives from each of four wards. Their plan permitted employing a professional manager to oversee the administration of the city, but the stature of the manager would be much reduced, as he or she would serve as the administrative assistant to the mayor.

Most of the debate regarding this issue concerned principles regarding the desirability of more citizen involvement and the criteria to be used in resolving issues.[4] Supporters of the WARDS proposal — primarily younger people who lived in lower-income neighborhoods and who identified themselves as liberals — articulated public-involvement principles. They argued that citizen participation, particularly through elections, would be enhanced because of the visibility of the mayoral elections and because the creation of wards would stimulate grassroots organization and activity. Proponents of the council-manager system — mostly older persons who lived in middle- and upper-income neighborhoods and who identified themselves as conservatives — responded in two ways to these arguments. First, they refuted the argument that the mayor-council plan would enhance citizen participation. According to Commissioner Barkley Clark, "Any argument that you'll get more participation with the mayor-council form just doesn't jibe with the facts."[5] Clark presented statistics of abysmally low voter turnout rates in the four Kansas communities having the mayor-council form. Second, proponents claimed that the council-manager system provided for "stronger, more qualified leadership" than would the proposed change. However, they remained silent on the question of whether such leaders would exercise independent judgment in making policy decisions rather than acting as instructed agents of the public. Given the subordinance of Burkean principles to Jeffersonian ones among Lawrence citizens, the silence was probably prudent. As shown in Table A in the appendix, participant allegiance to public-involvement principles (DEMO) was positively related to support for the WARDS proposal ($B_p$ = .39); among citizens, such principles were also significantly (though more weakly) related to their preferences about the form of government ($B_c$ = .16). Thus, dominant cultural norms calling for more public involvement in the policy process were relevant to the WARDS issue.

Principles about appropriate policymaking criteria were also relevant to the WARDS proposal. Opponents of wards — especially the sitting representatives, City Manager Watson and his staff, and community notables — argued that the existing council-manager system reduced political conflict and enhanced planning, professionalism, and economic efficiency. They stressed the logical connection between at-large representation and achieving policies reflecting the utilitarian criterion of benefiting the community as a whole. In contrast, proponents of wards argued that the current system gave undue emphasis to economic and utilitarian criteria. They argued that the policy recommendations of the city manager were based almost solely on economic and business concerns, as the manager was too insulated from legitimate political concerns, especially those coming from neighborhood and working-class people. A directly elected mayor, they argued, would serve as a useful antidote, since electoral accountability would provide incentives for the mayor to be more attentive to political opposition. It was also suggested that the creation of wards would give greater importance to distributive criteria in the resolution of issues; according to Mark Kaplan, a leader of Citizens for Mayor-Council Government, wards "would protect parochial interests"[6] in the policy process. As shown in Table A, participants whose principles emphasized the importance of ECONOMic criteria tended to oppose the WARDS proposal ($B_p$ = − .35), though they did not significantly relate their conceptions of justice (AGG) to the issue. Thus, by the procedures adopted in this study for determining the relevancy of various principles to concrete issues, dominant community values emphasizing the importance of economic criteria are relevant to the WARDS issue, but dominant utilitarian principles are not.

The referendum resulted in 70 percent of the voters rejecting the WARDS proposal. Given the distribution of support for wards among participants, this outcome was a victory for Country Clubbers, Seniors, Hometowners, Conservatives, and Managerialists and a loss for their counterparts (Cellar Dwellers, Rookies, Visitors, Liberals, and Politicos).[7] Because most representatives, bureaucrats, notables, mobilizers, and individual activists shared the dominant views of citizens on the issue, Level 10 (consensus) on the scale of responsible representation presented in Chapter 2 was achieved.

Table 5.1 shows the principles relevant to this issue and whether rejection of the WARDS proposal was consistent with dominant principles in the community. Most Lawrence citizens believe that economic criteria are more important than are political ones; by rejecting WARDS, they achieved an outcome consistent with their preference for ECONOMic criteria. Lawrence citizens also hold citizen participation principles, however, and they related such principles to the wards issue; by rejecting WARDS, they produced a result that was inconsistent with their widespread Jeffersonian principles (DEMO). A survey conducted in the immediate aftermath of the 1977 election revealed that most people considered the manager form of government efficient and the mayor form responsive to citizen concerns, but ultimately citizen concerns about efficiency outweighed those about participation and responsiveness.

It is debatable whether people must choose between economic and participatory concerns when resolving form-of-government issues. Separate questions regarding various aspects of governmental structure can be presented to voters, as was done in surveys conducted in 1977, 1984, and 1986. As shown in Table 5.2, in each survey, voters registered strong support for the city manager component of the council-manager plan, but they also showed support for a directly elected mayor and for the creation of wards. Because the community strongly wants its local government run on an efficient businesslike basis, it opposes proposals that reduce the professional manage-

Table 5.2    Citizen Support for Various Governmental and Electoral Structures (in percentages)

| Structure | 1977 | 1984 | 1986 |
|---|---|---|---|
| Retaining a city manager | 67 | 70[a] | 59[a] |
| Having a popularly elected full-time mayor | 55 | 71 | 54[b] |
| Creating wards | 55[c] | 75 | 54[b] |
| Having partisan ballots | 16 | 37 | — |

[a]While the 1977 survey measured support for the office of the city manager, the 1984 and 1986 surveys measured support for the incumbent city manager.

[b]The 1986 survey asked respondents a single question, mirroring the 1977 referendum question about their support for *both* a popularly elected, full-time mayor and the creation of wards.

[c]Includes support for wards only (34%) and for a mixture of wards and at-large representation (21%).

ment component of local government, but because the community also wants more citizen involvement, it supports a directly elected mayor and wards.

Given the dominant principles about businesslike efficiency and democratic involvement in the community, principle-policy congruence might be furthered by modifying the community's form of government to include these more politicized governmental institutions, as well as by retaining its commitment to city management. Unfortunately, Lawrence has not had the opportunity to adopt such hybrid institutions. Subsequent issues have thus been resolved within institutions that minimize the role of citizen participation while giving priority to economic criteria.

## CHOOSING THE "RIGHT MAN" TO LEAD THE COMMISSION: THE MAYORAL SELECTION ISSUE

In the aftermath of the 1977 referendum, suggestions were occasionally made that the office of mayor could be strengthened by changing the method by which the mayor was selected. By tradition, those commissioners who had received the most and second-most votes during an election rotated into the office of mayor for one-year terms. In 1980 Ed Carter, who was in line to become mayor in a few weeks, proposed that commissioners simply vote for the person they wanted to serve as mayor during the next year. It was argued that this change would permit commissioners to select as their leader the person "most qualified," who "best represented the dominant orientation" on the commission, or who "represented its ideological center." Additionally, this method would allow for the possibility that such a leader could be reelected as mayor, thus providing more continuity and visibility to the office.

There was another consideration underlying Carter's proposal. If the traditional method remained in effect, Marci Francisco would rotate into the mayor's office in 1982. Because of the mayor's role in representing the community in dealings with firms considering moving to Lawrence and because Francisco was not an advocate of growth, several commissioners, as well as various members of the Growth Machine, viewed that eventuality unfavorably.

Although several proponents of the Carter proposal admitted (in interviews for this study) that concerns about economic growth prompted their desire to abandon the traditional method of selecting the mayor, Table A shows that economic-GROWth principles had no significant impact on preferences on the MAYORal selection issue; thus, the relevance of such principles to this issue has not been clearly established.[8] Instead, democratic-process principles seem to have been most relevant to the issue. Opponents of Carter's proposal argued that it would "remove the voters one step" from the policy process. Because the rotation system had given the voters an indirect role in the selection of the mayor, Francisco supporters claimed that her second-place finish in the 1979 election provided a public mandate for her to become mayor in 1982. As shown in Table A, support for the Carter proposal was directly related to principles about DEMOcracy, since those participants supporting more citizen involvement tended to oppose efforts to abandon the traditional rotation system.

As shown in Table 5.1, abandoning the rotation method of selecting the MAYOR was inconsistent with dominant citizen-involvement principles (DEMO). Because there is insufficient evidence that the new method of selecting the mayor was consistent with other dominant cultural principles (such as promoting economic GROWth), principle-policy congruence was not achieved on the issue. Furthermore, abandoning the traditional method of selecting the mayor was a loss for women, Cellar Dwellers, Rookies, Liberals, and other interests who frequently lost to their counterparts on community issues, thus contributing to increased simple inequalities of responsiveness to various segments of the community.[9] Nevertheless, Level 8 (majority will) of responsible representation was attained on the issue; there was little public opposition to the desire of most commissioners to change the method of selecting their leader.[10]


FIRING THE MANAGER:
THE BUFORD WATSON ISSUE REVISITED

In Chapter 1, I discussed Commissioner Tom Gleason's efforts to fire the city manager. It is necessary here only to evaluate democratic performance on the issue.

Although Buford Watson's detractors alleged various misdeeds, and his supporters stressed his many accomplishments, the controversy was rooted in the question of whether the principles that Watson both embodied and symbolized would continue to be reflected in the outcomes of future issues. Principles of the democratic process were foremost in the minds of many people. On the one hand, for those holding Hamiltonian principles, that the art of governing should be delegated to experts, Watson was "a strong leader" and a "seasoned professional." On the other hand, for those holding Jeffersonian principles that citizens should be more involved in the governing process, Watson's style of "turning information the way he wants it to go makes it hard for the public to be heard." As shown in Table A, support for firing the MANAGER was most pronounced among those participants and citizens who championed public-involvement principles (DEMO).

Notions about the appropriate criteria to be used in resolving policy issues were also at stake in the Watson controversy. Watson's political principles gave priority to economic and aggregative criteria, and he was often cited for his managerial skills, his ability to run the city efficiently and economically, and his commitment to projects that benefited the city as a whole, even when certain groups protested against these projects. However, Watson's opponents claimed that his economic and utilitarian principles left him unreceptive to the concerns of the neighborhoods, lower-income people, and minorities. Thus, as shown in Table A, support for the MANAGER was greatest among those persons whose principles gave priority to (ECONOMic concerns and) AGGregative principles of justice.[11]

Also at stake in the Watson controversy were the policy directions of the city; Watson's opponents objected to his policy objectives. Primarily, he was seen as a leader of the Growth Machine, and he pursued its interests in several ways. First, he supported subsidies and tax exemptions for new and expanding businesses. Second, he encouraged the planning department to develop land-use policies that permitted "orderly growth." Finally, he sought to keep tax burdens low, even if certain types of city services had to be limited. Each of these orientations ran afoul of those with different principles. Preservationists argued that Watson should have wrung concessions from developers — "as the price of doing business in Lawrence" — rather than recommending subsidies for them. They also complained that he was antineighborhood; the planning department often urged zoning changes that permitted business and higher-density land uses despite the objections of nearby residents. Others claimed that Watson was hostile to "people programs" and social-service agencies. These concerns were evident in the way people related their principles to their position on Watson. In general, the more people favored economic growth, property rights, lower taxes, and limited provision of welfare, the more they supported Watson. As shown in Table 5.1, ECONOmic-growth, public SERVice, and public-WELFare principles were at stake on the MANAGER issue.

The commission's decision to retain Watson was responsive to those interests that usually prevailed in the resolution of Lawrence issues; men, Country Clubbers, Seniors, and fiscal conservatives were among the winners of the city MANAGER issue. Because most participants and citizens supported Watson, the commission also achieved a high level of responsible representation. However, it is less clear that the outcome achieved the ideal of principle-policy congruence. As shown in Table 5.1, those who supported Watson could claim that his retention was consistent with dominant economic-GROWth and AGGregative principles, but those who opposed Watson would claim that his retention was inconsistent with dominant principles regarding the provision of public SERVices, WELFare, and citizen-involvement (DEMO). Unless one can claim that certain principles are superior to others — for example, that the principle of economic growth should take priority over that of citizen involvement — the Watson issue could not be resolved by any simple reference to those principles that prevailed in the political culture of Lawrence.

## CONCLUSIONS

In Lawrence, issues of structure and leadership have been resolved in ways consistent with dominant principles that local government is like a business and thus ought to give priority to economic efficiency and utilitarian criteria. However, these issues have also been resolved in ways inconsistent with dominant citizen involvement principles. Such resolutions have also reflected economic-growth principles more than other policy principles dominant in Lawrence.

Citizens directly controlled the 1977 referendum on wards, and polls showed that most citizens supported the outcomes of the mayor and manager issues. This suggests that, overall, citizens in Lawrence want local governments to be efficient providers of public services and promoters of orderly growth. Structures and leaders that provide these goods on a routine basis are supported, even if this involves some sacrifice of citizen participation. However, citizens have not thereby abandoned their Jeffersonian principles. On major substantive issues, most citizens want to be consulted, and the failure to provide for adequate citizen participation can lead to strong protests and efforts to overturn the decisions of representatives, as will be shown when considering subsequent political issues.

# 6

# Developing the Local Economy

Although economic growth should occur in capitalist societies without the intervention of government, local officials have discovered that public and private partnerships between local governments and business can stimulate growth.[1] In this chapter we will consider five issues in which local governments were asked to play significant roles in attracting industry to Lawrence.[2] These issues involve efforts to improve the community airport and the road that serves as the gateway to the city, to build a rail-served industrial park and a research park, and to provide industrial revenue bonds to new and expanding businesses.

In addition to promoting growth, local governments also regulate business, sometimes in ways that may curtail growth. Thus, it is also useful to consider here a sixth issue, the regulation of billboards and signs, where the city commission had to balance economic-growth principles with aesthetic concerns. Because economic-growth principles are dominant in Lawrence, it might be expected that these issues would be readily resolved in favor of growth. Though this was sometimes the case, several economic-growth projects encountered considerable protest, and the Growth Machine did not always prevail.

## FROM BUSH LEAGUE TO DOUBLE-A BALL: THE AIRPORT IMPROVEMENT ISSUE

According to Dolph Simons, Jr., the editor of the *Lawrence Journal-World*, Lawrence has suffered from "bush league" airport facilities.[3] In 1973, Lawrence voters rejected issuing $664,000 in general obligation bonds to be used as local funds to capture Federal Aviation Agency (FAA) matching grants for airport improvements. Undeterred, city officials adopted an airport plan in 1975 and during the next twelve years spent almost $5 million on it. Most of this money came from FAA grants, with the city contributing portions of its revenue sharing funds to improve the runways, taxiways, and public access to the airport. A new terminal was financed by a lease-purchase agreement with a private investor, and a new hangar was financed through general obligation bonds. Thus, by 1987, the proponents of improving the airport — primarily the upper class and Country Clubbers — had prevailed.

The dominance of liberal public-service principles in Lawrence might seem to justify the development of a convenient, safe, and attractive airport. Table A shows, however, that neither participants nor citizens significantly related their public-SERVice principles to their position on the AIRPORT issue (primarily because many liberals viewed the airport as a special benefit for a few jet-setters rather than as a public facility of use to most citizens). Thus, Table 6.1 shows that dominant public-service principles are irrelevant to the issue.

Justification for the airport improvements can be found, however, in the prominence of economic-growth principles in Lawrence. According to a spokesman for the Lawrence Chamber of Commerce (LCC), an upgraded airport would benefit Lawrence's economy because "the airport is a factor in attracting new industries and new jobs to the city; we've had a number of industrial prospects that have been unable to land their corporate planes at the airport."[4] Those prospects that were able to land received a miserable first impression of the community from the archaic terminal. Because suppport for airport improvements was significantly linked to economic-GROWth principles among both participants and citizens (see Table A), dominant economic-growth principles were relevant.

Principles regarding the importance of economic criteria and citizen involvement were also relevant. Opponents of the airport have maintained that these improvements were an economically inefficient use of tax dollars. They also argued that the results of the 1973 referendum constituted a public mandate against proceeding with the airport improvements, that the public preferred allocating revenue sharing funds for more pressing community needs, and that the financing of the terminal through the lease-purchase agreement was an "end run" of state statutes requiring a public referendum on public financing of such facilities. In contrast, supporters of the airport improvements have maintained that commissioners had appropriately used their discretion, since one of the main purposes of revenue sharing was to enable city officials to make capital investments that might otherwise be rejected by tax-conscious voters. As shown in Table A, citizen opposition to AIRPORT improvement was enhanced by widespread attachment to principles emphasizing the importance of ECONOMic criteria and citizen participation (DEMO) in resolving major issues.

Table 6.1 shows that principle-policy congruence on the airport improvement issue was achieved with respect to pro-GROWth principles but was denied with respect to ECONOMic criteria and DEMOcratic participation. Although the

Table 6.1   Principle-Policy Congruence on Six Economic-Development Issues

| Issues | Principles | | | | | | | | |
|---|---|---|---|---|---|---|---|---|---|
| | GROW | NEIGH | SERV | WELF | USETAX | LIB | ECON | AGG | DEMO |
| AIRPORT improvement | + | NR | [+] | NR | NR | NR | − | [+] | − |
| North Second Street Improvement (N2ST) | + | NR | + | NR | NR | NR | NR | NR | NR |
| Develop RAIL-served industrial park | − | [+] | NR | NR | NR | NR | NR | − | + |
| Develop RESEARCH park | + | [−] | NR | NR | NR | NR | + | NR | − |
| Nonrestrictive issuance of industrial revenue bonds (IRB) | + | − | NR | NR | NR | NR | NR | + | NR |
| Regulation of billboards and SIGNS | [−] | + | + | NR | NR | NR | NR | + | NR |

NR : Alternative principles not relevant to issue.
 + : Outcome consistent with dominant principle, as specified in heading.
 − : Outcome inconsistent with dominant principle.
[ ] : Alternative principles were articulated in interviews, but such principles were not significantly and directly related to the policy preferences of participants or citizens.

conflicting guidance provided by dominant relevant principles resulted in limited principle-policy congruence, policymakers fared well on another important democratic ideal. Because most participants and citizens supported the commission's policies, a high level of responsible representation was achieved.

## MAKING A GOOD FIRST IMPRESSION: NORTH SECOND STREET IMPROVEMENTS

According to Gary Toebben, president of the LCC, "first impressions" are vital for attracting new commerce to the community, and Lawrence has suffered because North Second Street, the main entrance to Lawrence from the airport and for westbound traffic on I-70, was a "visual gutter."[5] In 1979, the Chamber of Commerce formed the North Second Street Task Force to consider ways of improving the area, and the city employed a local architectural firm to make policy recommendations.

    These efforts were initially met with apprehension. Small-businessmen along North Second Street were concerned that they might be required to bear the

costs of new property regulations or be assessed for sidewalks and other improvements on their rights-of-way. Neighborhood activists feared that the costs
of public improvements along the thoroughfare would be financed from federal
Community Development Block Grant (CDBG) funds; in their view, such
funds should be allocated to improve low-income neighborhoods, not a business district. Opposition faded, however, as residents were assured that most
improvements could be funded with state and federal grants and that private
improvements would be encouraged with the carrot of low-interest loans rather
than with the stick of property regulations or special assessments.

By 1985, North Second Street had a new asphalt overlay, the curbs and
gutters were repaired, the rights-of-way were landscaped, drainage in the area
was improved, some businesses made aesthetic improvements, and a few
new developments were built. Most proponents of improving the area were
"moderately satisfied" with the gains that were made, and there was little
dissatisfaction.

As shown in Table 6.1, only economic-GROwth principles seemed to be at
stake on the North Second Street (N2ST) issue. The limited scope of the project permitted city officials to act in ways consistent with dominant progrowth
principles in the community without involving other conflicting principles.
By sprucing up the appearance of "the front door to the community," the
issue was resolved consensually, providing a modest victory for the Growth
Machine.

## SEARCHING FOR THE RIGHT SITE:
## THE RAIL-SERVED INDUSTRIAL PARK ISSUE

In 1967, the Santa Fe Industrial Park in northwest Lawrence opened; within
fifteen years, fourteen plants had been built there, resulting in almost 2,000
jobs and a substantial increase in the economic base of the community. Because few vacancies remained in Santa Fe Park by 1982, the Chamber of Commerce endorsed a proposal for a new 275-acre industrial park at a location
two miles north of Lawrence providing immediate access to I-70, the airport,
and railroads.

In order to extend water and sewer lines to the proposed park, the city had
to annex the site. Under Kansas state law, county commissions must concur
with decisions by city commissions to annex such islands of land not adjacent to existing city limits, but in January 1983, the Douglas County Commission unanimously rejected the rail-served park proposal, providing a victory for Preservationists who opposed the project.

The industrial park proposal was clearly an economic-growth issue. Its
supporters — such as Martin Dickinson, then president of the LCC — argued
that more industry was needed to expand the tax base and generate new job

opportunities, reduce unemployment, and keep young people in the community.[6] Its opponents—such as Tim Miller, who published an occasional newspaper (*The Plumber's Friend*) criticizing "the Los Angelization of Lawrence"—argued that the industrial park would bring to Lawrence such "fruits of expansion [as] increased congestion, increased pollution, higher crime rates, more traffic, higher taxes, and all of the other things characteristic of larger cities."[7] As indicated in Table A, those activists and citizens who shared Miller's anti-GROWTH principles also tended to oppose the RAIL-served park proposal, and those who shared the chamber's pro-growth principles supported the park. The rejection of the rail-served park was thus incongruent with dominant pro-growth principles in Lawrence. In addition, those participants with a strong AGGregative conception of justice were particularly committed to the industrial park; they saw economic growth as beneficial to the city as a whole. Because aggregative principles are also dominant in the community, the question arises, Why did the rail-served park get derailed?

The data in the DEMO cell of Table 6.1 suggest that part of the answer is the community's commitment to citizen participation; those people with stronger citizen-participation principles tended to oppose the park, making democratic-process principles relevant to the issue. By listening to participants protesting the project, county commissioners achieved some principle-policy congruence.

Rejection of the rail-served park was also connected to the community's strong commitment to land-use regulations.[8] First, county commissioners were sensitive to the fact that the proposed site was in a flood plain; because stormwater was naturally retained in the low lying area, expensive drainage systems would be required. Second, commissioners responded to the concerns of environmentalists and farmers that the proposed park would lead to the industrial and commercial development of the entire area between the existing city limits and the site, which occupied some of the best farmland in the county.

Thus, on this issue pro-growth principles were less potent than were citizen-involvement and restrictive land-use principles. However, as County Commissioner Beverly Bradley insisted, the vote against the rail-served park "should not be interpreted as anti-growth."[9] Like most notables, bureaucrats, activists, and citizens who supported the proposal because of its growth potential, the county commissioners also supported economic growth in principle. They simply preferred to search for a more appropriate site, even if they had to act as unsupported trustees. In January 1986, the county commission—as well as the city commission and the Chamber of Commerce—supported an Eastern Hills Industrial Park at a less controversial site just east of Lawrence. Thus, while the Growth Machine lost the 1982–83 industrial park battle, it ultimately won the war.[10]

COMPETING WITH SILICON VALLEY:
THE RESEARCH PARK ISSUE

Stories of North Carolina's Research Triangle Park and California's Silicon Valley reached Lawrence in the early 1980s, and the Growth Machine and university administrators hoped that Lawrence might attract similar "clean growth," providing better jobs for the community's well-educated population and consulting and entrepreneurial opportunities for professors working on the cutting edge of technological advances. As a result, Bob Billings, the top economic notable in the community, proposed developing a "research park" on 296 wooded acres west of Lawrence. The major problem for the Billings proposal was not local opposition but national competition; almost every city in America wanted a similar project and could be expected to compete with the city in attracting high-tech firms to the park. Nevertheless, city officials believed that Billings controlled enough land, capital, and clout to make the project a success and moved expeditiously to rezone Billing's property and bring roads and public utilities to it. Thus, the issue was resolved consensually and resulted in an important victory for the Growth Machine.

As shown in Table 6.1, development of the RESEARCH park was consistent with the community's dominant economic-GROWth and ECONOMIC-criterion principles. However, the outcome was also inconsistent with dominant citizen-participation principles (DEMO) in the community; those citizens opposing the project believed that a referendum should have been held on such a significant project.

Restrictive land-use principles may also prove to be relevant to the issue. One of the few opponents of the research park was Commissioner Nancy Shontz,[11] who thought that the hidden agenda behind the proposal was to create "a second city" by opening up for further development almost 1,000 additional acres of land controlled by Billings.[12] Shontz also feared that Billings's optimism about locating research firms in the park could prove to be unfounded; the research park could thus become a mere "office park," and businesses currently located in the Central Business District (CBD) could relocate there, contributing to the deterioration of the CBD. Shontz's fears may have been justified; in 1987 Billings requested and city commissioners approved a change in zoning provisions that permits, for example, the development of accounting, legal, and insurance offices in the research park. But such effects of the research park on the CBD were not immediately visible, and no organization attempted to mobilize people on behalf of protectionist principles. This enabled dominant economic-growth principles to prevail easily.

## REDUCING THE COSTS OF ECONOMIC DEVELOPMENT:
## INDUSTRIAL REVENUE BOND ISSUES

In order to attract new industries to town and induce existing firms to expand their facilities, the Lawrence City Commission issued forty-one Industrial Revenue Bonds (IRBs) totaling just over $100 million between 1966 and 1986. IRBs stimulated private investment in two ways. Under federal law, local governmental approval of IRBs enabled businesses to pay lower interest on bonds to finance capital improvements because interest on IRBs was exempt from federal income taxes.[13] Under Kansas state law, the land or buildings purchased with IRBs could be exempted by local governments from local property taxes for up to ten years.[14]

The Lawrence City Commission placed several restrictions on the issuance of IRBs. For example, in 1977 the commission required recipients of IRBs to comply with the affirmative-action and land-use regulations of the city. In 1980 the commission restricted the use of IRBs for equipment unless such equipment purchases were tied to building expansions. And in 1981 the commission restricted issuing IRBs to businesses that compete with other local firms — unless the expansion financed by IRBs added significantly to the diversification of the economy or helped downtown redevelopment. Despite these restrictions, the commission generally used IRBs in a relatively aggressive manner to encourage growth. As a result, IRB supporters were more satisfied with the outcome of IRB issues than were their opponents, and the resolution of IRB issues were victories for the Growth Machine.

As shown in Table 6.1, the aggressive use of IRBs has been congruent with dominant pro-GROWth principles in the community. However, the use of IRBs has sometimes been incongruent with dominant land-use principles (NEIGH). For example, some participants have opposed issuing IRBs for projects that fail to conform with Lawrence's comprehensive plan (Plan 95).

Most often opponents of the IRBs have argued that IRBs are unjust, as shown in the AGG cell of Table 6.1. Even if the provision of IRBs stimulates growth benefiting most citizens in the community, such growth can come at the expense of existing firms that must compete in the market with IRB recipients whose business costs have been reduced by low interest rates and tax exemptions. However, utilitarian principles are dominant in Lawrence, and congruence with dominant utilitarian principles was achieved by the nonrestrictive issuance of IRBs.

Representatives expressed some sensitivity to the injustice argument. For example, despite approving (at least in part) all previous IRB requests, in 1983 the commission rejected an application from Robinson Shoes when competing retailers objected. Indeed, most representatives indicated in interviews their general opposition to providing IRBs to businesses competing with local firms; however, when confronted with specific IRB requests, a majority of commis-

sioners usually deferred to arguments that the overall economic benefits of providing the IRBs outweighed the unfairness to competing firms. Thus, responsible representation has been diminished on the IRB issue by such unwillingness
of commissioners to stand consistently by their broader independent judgments.

## HAWKING ONE'S WARES ARTISTICALLY:
## THE SIGN AND BILLBOARD ISSUE

Communities are more than marketplaces, and local governments sometimes
regulate business practices and private property in ways that increase business
costs, reduce trade, and curtail economic growth. Responding to Lady Bird
Johnson's beautification campaign, the Lawrence City Commission adopted
an ordinance regulating commercial signs and billboards in November 1966.
By deferring the full enforcement of these regulations until 1979, local businesses were permitted to phase in smaller, lower signs, but as the 1979 deadline approached, many businesses sought "sign variances," and the willingness
of the commission to grant such exemptions from its restrictive policies became
a significant community issue.

In general, city commissioners saw themselves as standing firm on signs.
The commission denied the Holidome's requests for a 260 square-foot sign
(which was three times larger than permitted) and an additional reader board
that could be visible from I-70. The commission even declared the red, white,
and blue striped paint job at Big Bob's Carpets a violation of the city's
ordinance.

Some participants also interpreted the 1966 ordinance to ban billboards
from the city, prompting city officials to ask Martin Signs to dismantle their
boards. After Martin threatened to file suit, an agreement was reached reducing the number of billboards in the city and requiring that the remaining
boards be lower and more aesthetically pleasing. Overall, the resolution of
the signs and billboards issue appears to have been a narrow victory for the
proponents of strict regulation. Some participants have been dissatisfied with
the commission's inability to eliminate billboards, and they believe that too
many sign variances have been granted, but most supporters of a restrictive
sign ordinance have been moderately satisfied.

Such an outcome may appear incongruent with the principle of promoting
economic growth; sign regulations often cost businesses thousands of dollars to
replace old signs and in lost customers (How many travellers have not spent the
night in the Holidome because its sign was not visible from I-70?). However,
neither participants nor citizens significantly linked their preferences on the
sign issue to their economic-growth principles. Thus, the community's dominant economic-growth principles were not especially relevant to the resolution.

More relevant to the issue have been the community's restrictive land-use, public-service, and utilitarian principles. The Douglas County Environmental Improvement Council (DCEIC) organized on the sign issue, urging the regulation of property rights in the public interest. As suggested in Table 6.1, its members succeeded in linking NEIGHborhood-protection principles with support for the SIGNS ordinance among participants. Dominant cultural principles calling for government to be more active in providing public SERVICES and to apply AGGregative criteria (that the commission put the public interest ahead of special interests) also contributed to public support for the regulations. With economic-development principles of questionable relevance to the issue, and with dominant neighborhood-protection, public-service, and utilitarian principles all supporting extensive regulations, a high level of principle-policy congruence was achieved. Because the majority of participants and citizens also approved of the regulations, the commission achieved a high level of responsible representation by standing firm on signs.

## CONCLUSIONS

Although city governments may have limited powers, it is sometimes suggested that they pursue economic-growth policies with an almost limitless zeal.[15] Lawrence officials have sought to encourage economic growth by investing in airport improvements, by sprucing up the gateway to the city (N2ST), by building roads, water, and sewer facilities to serve both an Eastern Hills industrial park and a research park, and by providing IRBs to all firms that could reasonably claim to contribute to the export economy of the city. Nevertheless, the commitment to economic growth of Lawrence officials has not been unlimited. In order to mollify opposition to airport improvements, few locally generated dollars were invested in the project. Opposition to North Second Street improvements was disarmed by minimizing the scope of that project. Despite the need for a new rail-served industrial park, several proposed sites were rejected because they generated opposition based on other principles. When issuing IRBs, the city commission showed some sensitivity to the notion that such inducements were intended to build the community's export economy and should not be granted to businesses competing with other firms in the city. Additionally, the city has pursued fairly strong regulatory policies on commercial signs and billboards, increasing the costs of doing business in the city.

This does not mean that Lawrence government, like other local governments, is unaffected by structural or systemic biases in favor of growth. Decision makers in Lawrence do attempt to promote growth, and they do so in accordance with the pro-growth principles dominant in Lawrence. Nevertheless, other principles and concerns often crosscut this commitment to growth, and concessions are made to these other principles.

Systemic bias toward growth is most pronounced when the relevance of other crosscutting principles is unforeseen or suppressed. Thus, the city vigorously supported the research park: few people other than Nancy Shontz perceived the relevance of land-use principles to the project. Also, the city managed conflict on the airport issue by financing these improvements through means intended to keep opposition to a minimum. When economic-growth projects seem to touch on other principles, such as neighborhood protection or keeping taxes low, activists holding such principles begin to mobilize others and demand more citizen involvement in the projects. As the scope of participation begins to broaden beyond the circle of representatives, bureaucrats, and notables most committed to growth, we can no longer assume that the outcome will favor the Growth Machine.

# 7

# Protecting the Neighborhoods

Governments and businesses often propose to build new expressways, office complexes, and other developments that threaten to alter the character of neighborhoods, affecting property values and social relationships. Because threats to neighborhoods touch people's immediate interests and values, residents of neighborhoods often overcome numerous obstacles to mobilization and create issues involving neighborhood-protection principles.[1] In this chapter, we will examine four neighborhood issues. In the Oread neighborhood, residents sought extensive downzoning of property to prevent the bulldozing of older homes and their replacement with apartment buildings designed for university students. In East Lawrence, residents also sought an extensive downzoning, in this case to maintain the single-family character of their neighborhood, which was being threatened by the construction of duplexes and other higher-density developments. A proposal to rezone and develop the Bluffs precipitated a battle between the developer and the residents of the adjacent neighborhood. Finally, when the Catholic Archdiocese of Kansas City sought to expand its student center and build a church on the edge of the University of Kansas campus, another neighborhood group lodged a protest. The dominance of neighborhood-protection principles sometimes facilitated victory or concessions to threatened neighborhoods, but other issues were resolved in ways that gave priority to competing principles.

## PROTECTING OLDER HOMES FROM BULLDOZERS: THE OREAD DOWNZONING ISSUE

Located just to the east and north of the University of Kansas, the Oread Neighborhood contains many large Italianate, Victorian, and American Four-Square houses built between the 1860s and early 1900s. In 1966, much of the neighborhood was zoned RD (residence-dormitory), the city's highest-density residential zoning category, stimulating the development of off-campus student housing in the neighborhood.

In 1977 the staff of the city planning department began work on the Oread Neighborhood Plan and quickly learned that one of the major concerns of the more permanent residents of Oread was downzoning; the residents wanted the RD classification replaced (for the most part) with a more restrictive duplex (RM-2) classification, allowing no more than duplexes on a single lot. According to Oread Neighborhood Association (ONA) activists, RD zoning encouraged landlords to divide their once-stately older buildings into as many as seven apartments, maintain them as little as possible, and then sell them at inflated prices to developers, who would raze the old buildings and build new apartments in their place. ONA leaders also argued that the increasing density of the neighborhood brought with it a variety of problems, such as high crime and inadequate parking, contributing to the sense of loss of neighborhood and accelerating the deterioration of this historic area.

Because of these concerns, the planning department submitted the Oread Neighborhood Plan, which called for the downzoning of much of the neighborhood. When city commission members voted to adopt the plan in 1979, however, they rejected the downzoning plank. The continued demolition of older homes in the neighborhood kept the issue alive until 1987, when the commission rejected another downzoning initiative. Although the subsequent passage of a historical preservation ordinance addressed some of the concerns of ONA activists, the overall result has been a loss for the Cellar Dwellers, women, liberals, Politicos, and Preservationists who sought downzoning.

The Oread downzoning issue was a classic case of conflict between property-rights principles and neighborhood-protection principles. According to one commissioner, downzoning in the Oread would have been "totally unfair to the landowner" who bought the RD zoning classification as well as particular parcels of land; in some instances the RD classification "cost people four times the actual market value of the land."[2] Nevertheless, by failing to downzone, the commissioners failed to protect the interests of many Oread residents who sought preservation of older homes, encouragement of single-family dwellings, and reduction of parking problems. They also failed to resolve the OREAD issue in a way consistent with dominant neighborhood-protection principles in Lawrence, as shown in the NEIGH cell of Table 7.1.

Nevertheless, it is difficult to argue that the commissioners acted irresponsibly on the issue. The judgment of most commissioners was that property rights had to be preserved. Community notables were also persuasive in arguing that dominant economic-GROWTH principles were relevant to the issue and should be respected. Though the Oread downzoning issue has been, overall, a loss for neighborhood interests, the subsequent passage of the historical

Table 7.1   Principle-Policy Congruence on Four Neighborhood-Protection Issues

| Issues | Principles | | | | | | | | |
|---|---|---|---|---|---|---|---|---|---|
| | GROW | NEIGH | SERV | WELF | USETAX | LIB | ECON | AGG | DEMO |
| OREAD neigh-borhood down-zoning | + | − | NR | NR | NR | NR | NR | NR | NR |
| EAST Lawrence downzoning | NR | + | NR | NR | NR | NR | − | − | NR |
| BLUFFS develop-ment | + ? | + ? | NR | NR | NR | NR | NR | NR | NR |
| CATHOLIC center expansion | NR | − | NR | NR | NR | NR | + | NR | NR |

NR : Alternative principles not relevant to issue.
 + : Outcome consistent with dominant principle, as specified in heading.
 − : Outcome inconsistent with dominant principle.
 [ ] : Alternative principles were articulated in interviews, but such principles were not significantly and directly related to the policy preferences of participants or citizens.
 ? : The BLUFFS outcome was resolved as a virtual tie between pro-growth and neighborhood-protection forces.

preservation ordinance illustrates the kind of adjustments that policymakers in pluralist communities often make to resolve issues when important cultural principles are in conflict and when participants are strongly divided.

## PRESERVING A SINGLE-FAMILY NEIGHBORHOOD: THE EAST LAWRENCE DOWNZONING ISSUE REVISITED

Although there were some practical differences between the proposals to downzone the Oread and East Lawrence neighborhoods, the two issues were similar in that each involved conflict between property-rights principles and neighborhood-protection principles, as shown in the NEIGH cells of Table 7.1. Property-rights principles prevailed in the resolution of the OREAD issue, but neighborhood-protection principles prevailed when EAST Lawrence was downzoned. These different outcomes might be explained in two ways.

First, the different contexts surrounding these issues may have made property-rights principles seem more relevant in the Oread while neighborhood-protection principles may have seemed more relevant in East Lawrence. In contrast to the Oread, East Lawrence contains mostly smaller, single-family, owner-occupied dwellings appraised below $50,000. While the Oread is largely occupied by students (who, according to one commissioner, may be "able to tolerate the mess there"), East Lawrence is occupied by "the working class" and many minorities (who may have "viewed intrusive developments there as particularly objectionable"). Though developers and landlords had extensive investments at stake during the Oread controversy, such people were less heavily invested in East Lawrence. As a result, property rights may have been less threatened by the East Lawrence downzoning proposal than by the Oread proposal.

Another reason why downzoning occurred in East Lawrence, but not in the Oread, could be that different city commissioners, having different political principles, resolved these issues. While downzoning was consistent with dominant NEIGHborhood protection principles, it was inconsistent with dominant concerns for emphasizing ECONomic and AGGregative principles, as shown in Table 7.1. The commissioners who supported East Lawrence downzoning (Shontz, Gleason, and Francisco) held strong neighborhood-protection principles, and they were less committed than were other commissioners (who resolved the Oread issue) and the public to the importance of economic and aggregative criteria. They were thus easily persuaded that the new developments in the neighborhood affected noneconomic values by attracting renters who were out of character with the neighborhood, by increasing traffic and crime, and by destabilizing the neighborhood generally. They also thought that the new developments burdened residents immediately adjacent to them more than such developments would contribute to the public interest. Thus, the commissioners acted responsibly by downzoning East Lawrence on the basis of *their* dominant principles. However, because the public at large did not generally share their concerns about the importance of political and distributive criteria, principle-policy congruence was limited.

## A BIG BATTLE OVER A LITTLE HILL: THE BLUFFS ISSUE

Between 1979 and 1982, the Bluffs, a rocky hill of five acres described by Preservationists as one of Lawrence's "most beautiful natural resources," was the site of controversy, pitting Duane Schwada, a leading member of the Growth Machine, against residents of the Pinckney neighborhood. Although the land had been zoned for single-family residences, Schwada hoped to build some apartments and offices there. Nearby residents wanted the area to remain undeveloped open space.

In March 1980, city commissioners agreed to Schwada's request to rezone the land, prompting the neighborhood to organize and file suit against the city. Although the commission subsequently approved Schwada's site plans, it then did an about-face, rescinding his building permit because it was discovered that he had never filed a preliminary plat for the entire Bluffs area. This action prompted Schwada to file suit against the city commission, as the neighbors had done earlier. During the next nine months, the issue stayed in district court, with lawyers representing the developer, the neighborhood, and the city. In April 1982, the lawyers finally produced a settlement to which all sides could agree. The developer received his building permit and an additional change in zoning, permitting more extensive office developments. The neighbors were "buffered" from the densest developments on the site and were sheltered from increased traffic by an agreement to build a new road providing direct access to new developments. Proponents and opponents of the Bluffs developments both tended to declare themselves "moderately satisfied" with this outcome, and the issue can thus be considered resolved as a tie.

When issues are resolved as ties, they may be difficult to evaluate. A type of simple equality was achieved between the Growth Machine and Preservationists on the Bluffs issue, as both sides received a partial victory, but it is unclear how much responsible representation occurred on the issue. On the one hand, the quick reversals in policy suggest that commissioners were quick to abandon their independent judgments and were tugged to-and-fro by the competing demands placed upon them.[3] On the other hand, the judgments of the commissioners seem to have been mixed, and the distribution of preferences among participants and citizens prevented reaching consensus.

Principle-policy congruence was also elusive, as both dominant economic-GROWth and NEIGHborhood-protection principles were at stake, as shown in Table 7.1. A clear victory for Schwada would, of course, have facilitated growth, but at the expense of neighborhood protection. A clear victory for the adjacent homeowners would have been consistent with neighborhood protection, but at the expense of growth. Perhaps the compromise enabled as much principle-policy congruence as possible in this situation. Pinckney neighbors received some protection, and the developer delivered on his economic-growth principles by building the regional headquarters for the Student Loan Marketing Association (Sallie Mae) on the site.

## FIGHTING THE CHURCH:
## THE ST. LAWRENCE CATHOLIC CENTER ISSUE

In September 1983 plans were announced to build – in the midst of the affluent West Hills residential area – a 424-seat church, a 100-seat chapel, and a student center for the 4,500 Catholic students attending the University of Kansas. Shortly thereafter, thirty-seven families formed the Crescent-Engel Neighborhood Association (CENA) to protest the project. Although the area was zoned for single-family dwellings, Lawrence ordinances permit churches in residential areas if they "do not create significant objectionable influences" on the neighborhood. CENA found a number of things objectionable. They argued that the development was "far too vast" for the 2.26 acres of land available for the project. They were concerned that traffic to and from the complex and overflow parking would create further safety problems on their already overtaxed residential streets. Furthermore, they feared that the announced plans were just the beginning of additional church-related developments in the area, as rumors circulated that the archbishop had tried to purchase other houses in the area. Employing highly emotional rhetoric, CENA suggested that the proposed church would transform their neighborhood into a "sad and unsightly fringe of houses randomly arranged around the edge of a church parking lot."[4]

The city commission sought to address some of CENA's concerns by deleting the chapel from the site plans, trimming the size of the main church and the parking lot, and asking that the development be screened and landscaped in order to be better integrated into the neighborhood. Nevertheless, CENA filed suit in district court when the modified site plan was approved. The suit delayed development by almost a year and resulted in an out-of-court settlement containing two more concessions to CENA. First, the church agreed to a fifteen-year moratorium on any additional developments at the site. Second, the city agreed to restrict parking on the residential streets surrounding the project. Despite these concessions, most of the residents of the neighborhood remained unsatisfied, and participants in the issue rate the outcome as a greater victory for the church than for the neighborhood.

As shown in Table 7.1, the CATHOLIC Center issue was mainly concerned with NEIGHborhood-protection principles. By failing to side with CENA, the commissioners appear to have acted in a way that violated dominant principles in Lawrence that neighborhoods should be protected from disruptive developments. Even the *Journal-World*, which does not ordinarily side with neighborhoods in their fights with the Growth Machine, asked, "Why put it in the middle of one of the city's most attractive residential areas?"[5] From the viewpoint of city commissioners, the answer was simply that the community's zoning laws permitted it. They thought the issue was overpoliticized and objected to "being snowballed" on the issue by the heavy-handed actions of CENA. In their efforts to depoliticize the issue, they acted consistently with community norms that discount the importance of political values, as shown in the ECON cell of Table 7.1. They also responded positively to the dominant preferences of most participants and citizens and thus achieved a high level of responsible representation.

## CONCLUSIONS

Neighborhood protection entails social values that often compete with economic values, and injecting these social values into the policymaking process is often highly conflictual and "political." If only economic considerations and legal property rights were brought to bear when neighborhoods were threatened by new developments, there would be few constraints on these developments, and neighborhoods would be at the mercy of developers. When neighborhood-protection principles are introduced, issues are raised and developments become politicized. Because these issues hit close to home, they are highly controversial and emotional. While particular communities must resolve concrete land-use issues in ways that reflect their own understanding of the relative importance of property-rights principles and neighborhood-protection principles, the notions that politics is unseemly and that government should be run on a strict businesslike basis provide little opportunity for the consideration of neighborhood-protection principles in the resolution of community issues. This difficulty can be a great defect in the practice of pluralist politics, for neighborhood-protection principles are often widely shared and highly relevant to concrete issues.

# 8

# Restricting Individual Choices

Some people hold liberal individual-choice principles emphasizing personal freedom and declaring that governments ought not to legislate morality. Other people hold more conservative social-control principles and declare that moral standards can be ascertained and that "vices" that are harmful to the social fabric of the community should be prohibited. However, liberals sometimes argue that certain freedoms, such as the freedom to discriminate on the basis of race or sex, ought to be restrained. Conservatives sometimes argue that certain social controls, such as controls on private property, impose excessive limitations on individual rights. Thus, contrasting principles regarding individual choice and social control may only loosely constrain people's policy preferences on specific issues. When it is widely believed that particular acts violate community standards, laws may be enacted that impose social controls, even in communities — such as Lawrence — where most citizens hold individual-choice principles.

In this chapter, we will examine four issues that involve principles of individual choice and social control. First is the enforcement of Lawrence's environmental code, which restricts the right of individuals to maintain their premises as they wish. Second is the regulation of the sale of drug paraphernalia to minors. Third is an issue where some parents sought to eliminate from the public school curriculum a program dealing with moral issues. The final issue concerns an attempt to give expectant mothers freedom of choice in delivering their babies. Despite the prevalence of liberal individual-choice principles in Lawrence, each of these issues was resolved in a way consistent with conservative social-control principles.

## LIMITING FREEDOM AT ONE'S DOORSTEP:
## THE ENFORCEMENT OF THE ENVIRONMENTAL CODE

In 1975 Lawrence passed an environmental code largely concerned with elimi-
nating unsafe housing conditions but also addressing certain matters of aes-
thetics. When Gene Bernofsky decided to heat his home with wood and
accumulated a large, untidy woodpile, he was cited for violating the city's
environmental code. When Ron Lantz failed to maintain his property, city
crews trimmed his overgrown shrubs and trees. Because Mike Almond landscaped his yard with "a meadow lawn," he was cited for violating the community's weed ordinance. As a result, Bernofsky, Lantz, and Almond challenged the validity of the aesthetic aspects of the environment code.

To some extent, the environmental code was altered because of these challenges. When Bernofsky protested his treatment by the city staff, more formal procedures providing compliance deadlines and rights of appeal were
adopted. When Almond argued that his natural grasses should not be arbi-
trarily defined as weeds, the city revised its ordinance and specified about
seventy-five plants — ranging from dandelions to marijuana — that were prohibited from growing beyond twelve inches in length. Despite such changes,
most people involved in the issue do not think that the environmental code
was significantly softened. In general, those people who supported the strong
enforcement of the environmental code were more satisfied than were the code's
protesters. Because most citizens supported the commissioners' judgments
that the code should be strictly enforced, a high level of responsible representation (Level 8 or "majority will") was attained.

According to one commissioner, the issue pitted a small group of people
with a very strong conception of property rights — that people can take care
of their property as they wish — against most neighborhood associations,
whose leaders argued that some restrictions on property rights are an essential means of protecting neighborhoods from blight and thus protecting property values throughout the city. Accordingly, citizens related their preferences
regarding the enforcement of the ENVIRonmental code to their principles about
property rights and neighborhood protection. By strictly enforcing the code,
city officials acted consistently with dominant NEIGHborhood protection principles, as shown in Table 8.1.

For many participants who opposed the code, individual liberty was at
stake.[1] Bernofsky claimed that, by enforcing the code, the city legislated a
particular aesthetic viewpoint and "stamped out individuality" by telling people "how to live their lives, how to use their property, and how to take care
of their environment." According to Almond, "Any ordinance that requires
people to garden in a certain manner is an infringement of civil rights."[2] In
contrast, supporters of the environmental code believed that most people want

Table 8.1    Principle-Policy Congruence on Four Social-Liberty Issues

| Issues | Principles | | | | | | | | |
|---|---|---|---|---|---|---|---|---|---|
| | GROW | NEIGH | SERV | WELF | USETAX | LIB | ECON | AGG | DEMO |
| Enforcement of the ENVIRonment code | NR | + | NR | NR | NR | − | NR | NR | NR |
| Regulation of sales of DRUG paraphernalia | NR | NR | NR | NR | NR | [−] | NR | + | NR |
| End TRIBES value clarification program | NR | NR | NR | NR | NR | − | NR | NR | NR |
| Create BIRTHing room at hospital | NR | NR | [−] | NR | NR | − | [+] | NR | [−] |

NR : Alternative principles not relevant to issue.
 + : Outcome consistent with dominant principle, as specified in heading.
 − : Outcome inconsistent with dominant principle.
 [ ] : Alternative principles were articulated in interviews, but such principles were not significantly and
       directly related to the policy preferences of participants or citizens.

to keep the town tidy and that the code is necessary to enforce community-wide standards dealing with the maintenance of private property.

As shown in Table 8.1, strict enforcement of the aesthetic aspects of the ENVIRonmental code was incongruent with dominant community support of individual-choice (LIB) principles. However, there is not much agreement in Lawrence about the priority of social-control and individual-liberty principles or about how these principles applied to the environmental code. The data collected for Table 4.1 show that the percentage of citizens who agree with individual-choice principles (48%) is only slightly greater than the percentage of citizens who agree with social-control principles (40%),[3] and, as shown in Table A, support for individual-choice principles was not significantly related to preferences regarding the environmental code among citizens. For most citizens, the environmental code may have infringed upon people's liberties, but such infringements were not viewed as unnecessary impositions of morality. Lawrence citizens may generally be willing to grant their neighbors the right to do whatever they want inside their homes, but what occurs outside the home, even on an individual's own property, is often a matter of public concern and thus potentially a matter of public control.

## DISCOURAGING YOUNGSTERS FROM GETTING STONED:
## THE DRUG PARAPHERNALIA ISSUE

Early in 1980, a "head shop" posted a sign proclaiming a sale on bongs, water-filled devices for smoking marijuana and hashish. Commissioner Ed Carter happened to walk by the shop with his young son, became offended, and soon called for an ordinance to ban the sale of drug paraphernalia to minors and to restrict the display of such items. According to Carter, "We have a couple of places in town that are disgusting . . . and right next to a candy store!"[4]

Despite getting extensive media coverage, the drug paraphernalia issue was the least controversial issue in the sample, as other commissioners solemnly announced that they too were "for any and all drug control." Final action on the ordinance was deferred for six months while the Kansas State Supreme Court ruled on the constitutionality of a similar ordinance passed in nearby Overland Park, but almost no opposition surfaced. When the ordinance was consensually adopted, a high level of responsible representation was achieved.

As shown in the LIB cell of Table 8.1, individual-choice and social-control principles are not relevant to the DRUG paraphernalia issue, as there was little discussion of such principles. Those citizens who supported the regulation of drug paraphernalia were less likely to hold social-control principles than utilitarian ones. For them, the drug ordinance served the public interest, and its adoption was consistent with dominant AGGregative principles in Lawrence. Those who held individual-choice principles apparently did not perceive the ordinance as a serious threat to their principles, because it applied only to minors, its broader application would not seriously threaten individual choices, and it was merely a symbolic gesture intended to reaffirm the community's opposition in principle to widespread social practices that most citizens could not condone.

## DEALING WITH MORAL CHOICES IN THE SCHOOLS:
## THE TRIBES ISSUE

During the 1980–81 school year, the TRIBES Value Clarification Program[5] was being used experimentally in three Lawrence elementary schools. TRIBES, Teaming for Responsibility, Identity, and Belongingness in Educational Systems, was one of several educational programs used in Lawrence to examine human emotions and clarify value choices. While other programs were uncontroversial, a relatively small but vocal group of parents mobilized against TRIBES and some parents transferred their children out of schools where TRIBES was used.

The issue began when some youngsters conveyed to their parents that their feelings had been hurt by one of the TRIBES activities. When confronted with an imaginary situation where there was inadequate space on a lifeboat for all endangered people in a group, some students opted against staying together and chose to leave some of their classmates behind. Concerned parents sought out the TRIBES handbook and soon found other activities in the program objectionable. For example, another activity was designed to help fourth through eighth graders think about the value they placed on sexual pleasure. Teachers and school administrators generally agreed that such activities were controversial, and they were willing to abandon such activities. However, they contended that affective education was an important part of the curriculum and objected to censorship by parents.

In September 1981, the issue reached the school board, which ruled that TRIBES could be continued in the schools where it was presently used, but the board also discouraged its adoption in other schools in the district and urged teachers to use the program "selectively." As a result, teachers soon adopted other less controversial materials dealing with affective education, and TRIBES quickly disappeared as an identifiable program and did not become a permanent part of the curriculum in Lawrence schools. Overall, opponents of the TRIBES program indicated somewhat more satisfaction with this outcome than did its supporters.

As shown in Table 8.1, participants in the issue related their preferences on the TRIBES issue to their principles regarding individual choice and the regulation of morality (LIB). In general, those who valued individual choice supported TRIBES, and those who thought that government should regulate morality opposed it. On the surface, these relationships are surprising, as some people presented arguments that seemed to undermine their principles. In general, opponents objected to the schools' attempting to influence the values of their children, and argued that value clarification and moral choices should be taught by parents and churches. This argument seems compatible with liberal principles that local governments should not be involved in private matters of morality. However, most protesting parents held fundamentalist values and thus had little objection, in principle, to the regulation of morality, provided that "proper" moral standards were being regulated. Thus, they objected that the TRIBES program did not instruct students to distinguish right from wrong; its open-ended format encouraged students to accept "value relativism" and "secular humanism." In contrast, teachers and administrators did not view the TRIBES program as contributing to the regulation of morality. Rather, they insisted that affective education did not tell children what to believe but rather sought to instill in children moral capacities that would enable them to make responsible individual choices.

By permitting the TRIBES program to remain part of the affective education curriculum, but by not endorsing the program, the school board sought to find the middle ground on a concrete issue that touched on conflicting principles. For board members, it was important to resolve the issue in a way that indicated that they would not capitulate to fundamentalist demands or engage in censorship. To do otherwise would have risked offending those Lawrence citizens who held liberal values upholding individual choices on moral issues. However, by discouraging the use of TRIBES, the school board responded to the concerns of the fundamentalists, and the issue was resolved in a way that embodied conservative social-control principles more than it reflected dominant individual-choice principles.

## DELIVERING THE NEXT GENERATION OF CITIZENS: THE BIRTHING ROOM ISSUE

In 1978, an ad hoc group, the Lawrence Association of Parents and Professionals for Safe Alternatives in Childbirth (LAPSAC), organized over the issue of "providing freedom of choice in childbirth" at Lawrence Memorial Hospital (LMH).[6] Dissatisfied with the "terrifying" and "violent" methods of childbirth practiced by traditional medicine and inspired by visions of "gentle" and "natural" birth, LAPSAC sought a birthing room at LMH. Essentially the same equipment would be available to mother and child, but the entire birthing process would occur in the same bed in the same homelike atmosphere. In comparison with the childbirth procedures being practiced at LMH, it was thought that the creation of the birthing room would reduce the use of drugs during childbirth; avoid unnecessary fetal monitoring, episiotomies, and Caesarean sections; increase the presence of fathers, siblings, and friends at birth; keep mother and child together after birth; and shorten the stay in the hospital.[7]

The board of trustees at LMH initially supported the birthing room. However, when doctors in the obstetrics and gynecology (OB-GYN) unit of LMH voiced safety concerns, several board members reasoned that they would be acting outside their authority if they were to override doctors on questions of medical practice. As a result, the birthing room was shelved.

As shown in Table 8.1, the BIRTHing room issue involved contrasting individual-choice and social-control principles (LIB). While birthing-room proponents were "pro choice," opponents argued that the choices of mothers had to be constrained, both for their own good and that of their child.

Table 8.1 shows that other principles were also articulated on the BIRTHing-room issue, but these principles were insufficiently related to the preferences of participants or citizens to be considered relevant to the issue by the criteria employed here. For example, opponents of the birthing room claimed that the facility was unECONomical. The executive director of the hospital argued that the efficiency of the obstetrics ward could be significantly reduced if the birthing room were underutilized. Indeed, the different ways in which proponents and opponents of the facility viewed "demand" for the birthing room well illustrates the differences between economic and political criteria in decision making. For hospital administrators and doctors, demand meant primarily market demand, and they predicted that few expectant mothers would use the birthing room. Birthing-room supporters conceived of "demand" for the birthing room in more political terms, stressing widespread public support for the right of all mothers to have such a facility available.

Conflicting DEMOcratic-process principles were also articulated on the issue. While birthing-room supporters called on the board to be responsive to citizen preferences, most members of the board rejected the dominant cultural view that it was their role to be agents of citizens; instead, they viewed themselves as "trustees" and asserted that they had to be more concerned about the expert opinions of doctors than about citizen preferences. By finding the arguments of doctors persuasive, Level 6 (elite persuasiveness) on the scale of responsible representation was achieved.

In summary, the birthing-room issue was resolved in a way inconsistent with individual-choice principles prominent in Lawrence. Perhaps such principles would have prevailed had the issue been resolved by more political institutions. However, LMH is essentially a business, and the members of the board of trustees thought that they should apply economic criteria and defer to the expertise of the medical staff rather than respond to the political demands of citizens seeking more individual options in the public facilities available for the delivery of their children.

## CONCLUSIONS

The environmental code, drug paraphernalia, TRIBES, and birthing-room issues each involved individual-choice versus social-control principles, and none of these issues was resolved in a way consistent with dominant individual-choice principles in the community. Perhaps the failure to achieve principle-policy congruence on these social issues is due to the fact that, in Lawrence, there is no widely accepted understanding of the priority of these principles. Furthermore, people often do not strongly relate such principles to those concrete issues in which the principles are at stake. For example, many persons with strong individual-choice principles did not find these principles threatened by the enforcement of the environmental code or by a largely symbolic ordinance regulating the sale of drug paraphernalia. People may generally support individual-choice principles but not object to particular laws that restrict behaviors that are widely recognized as inappropriate or that might harm others in the community. Like all principles, individual-choice principles provide their adherents with initial predispositions about certain issues, but these predispositions can be overridden by specific proposals to restrict individual choices in order to further some community good.

# 9

# Providing Public Services and Welfare

As in other American communities, certain goods and services — such as fire and police protection and public education — are provided through governmental or quasi-governmental organizations to all Lawrence citizens, regardless of their ability to pay for them or of the amount of taxes they pay. Proposals that local governments extend or cut back the quantity or quality of such communal goods often become controversial issues in community politics.[1] In Lawrence the development of a comprehensive stormwater-management system was rejected in a public referendum in 1982. School administrators proposed closing three elementary schools in 1981, but parents successfully protested the transference of their children to other schools. A program providing lifeline gas rates for the needy was debated in 1982, and increasing or reducing governmental appropriations for social services has been a continuing issue in Lawrence.

Communal-provision principles asserting that local governments ought to provide more services and welfare, even if taxes must be raised, are more widespread in Lawrence than are contrary principles. Thus, in order for Lawrence government to achieve principle-policy congruence on communal-provision issues, it needs to respond positively to various demands for program expansion and reject proposals for program cutbacks. However, effective pluralist governments do not respond positively to every demand for more communal goods, even in communities such as Lawrence, where liberal communal-provision principles are dominant. Each demand — whether for more extensive stormwater-management systems, maintenance of neighborhood schools, or lifeline gas rates — must be decided by community members based on their understanding of the rights of citizenship in their community. On the one hand, if most people reject the provision of more extensive stormwater-management facilities and controls, then the criterion of responsible representation — asserting that policy decisions should reflect issue-specific

104

public preferences — would weigh against the stormwater-management proposal. Perhaps in this case, the criterion of principle-policy congruence should yield to that of responsible representation, resulting in the rejection of the proposal. On the other hand, if most people believe that citizens have a right to heat during the cold winter months, then the criterion of responsible representation would complement that of principle-policy congruence, and the case for passing the lifeline program would be more urgent. Thus, both public support for public-service principles and issue-specific public preferences need to be considered on communal provision issues.

The provision of more communal goods requires not only a willingness of citizens to bear additional taxes to pay for public services and welfare but also citizen support for particular types of taxes that are proposed and levied. Discovering acceptable methods of taxation can thus be a formidable obstacle to the provision of communal goods in communities such as Lawrence where there is little agreement about tax-distribution principles. This difficulty is apparent on three additional issues in the Lawrence sample that are discussed in this chapter: a proposal to tax videogames, a referendum on the intangibles tax, and the reappraisal of real estate as a basis for levying property taxes.

## THE RIGHT TO A DRY BASEMENT:
## THE STORMWATER-MANAGEMENT ISSUE

As depicted in *The Wizard of Oz*, violent storms often descend on the Kansas plains. However, eastern Kansas is not as flat as popularly believed, and Lawrence is built on a series of gently rolling hills. As a result, thunderstorms can result in street flooding, inundated basements, and a variety of drainage problems. At the urging of the DCEIC and the Lawrence League of Women Voters (LWV), the city commission hired a consultant to conduct a stormwater-management study in December 1980. The cost of the study, estimated at $140,000, would be paid by adding 50 cents to monthly water bills for a two-year period.

There was little controversy about the matter until the following spring when newly elected Commissioner Nancy Shontz sought to modify the tasks of the consultants to include considering "development controls that protect the natural drainage system."[2] Developer Duane Schwada claimed that Shontz's real agenda — curbing economic development — was now apparent, and builders and developers began to mobilize against the stormwater-management proposal.

In October 1981, the developers received an assist from Buzz Zook, a retired official with the Chamber of Commerce who champions Market Provider values. Zook alleged that the fifty-cent monthly fee was illegal because, by state law, water bills are user fees, based solely on the amount of water used.

With the help of developers and an ad hoc antitax group, Zook collected enough signatures on a petition to force a referendum on the issue. In a special election in May 1982, only 36 percent of the voters supported the fifty-cent fee on their water bills. The city commission interpreted the results of the referendum as a mandate to discontinue the stormwater-management study, which could have been financed by other means.

As shown in Table 9.1. public-SERVICE principles were central to the STORMwater-management issue. Even though Lawrence citizens are generally inclined to support increased city services (and taxes), the public voted for an outcome that was incongruent with their dominant communal-provision principles. Perhaps they agreed with Zook's argument that there was no widespread public need—that only a miniscule percentage of the city's population complained to the city, even when flooding problems were most severe. Such an argument misunderstands the characteristics of goods that are communally provided, however. In order to be a communal good, there must be widespread recognition by the public that all people in the community are entitled to the good simply because they are members of the community. Perhaps only some people need the good, but governments are obligated to provide the good if particular individuals are not responsible and are unable to satisfy their need through individual action. For example, the buildings, roads, and parking lots on the university campus atop Mount Oread cause runoffs that end up in the basements in the Schwegler neighborhood at the bottom of the hill. As one homeowner stated, "I have done everything I can to try to correct the problem, but this is a situation which individual homeowners cannot correct. Only the city can correct it."[3] Such communal needs seem to be widely recognized in Lawrence. A 1984 public opinion poll showed that 68 percent of Lawrence citizens having an unambiguous preference believed that local government ought to address the stormwater problem. This suggests that some people abandoned their communal-provision principles, not because they rejected stormwater management as an appropriate area for governmental involvement, but because the city commission's handling of the problem conflicted with other principles that they held.

When a variety of principles are relevant to an issue, people's commitment to one principle may be outweighed by their commitments to other principles. On the stormwater-management issue, people argued that the approach the city commission took conflicted with dominant principles regarding economic development ("Some commissioners were eager to use the stormwater issue to place new regulations on developers"), tax distribution ("Water bills should be user charges"), and citizen involvement ("The public was kept from having a voice" until a referendum was held). Table A shows that only citizen-involvement principles (DEMO) were significantly related to citizen preferences on the STORMwater issue, but particular people could, of course, find justification in any

Table 9.1   Principle-Policy Congruence on Seven Communal-Provision Issues

| Issues | Principles | | | | | | | | |
|---|---|---|---|---|---|---|---|---|---|
| | GROW | NEIGH | SERV | WELF | USETAX | LIB | ECON | AGG | DEMO |
| STORMwater management | + | − | − | NR | [+] | NR | NR | NR | + |
| CLOSE three elementary schools | NR | NR | + | NR | NR | NR | NR | − | + |
| Authorize LIFELINE gas rates | NR | NR | NR | − | [+] | NR | NR | + | NR |
| Fund SOCIAL services | NR | NR | NR | ? | NR | NR | NR | NR | NR |
| Tax VIDEOgames | NR | NR | NR | NR | + | [+] | + | NR | NR |
| End INTANGIBLES tax | NR | NR | [−] | NR | + | NR | + | NR | NR |
| REAPPRAISE real estate | [+] | NR | NR | NR | NR | NR | NR | NR | NR |

NR : Alternative principles not relevant to issue.
 + : Outcome consistent with dominant principle, as specified in heading.
 − : Outcome inconsistent with dominant principle.
 [ ] : Alternative principles were articulated in interviews, but such principles were not significantly and directly related to the policy preferences of participants or citizens.
 ? : The SOCIAL services issue was resolved as a virtual tie, making it unclear whether the outcome better reflected dominant public-welfare principles or subordinate private-giving principles.

one of these principles for abandoning their liberal public-service principles and their preference for more stormwater management.

Although the resolution of the STORMwater-management issue was inconsistent with dominant liberal public-SERVice and with NEIGHborhood-protection principles, the outcome was consistent with dominant economic-GROWth and citizen-involvement (DEMO) principles, as shown in Table 9.1. Thus, the stormwater issue illustrates an important obstacle to achieving principle-policy congruence on public-service issues: a variety of additional principles can be relevant to these issues, and these principles may prompt those with liberal public-service principles to reject specific communal-provision proposals.

## THE RIGHT TO NEIGHBORHOOD SCHOOLS: THE SCHOOL-CLOSING ISSUE

In the fall of 1981, school administrators, concerned with the dual problem of declining enrollments and shrinking economic resources, proposed the closing of three rural elementary schools: Grant, India–Kaw Valley, and Riverside. During public hearings in January 1982, the parents of students enrolled in these schools protested. The school board thus had to choose between school administrators and those constituents with children attending the endangered schools.[4] By a vote of five to two, they rejected the school closings and achieved Level 7 (minority persuasiveness) on the scale of responsible representation.

Of course, the school-closing proposal did not threaten to remove the communal provision of education to the affected students. Rather it threatened the right to an education within the context of neighborhood schools.[5] For opponents of the school closings, the removal of this right was not worth the small savings (of about $115,000 annually) that would be achieved. However, citizens who wanted to cut taxes tended to support the school closings, making public-SERVICE principles relevant. In Lawrence, liberal public-service principles are dominant, and the school board resolved the issue in a way congruent with dominant communal-provision principles. In doing so, however, they had to violate the AGGregative conception of justice that prevails in Lawrence. As shown in Table 9.1, the protesting parents tended to hold distributive principles. For example, one parent urged the school board to "take a stand for the one kid who may be just part of a crowd or lost in the shuffle" when transferred to one of the other schools.[6] Although the culture of Lawrence is not very receptive to such distributive arguments, the school board recognized the claim that closing the neighborhood schools would be unjust to the affected parents and students.

## THE RIGHT TO HEAT:
## THE LIFELINE GAS PROPOSAL

The winter of 1981 had been unusually harsh, straining the budgets of those social-service agencies that helped Lawrence residents who were unable to pay their heating bills. With the cost of natural gas expected to rise by 30 percent before the following winter, advocates for the poor and social-service workers proposed that Lifeline gas rates be adopted. Under their proposal, families having incomes that placed them near the official poverty line would be eligible for up to 50 percent reduction on their heating bills. In order to generate $250,000 to finance this subsidy, other residential gas consumers would have a surcharge, averaging about $7.50 annually, added to their gas bills. In November and December 1982, the commission expressed its interest in the Lifeline concept and unanimously approved an ordinance to establish the program.[7]

The Lifeline proposal violated the antiwelfare principles of most notables who asserted that the needs of the poor should be addressed by private charity. In order to forestall the Lifeline program, they formed a private organization, Warm Hearts, and collected over $65,000 in voluntary contributions by mid-December. The perception that Warm Hearts was an adequate response to the problem prompted more than 2,000 residents — mostly conservatives, men, Market Providers, Seniors and Veterans, Privates, and Hometowners — to sign a petition protesting Lifeline. Such protest prompted reconsideration and defeat of the Lifeline program in January 1983, as Commissioners Barkley Clark, Marci Francisco, and Nancy Shontz withdrew their initial support for the program.

Like the stormwater-management and school-closing issues, the Lifeline issue invoked communal-provision principles, but while the goods of dry basements and neighborhood schools are distributed in ways that cut across class lines, Lifeline would be available only to the poor. As shown in Table 9.1, people thus brought their WELFare principles to bear on the LIFELINE issue. Supporters argued that public assistance was required because, "Natural gas is a necessity in winter just as food and shelter is."[8] Some opponents rejected such claims outright; one irate citizen told the commission, "I don't intend to give nothing to nobody who doesn't deserve it. . . . That's not the American way. That's the communist way."[9] However, most opponents made the more limited claim that such needs of the poor should be handled through charity. In a letter to the editor, Debbie and Pat Hodges expressed these private-charity principles. "Surely the issue here is not that of letting the poor freeze to death; rather that charity must be legislated by the commission. . . . the imposition of this kind of tax seems to imply that the City Commission has a lack of faith in the churches and charitable organizations of Lawrence."[10] Supporters of Lifeline did question the ability of charitable organizations to meet the need; as one person put it, "Warm Hearts is fine, but what about next year? What is needed is a more institutionalized, more dependable way, of helping the needy."

In addition, supporters of Lifeline may have believed that "there is a fundamental difference between aid that is provided as a charitable gesture and aid that is provided as a legal right."[11] The existence of charity provides no rights. Needy persons must request aid from those who may turn them down if they are deemed unworthy. In contrast, the Lifeline program would be a legal right of all persons who had resided in Lawrence for at least three months. Citizen surveys indicated that most Lawrence residents thought that the "right to heat" should be supported by governmental programs financed by mandatory taxes.

Supporters of the Lifeline program thus had on their side dominant cultural principles supporting public welfare and citizen support for the provision of heat in particular. Why, then, were the commissioners persuaded by a vocal minority to abandon the Lifeline program?

One possibility is that conflicting principles of justice were also relevant to the LIFELINE issue, as shown in the AGG cell of Table 9.1. Because the Lifeline program would improve the condition of the poorest people in the community, Rawlsian distributive principles — that the least advantaged should be given special consideration in the formulation of public policy — were at stake on the issue.[12] While the amount of support for specifically Rawlsian distributive principles in the community is unknown,[13] what the commissioners heard from activists were not Rawlsian principles. Instead, differentiating conceptions of justice associated with utilitarianism — people should only get what they earn — were widely articulated.[14] By capitulating to such views, commissioners responded to the dominant aggregative conceptions of justice in the community.

Tax-distribution principles were also articulated on the Lifeline issue and, though such principles did not have a significant direct effect on preferences generally, they may account for its rejection. Commissioners Francisco and Shontz were concerned that the Lifeline proposal would not tax people on the basis of their ability to pay. Francisco objected to the fact that businesses would be excluded from the surcharge on gas bills, and Shontz objected to the ordinance's failure to exclude those people just above the poverty line from subsidizing those just below it. Thus, tax-distribution principles did concern the dissenting commissioners. Although Lawrence residents have rather mixed views about appropriate tax principles, the Lifeline program did not contain tax principles acceptable to the wavering commissioners.

In summary, the Lifeline issue was highly controversial. Although most citizens support liberal public-welfare principles, which in turn supported lifeline, a significant number of people do not share these principles. Rawlsian distributive principles supporting Lifeline are probably not strong enough in Lawrence to command the attention of policymakers. Progressive tax principles were not clearly furthered by Lifeline, and attachment to progressive tax principles is not particularly strong in Lawrence. Thus, the "right to heat" remains unestablished in the community, despite its support from most citizens.

## EXTENDING THE SAFETY NET:
## THE PROVISION OF SOCIAL SERVICES

According to many community leaders and social workers, Lawrence is "a caring community"; there is a broad variety of nonprofit social-service agencies providing assistance to people with needs that they cannot afford in the marketplace. The services provided by such agencies are funded from a wide variety of sources including federal and state grants and private contributions, especially those administered by the United Fund.

Local governments also contribute to the provision of welfare. Some non-controversial social services — such as public health and homes for the mentally retarded—are included in the base budgets of the county or city and continuously funded. Other agencies providing less established programs—such as Women's Transitional Care Services, which aids battered women, or the Douglas County Child Development Association, which helps fund child care for lower-income mothers—have depended on the city and county commissions to allocate part of their discretionary federal revenue sharing or CDBG funds for social services. Until 1980, the city allocated less than $100,000 (or about 12 percent) annually of its revenue sharing budget to social services. During the early 1980s, revenue sharing funding for social services increased dramatically, reaching almost $200,000 (or 28 percent) in the 1984 budget. Though CDBG funds were allocated for neighborhood and capital improvement projects until 1981, as much as 12 percent of these funds ($87,000 in 1984) went to social-service agencies thereafter. Such support for social-service agencies has declined since 1984 and received a major setback in 1987 when federal revenue sharing was discontinued.

The question of the extent of city (and, to a lesser extent, county) governmental contributions to social services has been an ongoing community issue having no clear resolution. Occasionally someone made a clear proposal, such as adding three or four mills to the city property tax to support social services[15] or having "municipal government get the hell out of social services."[16] However, such proposals died quickly, as the commission has instead dealt with social service funding in an incremental way. Each year when the city and county commissions allocated their revenue sharing and CDBG funds, various provisions were made for social-service agencies. The outcome of the funding of the social-service issue has been scored as a "tie," because proponents and opponents of public welfare expressed about equal levels of satisfaction and dissatisfaction with these decisions.[17]

As shown in Table 9.1, only contrasting WELFare principles have been relevant to the SOCIAL service issue. Perhaps the indecisive outcome of this issue is an appropriate response to the cultural ambivalence that exists regarding welfare principles in Lawrence. However, most citizens support public welfare in principle. Municipal funding for social services has declined sharply since 1983–84 (when both supporters and opponents of governmental funding provided mixed assessments about the adequacy of social service funding). Since 1984 the United Fund has sought higher levels of private contribution, but target goals have not been met. A one-cent local sales tax—with revenues partially earmarked for social service agencies—has also been rejected in a countywide referendum. Such occurrences lend credibility to the claim that social service funding policies are no longer consistent with the liberal public-welfare principles that prevail in the local culture.

## PAC-MAN AS THE TAX-MAN: THE VIDEOGAMES ISSUE

In May 1982, a town meeting was held to discuss social service issues. During a discussion of how to generate revenue for such services, someone suggested that the city tap into the videogame fad. Commissioners expressed interest in the idea but soon discovered that they lacked jurisdiction to impose a tax on the gross receipts from any business beyond the sales tax already being collected. Their only option was to collect licensing fees. After it was discovered that Kansas City, Kansas, charged fifty dollars for an annual licensing fee on each amusement machine, Lawrence drafted a similar ordinance.

When the issue was placed on the agenda in September 1982, a well-organized and well-prepared group of opponents of the tax — mostly videogame operators — greeted commissioners. The operators argued that licensing fees were intended for businesses such as taverns and dance halls, to pay the costs of averting crowd-control problems. Because crowd control was not a problem with videogames, the need for regulation was questioned. The operators also argued that the licensing fee would not generate significant revenue; in fact, a chamber spokesman calculated that the ordinance would cost more to implement than it would collect in licensing fees. The only person at the commission meeting to argue for the licensing fee conceded that it might not raise much revenue but urged regulating videogames as a means of discouraging the corruption of youth. Thus, the effectiveness of the lobbying effort by videogame operators, the lack of support for regulating videogames, and the limited revenue potential of the licensing ordinance weighed strongly against the proposal, and it was unanimously abandoned.

By rejecting the VIDEO tax, the issue was resolved in a way consistent with the dominant principles in Lawrence that were relevant as shown in Table 9.1. Though participants with public-WELFare principles initially supported the tax, they abandoned the issue when it became apparent that it could not generate significant revenues for social services. Thus, public-welfare principles were not at stake. Even though subsequent arguments for the tax stressed the need to exercise social control over a "public nuisance," people did not relate their individual-choice and social-control principles to the issue. Thus, dominant individual-choice principles (LIB) were also irrelevant to its resolution. Participants who opposed the video tax tended to hold benefits-received tax principles (USETAX). Because they and the users of videogames would receive no public services in return for their tax contributions, they argued that the original video tax and licensing fee were unfair. Participants who opposed the video tax also tended to believe in the importance of ECONomic criteria, and they agreed that the proposal made no sense economically. Because the video tax proposal did not reflect benefits-received tax principles and because economic criteria seemed to weigh against it, its rejection achieved principle-policy congruence.

TAXING PEOPLE'S INTEREST:
THE INTANGIBLE TAX ISSUE

As citizen tax-revolt movements spread from California to other states in the late 1970s, the Kansas State Legislature passed a bill permitting local governments to repeal their tax on intangibles. When the issue arose in Douglas County in 1980, the intangibles tax under consideration amounted to a 3 percent levy on income from interest and dividends that people received from their investments, and it generated about $300,000 each year for the City of Lawrence and about $125,000 each year for Douglas County.

In the spring of 1980 the ad hoc Committee to Repeal the Intangibles Tax was formed and quickly obtained 2,000 signatures on a petition demanding a referendum on the issue. Although commissioners made clear that repeal of the intangibles tax would inevitably lead to higher property taxes to make up for the lost revenue, there was no organized opposition against its repeal. Thus, it came as no surprise when 75 percent of the voters in Lawrence and Douglas County voted against the tax.

Participants involved in the INTANGIBLES-tax issue articulated public-SERVICE and tax-distribution (USETAX) principles, as shown in Table 9.1. Some activists wanted to abolish the tax simply because they held conservative public-service principles and thought that citizens were overtaxed. Others — especially bureaucrats[18] — thought that the intangibles tax was an important means of financing communal goods and services. However, the commission's declaration that the overall level of taxation would not be affected by the outcome of the intangibles-tax issue reduced the link between public-SERVICE principles and positions on the tax, and such principles became irrelevant.

There was some discussion of the tax-distribution principles at stake on the issue. According to a leader of the antitax group, the intangible tax was "unfair," as it "hurts the elderly and low-income groups that live from interest on their savings."[19] However, supporters of the intangibles tax rejected such claims, arguing that the intangibles tax was progressive since it was borne primarily by wealthy individuals who were the primary recipients of interest and divident income. As shown in Table 9.1, participants on the issue were able to sort out these competing claims, since opponents of the intangible tax were less likely to hold progressive tax principles than were its supporters.

Because participants related their tax principles to their position on the intangibles-tax issue, and because progressive-tax principles are not dominant in the community, it can be argued that the resolution of the intangibles-tax issue was congruent with prevailing tax-distribution principles. Nevertheless, if such congruence was achieved, it occurred without voters significantly relating their tax principles to their positions on the issue. Because analysis by activists, public officials, and the newspaper about the tax-distribution principles at stake was inadequate, it was relatively easy for those irritated with the tax to mobilize citizen support on behalf of their interests. As one supporter of the tax said, "Give the average citizen a chance to vote against a tax, and he will."

This outcome can, of course, be interpreted as an unprincipled capitulation to the demands of special interests and to poorly informed public prejudice. In contrast, the issue might also be interpreted as a strategic retreat by governmental officials concerned with the long-term well-being of local government. As Commissioner Barkley Clark noted, "The tax revenues involved were small and replaceable. If such a tax is an irritant, it's best to get rid of it, maintain citizen support, and keep government running."[20] Thus, though opposition to the intangibles tax was most pronounced among those citizens who wanted to apply efficient ECONOMIC criteria, the outcome may also have been politically prudent. Certainly, Lawrence officials have had a much easier time dealing with the limited discontent directed at the intangibles tax than officials elsewhere have had dealing with wholesale tax revolts.


TOO HOT TO HANDLE LOCALLY:
THE REAPPRAISAL OF PROPERTY

Lawrence city government obtains 17 percent of its operating expenses from property taxes. Douglas County government and the local school district are even more dependent on property tax revenues, as they receive 37 and 69 percent respectively of their operating expenses from property taxes. The central role of property taxes in municipal finance raises the question of whether property tax burdens are distributed fairly or equitably.

Although the Kansas State Constitution specifies that all property was to be assessed uniformly and equally for tax purposes, certain inequities in property-tax collections were apparent during the late 1970s. For example, a study completed in 1980 by the State Legislative Research Department estimated that throughout Kansas, agricultural land was being assessed on the average at 6 percent of its market value, residential property at 11 percent, locally assessed commercial and industrial property at 17 percent, and utilities, railroads and personal property (e.g., automobiles, business equipment, and farm machinery) at 30 percent. Within Douglas County there were also wide and systematic inequities in the appraised values of homes. For example, most newer homes were appraised at 15 percent or more of their market value, but most older homes were appraised at 10 percent or less of their market value.[21]

Nevertheless, there was little demand at the local level for the reappraisal of property. Even though local leaders were aware of the issue, they preferred to sit back and let the state legislature deal with it.[22]

For many years, the state legislature failed to resolve the issue, principally because of partisan disagreement about the "classification" of property. On the one hand, Democrats wanted statewide reappraisal to occur only after passage of a constitutional amendment allowing classification of property; rather than having all property appraised "uniformly and equally," they wanted utility, industrial, and commercial property taxed at one rate (for example, 30 percent of market value), residential property taxed at another rate (e.g., 12 percent of market value), and farm property taxed at another, still lower, rate. On the other hand, Republicans generally believed that property should first be reappraised so its effects could be better understood; if the effects were as startling as farmers and homeowners projected, classification amendments could then be entertained. Finally, the 1985 legislature broke this logjam by ordering reappraisal, but they did not make it effective until three years after voters were given the opportunity to vote on a classification amendment. Such an amendment was passed in November 1986, and all homes in Douglas County were reappraised by 1989.

How should the outcome of the reassessment issue be interpreted? Prior to state legislative action in 1985, supporters of reappraisal in Lawrence — primarily Country Clubbers and Split Levellers — were much less satisfied than were opponents of reappraisal, but such assessments fail to take into account the subsequent actions of the state, the approval of classification, and the impacts of reappraisal on taxpayers. For these reasons and, more importantly, because the issue was not resolved at the local level, the reappraisal issue is omitted from certain comparative-issues analyses in Chapters 12 and 13. Nevertheless, it is useful to consider the principles at stake on the reappraisal issue.

Table 9.1 shows that although some principles were said to be at stake, participants did not significantly relate their positions on reappraisal to broader political principles. The Chamber of Commerce was a strong proponent of reappraisal at the state level; the chamber argued that economic growth was inhibited because business — and especially business equipment — was relatively overassessed. The classification amendment placed the real estate of business in the highest tax category, but it reduced taxes on business equipment. Although the Growth Machine thus has mixed views about the implementation of reassessment, the adoption of the reappraisal policy was congruent with articulated pro-GROWTH principles.

Both proponents and opponents of reappraisal also talked about tax principles (mostly the need for "fairness" in taxation), but proponents of more progressive tax principles were on both sides of the reappraisal question. Opponents of reappraisal argued that existing practices giving tax breaks to the residents of older homes were progressive, as they favored Seniors and Cellar Dwellers. Supporters of reappraisal argued that many of the existing inequities were random; different tax liabilities were imposed on people with similiar levels of wealth and income. In the final analysis, the reappraisal issue probably raised the tax principle of "equity" — equal taxes for equal property values — rather than the tax principle of "progressivity" — higher taxes for those with the greater ability to pay. After all, the progressivity of property taxes generally has been a controversial matter,[23] and the progressivity of lower taxes on older homes is also questionable, given the gentrification of older neighborhoods by upper-middle class professionals.

Thus, the reappraisal issue has been significant for Lawrence, but the principles examined here do not appear to have played a significant role in its resolution. Neither Lawrence leaders nor ordinary citizens took the opportunity provided by the inequities in property appraisals to think through appropriate tax principles. Reappraisal provides for more equity, as similarly situated taxpayers will be treated more equally, but state-level decisions about how heavily to rely on property taxes (compared, for example, with more progressive income taxes), or how to tax various classifications of property were made on incremental grounds that involved minimal disturbance of the status quo.

## CONCLUSIONS

Lawrence citizens have relatively liberal communal-provision principles as they express a willingness to incur higher tax burdens to provide better public services and, to some extent, more public welfare. Nevertheless, concrete issues are seldom resolved in ways that involve increasing taxes to increase communal provisions in Lawrence. When citizens have been asked to pay for new public services (such as stormwater management) or new welfare programs (such as Lifeline gas rates) or when they are given a chance to eliminate a tax (such as the intangibles tax), outcomes have been consistent with conservative communal-provision principles.

This incongruence between dominant communal-provision principles and outcomes does not appear to be due to citizen rejection of specific programs; surveys showed strong majority support for governmental responsibility in stormwater management, the Lifeline program, and increased funding for social services. Instead, such incongruence seems to be rooted in questions of tax distribution. Citizens did not like the idea of paying for the stormwater management study through a surcharge on their water bills. City commissioners were uncomfortable paying for Lifeline gas rates through a surcharge on citizens' heating bills. A tax on videogames did not prove to be a feasible way to generate revenue for social services. On the whole, citizens prefer taxes based on benefits-received principles (such as user fees). Public services such as stormwater management and welfare services, however, cannot be paid for by user fees because they are inherently indivisible or redistributive.

Thus, in order to provide more services and welfare, there needs to be not only a willingness to pay more taxes but some understanding of how to levy such taxes. As the community searches for new revenue sources, the question of drawing upon relatively progressive or regressive taxes can profitably be elevated to an important issue and thus debated. The prevailing assumption — that the relatively regressive sales tax is most acceptable politically — has made the use of more progressive taxes a nonissue in Lawrence, perhaps because the interests of the upper class are furthered by its suppression. The current distribution of support for ability-to-pay principles means that many people will be skeptical of progressive-tax proposals, but the current distribution of support for any principle is not etched in stone. When confronted with concrete alternatives, people can be persuaded to support policies that are at odds with their principles, and they can modify their principles. Because neither the intangibles-tax issue nor the problem of inequitable appraisal of property prompted any serious discussion of tax principles, there is little basis for assuming that prevailing tax principles are carefully considered features of the political culture of Lawrence.

# 10

# Saving the Downtown

Lawrence has an attractive and vital downtown, which has been made historical by its 125 years as the commercial center of the community, green and
natural by its trees and plantings, and prosperous by attention from downtown businessmen and the local government. In 1978 a proposal to build an
enclosed shopping mall on the outskirts of town was immediately viewed as
a threat to the downtown. To foreclose the possibility that shops and shop-
pers would abandon the downtown and take their business to the Cornfield
Mall, several downtown shopping malls were proposed, but each was defeated.
This chapter considers five issues concerning the downtown—issues that have,
in many ways, dominated Lawrence politics during the period of this study.
Lawrence leaders and citizens have been deeply committed to "saving the
downtown," but they have been deeply divided on what that means and on
how to achieve it.

## SETTING THE AGENDA:
## THE CORNFIELD MALL PROPOSAL

In October 1978 Jacobs, Visconsi, Jacobs (JVJ)—a Cleveland-based developer
of shopping malls—proposed building a large suburban shopping center on
a sixty-two-acre tract just beyond the southern city limit. Opposition to the
Cornfield Mall materialized immediately among representatives and notables
who expressed concern that the proposed mall would inevitably lead to the
deterioration of the CBD. Six months later, Lawrence citizens elected three
opponents of the Cornfield Mall to the commission, and shortly thereafter
the commission denied JVJ's request that the land be zoned to permit commercial development. Because most participants and citizens had reservations
about the Cornfield Mall, the commission achieved a high degree of respon-

sible representation by rejecting that proposal. Did the commission also act consistently with dominant cultural principles relevant to the issue?

As shown in Table A, supporters of the CORNFIELD Mall were particularly committed to economic-GROWth principles.[1] According to a 1981 staff report of the planning commission, the Cornfield Mall would provide significant economic benefits for Lawrence: it would employ more than 600 people; annual sales of $40 million were projected; and property tax and sales tax collections would contribute more than $500,000 to local governments annually. Rejection of the Cornfield Mall was thus inconsistent with dominant economic-growth principles in Lawrence.

However, most opponents of the Cornfield Mall held protectionist land-use principles; as shown in the NEIGH cell of Table 10.1, protecting the CBD from the CORNFIELD Mall was consistent with such principles. Lawrence's comprehensive plan (Plan 95) designates the CBD as the main shopping area in the community. It was feared that the Cornfield Mall would simply redistribute sales, jobs, and tax collections from the CBD to the outskirts of town, resulting in boarded-up storefronts and blight downtown. For many citizens, the existing downtown is the "heart" of the community; their cultural, historical and aesthetic values were thus at stake in the struggle to save the CBD from a cornfield mall.[2]

Because public costs for the CORNFIELD Mall would be limited to making minor improvements to roads and other facilities serving the site, it was supported mainly by those with conservative public-SERVice principles (see Table A). However, liberal spending-and-taxation principles are dominant in Lawrence, giving credibility to the argument that citizens were — at least in principle — willing to incur the public expenditures necessary to locate an appropriate shopping mall in the CBD in order to save the downtown.[3]

Although a high degree of responsible representation and a significant degree of principle-policy congruence was achieved by the rejection of the initial Cornfield Mall, the threat of a suburban mall has persisted. Each time a downtown mall proposal faltered, new cornfield mall proposals emerged. By rejecting such proposals due to widespread opposition to them, representatives continued to act responsibly. By exploring a variety of downtown redevelopment proposals, they sought to respond to dominant cultural principles calling for economic growth and protection of the downtown through public spending.

## KNOCKING OUT JVJ AND COMMUNITY NOTABLES IN ROUND TWO: THE BUNKER MALL PROPOSAL

In June 1979, business and governmental leaders formed an organization called Action 80 to explore with JVJ the possibility of locating a mall downtown.

Table 10.1 Principle-Policy Congruence on Five Downtown Issues

| Issues | Principles | | | | | | | | |
|---|---|---|---|---|---|---|---|---|---|
| | GROW | NEIGH | SERV | WELF | USETAX | LIB | ECON | AGG | DEMO |
| Build CORN-FIELD Mall | − | + | + | NR | NR | NR | NR | NR | NR |
| Build BUNKER Mall | [−] | + | [−] | NR | NR | NR | NR | NR | NR |
| Build PARKing lot at 600 Mass. | + | − | NR | NR | NR | NR | NR | NR | − |
| Build SIZELER Mall | [−] | + | − | NR | NR | NR | NR | NR | NR |
| Build TOWN-CENTER Mall | − | + | − | NR | NR | NR | NR | [−] | + |

NR : Alternative principles not relevant to issue.
 + : Outcome consistent with dominant principle, as specified in heading.
 − : Outcome inconsistent with dominant principle.
 [ ] : Alternative principles were articulated in interviews, but such principles were not significantly and directly related to the policy preferences of participants or citizens.

A year later, JVJ proposed clearing a four-block area to accommodate in the downtown what was essentially a suburban-style mall—what critics called "the Bunker Mall." Attractive and historically significant buildings on the east side of Massachusetts Street (the main street of the CBD) would have to be torn down, and stores on the west side of Massachusetts Street would confront a massive brick wall. Only Action 80 and the Chamber of Commerce indicated mild support for the project. Other concerned groups and most citizens were appalled. Rather than endorse the project, the city commission hired a consulting firm—Robert B. Teska Associates—to evaluate the plan and consider alternative downtown redevelopment projects that would not destroy the existing CBD to save it from the continuing threat of a cornfield mall.

Like the Cornfield Mall proposal, the Bunker Mall proposal involved economic-growth, land-use, and spending-and-taxation principles. Teska asserted that a downtown mall, like a suburban mall, would contribute to the economic growth of the community because it would recoup sales leakages to other cities and generate jobs. Nevertheless, arguments based on pro-GROWth principles did not seem to contribute to support for the BUNKER Mall, as shown in Table A. Because many people with pro-growth principles supported the search for more attractive redevelopment alternatives, pro-growth principles were not relevant to the resolution of the Bunker Mall proposal.

Teska also claimed that the Bunker Mall was inadequate in terms of land-use principles; the consultants criticized its lack of integration with the rest of the downtown and East Lawrence (which would be "invaded" by the parking ramps associated with the project). As shown in Table 10.1, participant preferences regarding the BUNKER Mall were influenced by their NEIGHborhood protection principles. In order to respect dominant land use principles, commissioners needed to reject the mall.

Furthermore, the Bunker Mall proposal raised issues regarding the level of governmental SERVices and taxation. Teska estimated that the municipal government would have to spend $25 million to prepare the site to JVJ's specifications. Even if some federal funding were obtained, the public at large would have to foot much of the bill to pay off bonds for such improvements as parking ramps, utility relocations, and street construction. Although the dominant policy principles in the community include a willingness to increase taxes for service improvements, these principles did not translate into support for the Bunker Mall. Thus, the search continued for a downtown project that would provide economic growth, protect the downtown, and tap citizens' willingness to impose new tax burdens on themselves in return for desired public improvements.

## GETTING CITIZENS INVOLVED:
## THE PARKING LOT ISSUE REVISITED

As Lawrence citizens were despairing over the Bunker Mall proposal, the parking lot issue also came to a head. The combined specter of outside developers tearing up the east side of Massachusetts Street to build the Bunker Mall and city commissioners tearing down Bryan Anderson's "toy factory" to build a parking lot convinced many citizens that the downtown was being buffeted by projects that threatened its character. The PARKING lot issue was relatively insignificant in terms of the changes it wrought on the downtown, but the issue was important because it stimulated people to realize that downtown redevelopment affected their citizen-participation principles as well as their economic-GROWTH and land-use principles, as suggested in Table 10.1.

The parking lot issue was most supported by those who valued economic growth; the Growth Machine hoped that the project would stimulate a major development in the 600 block of Massachusetts Street[4] or simply serve as one of several small-scale parking facilities needed to encourage the continued redevelopment in the area. Downtown redevelopment could not occur without adequate parking, or, more importantly, if the city was unwilling to use its power of eminent domain to condemn and demolish buildings that stood in the way of progress. The PARKing lot was most opposed by those having protectionist principles (NEIGH). Although the parking lot did not intrude on residential neighborhoods or fundamentally alter the character of the downtown, the issue demonstrated that public authority could be used to inflict more sweeping changes on the downtown. According to Commissioner

Nancy Shontz, the issue showed that commissioners were willing to let the downtown "be picked to death."[5]

Most significantly, the parking lot issue raised questions about DEMocratic principles. According to its opponents, the parking lot issue demonstrated "a lack of openness by decision-makers." Commissioners agreed that there were ten opponents of the project for every supporter, but they did not give an inch. Commission meetings were sufficiently open to allow for an avalanche of protest, but that protest was not influential. Opposition to the parking lot and commitment to more Jeffersonian principles of democratic involvement thus went hand in hand.

By proceeding with the parking lot, the city commission gave priority to dominant economic-growth principles in the community. Even though the resolution of the immediate issue was inconsistent with protectionist land-use and citizen-involvement principles, the commission was not totally insensitive to these aspects of the political culture of the community. In response to citizen protest on the parking lot issue, the commission initiated an open process to develop a comprehensive plan, which it hoped would demonstrate its own commitment to saving the downtown.

## THE FAILURE OF PUBLIC PLANNING:
## THE SIZELER MALL PROPOSAL

The JVJ experiences convinced many participants that the community should initiate its own redevelopment plans rather than simply react to the plans of outside developers and to market forces. As a result, the city retained Teska in March 1981, to develop a comprehensive downtown plan based on the extensive involvement of interested citizens in the planning process.

In December 1981, a comprehensive plan was approved. It emphasized "adaptive re-use and in-fill rather than wholesale demolition," and nine months later Sizeler Realty Company was selected as "developer-of-record" to provide the city with development options that corresponded to the comprehensive plan. In January 1983, Sizeler proposed a somewhat smaller development than the Bunker Mall and suggested that its mall be located one-half block east of Massachusetts Street, minimizing disruption to the existing downtown.

Although the commission was initially favorable toward the Sizeler proposal, the public was less enthusiastic. Perhaps city commissioners could have rallied public support behind the project, but four of the commissioners who had nurtured the redevelopment process left office soon after the Sizeler plans were revealed.[6] Newly elected Commissioners David Longhurst and Mike Amyx — citing design flaws, cost considerations, and lack of public support — requested additional downtown proposals, prompting a group of local developers, engineers, and architects to propose the Towncenter Mall (which will be discussed below). In November 1983, after six weeks of discussion of the relative merits of the Sizeler and Towncenter proposals, the commissioners voted to abandon Sizeler. Most commissioners who participated in that decision thought that the Sizeler project had a great deal of merit, but they were concerned that the project had too little public support. By abandoning their independent judgments about the Sizeler project and responding to public opposition, the commission thus achieved Level 4, instructed delegation, on the scale of responsible representation presented in Chapter 2.

Although the proponents of the Sizeler Mall sought to develop a project that conformed to principles dominant in the community's political culture, the evidence in Table A suggests that participants and citizens were not convinced that they had succeeded in this endeavor. Like the CORNFIELD and BUNKER mall proposals, the SIZELER project promised economic GROwth in the form of $24 million in retained sales that were being lost to shopping centers in Topeka and Kansas City, in more than 700 jobs, and in increased tax revenues.[7] Nevertheless, many people who supported economic growth in principle opposed the Sizeler project because they perceived that the Towncenter proposal (or a cornfield mall) could provide equivalent levels of growth. Thus, economic-growth principles failed to become relevant to the resolution of the Sizeler issue.

Proponents of the Sizeler proposal claimed that the project offered much less disruption of the CBD than the Bunker Mall and that it protected the CBD against the threat of future cornfield mall proposals. Such arguments convinced the DLA to support the project[8] but had little impact on the preferences of participants or citizens generally. Indeed, as shown in Table A, most persons with protectionist principles (NEIGH) opposed the SIZELER project as an unneeded intrusion on the CBD. Thus, dominant restrictive land-use principles weighed against the development.

Finally, Sizeler proponents argued that the public expenditures associated with the project—estimated to be about $18 million—were significantly less than those of the proposed Bunker Mall and that these expenditures would protect the community against such "hidden costs" of a cornfield mall as the projected decline in the tax base downtown and the need to extend public utilities and roads to the site of a suburban mall. As shown in Table A, those participants with liberal spending-and-taxation principles (SERV) tended to support the SIZELER project. However, such participants could not persuade those commissioners (like Longhurst and Amyx) who were committed to keeping taxes low that the Sizeler project was a good public investment.

To the extent that the Sizeler proposal promised growth while protecting the downtown, the public's willingness to raise taxes for desirable projects might have led to its ultimate approval of general obligation bonds to finance the project. However, the new commissioners found little preexisting support for the project and were unwilling or unable to build that support by persuading the public that the Sizeler Mall conformed reasonably well to the community's economic-growth, land-use, and public-service principles. Although supported by the majority of commissioners who dealt with the issue, the project was abandoned because of perceived citizen opposition.

## JVJ STRIKES OUT: THE TOWNCENTER PROPOSAL

When city commissioners chose Towncenter over Sizeler, they picked a "pretty picture," a concept with the potential to correspond to community principles and values. Originally Towncenter was presented as a relatively small two-story development on a site at the north end of Massachusetts Street, which could be cleared with minimal disruption to the downtown. Furthermore, the public costs of Towncenter were originally estimated at $15.2 million ($3 million less than the Sizeler project), and the public would be responsible for only $3.4 million in general obligation bonds.[9]

Such attractions prompted the city commission to continue to assert its commitment to Towncenter for three and a half years. On several occasions, commissioners indicated their hostility to alternative cornfield proposals. They amended the developer-of-record contract to permit JVJ to enter into a joint venture with Towncenter in pursuit of the project. They also established the Urban Renewal Agency to determine that the area was legally blighted, to clear the area, and to arrange a financing package.

Like the Sizeler project, however, the Towncenter proposal could not sustain the enthusiasm of the public. Skepticism about the project was enhanced because the developers preferred to work privately, and announcements about progress on the mall — especially about securing the necessary commitments from major department stores — were slow in coming. Finally, in October 1986, Towncenter submitted site plans for the project, but these plans increased rather than decreased public apprehension. The small mall had grown, extending its footprint toward the Old West Lawrence residential neighborhood and requiring that additional streets be closed to accommodate the project. In general, the new design struck many people as more closely approximating those of typical suburban malls than of the pretty pictures they had seen three years earlier.

While the Towncenter proposal was slowly unfolding, the community became embroiled in another controversy: a proposal to build a trafficway south and west of town. By committing $8 million in city and county funds to the trafficway without holding a referendum, fears were sparked that representatives were proceeding with major projects without adequate public involvement. A group of activists thus mobilized as Citizens for a Better Downtown and collected petitions calling for a binding referendum on Towncenter. Although most commissioners thought that a referendum should be deferred until essential elements of the plan — such as the public costs — were clarified, they recognized that CBD leaders were successfully appealing to citizen-involvement principles and placed three advisory questions on the April 1987, ballot.[10]

The results of that vote were unambiguous; 56 percent of registered voters turned out shattering the community's previous best turnout record of 37 percent to indicate their unhappiness with Towncenter. Less than 30 percent of the voters cast pro-mall ballots on each of the three referenda questions. At the same time, voters turned out of office three commissioners who had been strong supporters of Towncenter and replaced them with three anti-mall challengers. Within a month, Towncenter was dismissed as the city's developer of record. Given the extensive opposition to the project, a high level of responsible representation was attained by this outcome, but was this outcome consistent with dominant community principles?

Most citizens of Lawrence support governmental subsidies to businesses for the promotion of economic growth. Because the Towncenter project was projected to have approximately the same positive impacts on growth as were other mall projects, it would seem that Lawrence citizens ignored pro-growth principles when they rejected the Towncenter Mall. Table A shows, however, that while participants related their positions on TOWNCENTER to their principles regarding GROWTH, citizens did not. Clearly, many citizens who support growth in principle voted against Towncenter, in part, because they were concerned with other principles.

Among the principles that competed with economic-GROWTH principles on the TOWNCENTER issue were those involving protecting neighborhoods and the downtown from disruptive developments, as shown in the NEIGH cell of Table 10.1. In public debate about Towncenter, arguments arose that the project would both save and cripple the downtown. On the one hand, supporters argued that Towncenter represented the community's last chance to avoid a cornfield mall and avert the deterioration of downtown projected to result from a cornfield mall. On the other hand, opponents claimed that the design of the mall and the location of the associated parking ramps were not adequately integrated into the existing downtown, the result being the Towncenter might harm, not help, the existing downtown. Such reasoning seems to have prevailed among participants, as those with stronger protection principles were most likely to oppose Towncenter.[11]

Voters thus had to weigh their concerns about economic growth with those about downtown and neighborhood protection. Also weighing against Towncenter was its cost. Although most Lawrence citizens hold liberal public-SERVice principles and are willing in principle to pay higher taxes for public improvements, they had to be convinced that the Towncenter Mall constituted a communal good worth the price of higher tax bills. Although public costs were difficult to determine at the time of the referendum, the original estimate that the mall would cost $3.2 million in general obligation bonds was clearly inadequate, both because of the increased size of the mall and because federal Urban Development Action Grants (UDAGs) were rapidly drying up.

In order to convince the public to support TOWNCENTER in accordance with their dominant liberal spending-and-taxing principles (SERV), TOWNCENTER supporters emphasized AGGregative criteria. According to Joel Jacobs, a leading community notable and the head of the Urban Renewal Agency, the Towncenter Mall should be viewed as the "Lawrence Mall,"[12] a public facility bene-fiting all Lawrentians. However, the fact that citizens did not significantly relate their widely held aggregative principles to their preferences on the issue probably contributed to the defeat of Towncenter.

The conflicting implications of the community's economic growth and pro-tectionist land-use principles, and the subjectivity involved in determining whether Towncenter served the public interest enhanced the argument that the issue could be resolved only by public vote. Although most supporters of TOWNCENTER held representative-discretion principles (as shown in the DEMO cell of Table A), the commissioners could not overlook widespread sentiment in the community that the public should be consulted on major community issues. By finally holding a referendum on Towncenter, the issue was resolved in a way consistent with the only principle that provided unambiguous guid-ance: letting the people decide.


CONCLUSIONS

The referendum did not put to rest the shopping-mall issue. Shortly after the rejection of Towncenter (and after completion of this study), the process of public planning was reestablished, but a new proposal — involving skywalks bridging various clusters of new stores scattered around the CBD — was quickly rejected. Developers proposed three more cornfield malls, but opposition to such malls had not subsided among most participants and citizens. Thus, these proposals were also rejected, saving the downtown — at least temporarily.[13]

Conflicting dominant community principles are a formidable, but not in-surmountable, obstacle to resolving the shopping-mall issue. The community supports both economic growth and the kind of land-use planning that pro-tects both the downtown and neighborhoods. Despite citizen rejection of pub-lic financing of the Towncenter project, Lawrence's communal-provision prin-ciples suggest that citizens can be persuaded to pay for public improvements that are necessary to resolve the downtown issue. To achieve such support, a project will have to be formulated in a way that incorporates dominant citizen involvement principles. Perhaps the most significant lesson of the Town-center issue is that Lawrence citizens are not content to allow developments affecting the "heart of the community" to be formulated without extensive citizen participation. In Lawrence, the failure to allow such participation leads to protest against the policymaking process as well as against the substantive proposals, and the distribution of power in the community makes it difficult for projects to succeed when there are even modest levels of protest.

# 11

# Political Culture: Principles, Preferences, and Policies

One important criterion for effective democratic government, principle-policy congruence, encompasses the notion that public policies ought to reflect the predominant, enduring values in the local political culture. In Chapter 4, data showed that the citizens of Lawrence have dominant principles supporting: governmental promotion of economic growth; neighborhood protection; more extensive communal provision of services and welfare financed through benefits-received tax measures; limited legislation of morality; the use of economic and utilitarian criteria in policymaking; and direct citizen participation in the resolution of key policy issues. By summarizing the analyses presented in Chapters 5 through 10, it is possible to evaluate the extent to which Lawrence governments have achieved policy outcomes congruent with these dominant principles and to determine which principles are most reflected in policy decisions.

## THE INADEQUACIES OF THE CULTURAL PERSPECTIVE

Urbanists sometimes adopt a cultural perspective to explain the policies of local governments.[1] By suggesting that dominant cultural values can account for policy decisions, they suggest that extensive principle-policy congruence is achieved at the local level.[2] There are two methods for summarizing the extent of principle-policy congruence in Lawrence and thus testing the adequacy of the cultural perspective; both methods involve tabulating the results presented in Tables 5.1, 6.1, 7.1, 8.1, 9.1, and 10.1.

First, the number of instances of principle-policy congruence (the +s in the cells of these tables) and principle-policy incongruence (the −s in these cells) can be compared. The results of this procedure show that on thirty-five occasions outcomes were clearly consistent with relevant dominant principles, but on twenty-eight occasions outcomes were inconsistent. These results suggest that the dominance of principles has little policy impact and that the criterion of having policies reflect dominant cultural values is not well attained on these issues.

A second procedure involves determining whether policy changes were more likely to occur on issues if proponents of change had a greater number of relevant dominant principles on their side than did opponents of change. To conduct such an analysis, an "index of cultural support" was calculated by first determining whether a policy change would have been consistent with each dominant principle relevant to the issue. Next, the number of relevant dominant principles supporting the status quo were subtracted from the number of such principles supporting change. For example, the cultural support score for the WARDS issue was "0" because creating wards would have been inconsistent with the relevant principle of emphasizing ECONOMIC criteria, though it would have been consistent with the relevant principle of enhancing citizen participation (DEMO), as shown in Table 5.1. The cultural support score for the SIGNS issue was "3" because that policy violated no dominant principle and was consistent with three dominant principles: protecting NEIGHborhoods, providing public SERVices, and emphasizing AGGregative criteria (as shown in Table 6.1). Higher cultural support scores are strongly and positively associated with policy changes when there are significant levels of principle-policy congruence, but, over the twenty-nine Lawrence issues, the correlation between cultural support and policy outcomes is only 0.16. Again, this suggests that the criterion of principle-policy congruence is not well achieved in Lawrence and that dominant cultural values provide less-adequate explanations of policy decisions than suggested by the cultural perspective.

The inadequacies of dominant cultural principles as explanations of policy outcomes seem to stem from two primary sources. First, the process of linking dominant cultural principles to concrete issues is problematic, as principles only weakly constrain the positions that people take on issues. Second, there are often a variety of competing dominant cultural principles relevant to concrete issues. Thus, policy decisions may reflect some dominant principles in a culture, but the presence of a variety of competing principles means that these same decisions will be incompatible with other widely held principles. In the remainder of this section, we will discuss these obstacles to the realization of principle-policy congruence before considering two alternatives to the cultural perspective: (a) a revision asserting that policies will reflect the most relevant or most dominant principles in a political culture, and (b) an economistic perspective asserting that policies will reflect economic imperatives regardless of the level of support for these principles within the political culture.

*The Problematic Process*
*of Linking Principles to Preferences*

In pluralist policy processes, the preferences and power of various actors are the main determinants of policy outcomes;[3] thus, the primary process for achieving principle-policy congruence would seem to require that principles influence preferences, which, in turn, influence policy outcomes.[4] This process may be thwarted, however, if people's preferences are derived from such factors as self-interest and group identification rather than from political principles.[5]

The analyses presented in Table A of the Appendix provide the basis for assessing the extent to which preferences are based on principles. To summarize the extensiveness of such linkage of principles to policy preferences, the average adjusted coefficients of determination for the twenty-nine issues have been calculated for participants and citizens. Such an analysis shows that about 36 percent of the variance in participants' preferences on concrete issues is explained by their principles. In contrast, the preferences of citizens on issues are only weakly explained by their specified principles, as the average adjusted coefficient of determination for citizens is only five percent.

Such findings point to a major obstacle to the realization of principle-policy congruence. In order to attain policies consistent with dominant cultural values, people need to base their policy preferences on their principles. Citizens do this only to a limited extent. Participants are much more likely to base their preferences on principles, but a good deal of variance in the preferences of participants remains unexplained by the principles considered here. Thus, when decisions reflect the preferences of citizens and participants, dominant cultural values may be ignored.

*The Policy Predicament*
*of Competing Dominant Principles*

Another major obstacle to the achievement of principle-policy congruence is the policy predicament of competing dominant principles. Most of the twenty-nine issues had at least two dominant, relevant principles that offered conflicting guidance. As a result, the violation of dominant community principles was often unavoidable. Table 11.1 summarizes this policy predicament by showing in the cells of the matrix those issues subject to the competing (and complementary) dominant principles listed in the column and row headings. When the name of an issue is followed by opposite signs ($+ -$ *or* $- +$), the dominant principles indicated by the column and row headings provided contrasting guidance about the resolution of that issue. The difficulty in achieving principle-policy congruence can be illustrated by discussing briefly a few of the more prominent clashes among principles dominant in the political culture of Lawrence.

Widespread community support for both economic-GROWTH and NEIGHborhood-protection is perhaps the greatest "contradiction" in the political culture of Lawrence. While economic-growth principles encouraged policymakers to issue IRBs in an unrestricted manner, to permit high-density developments in the OREAD and on the BLUFFS, to abandon STORMwater management, to build the PARKing lot at 600 Massachusetts Street, and to pursue the building of the TOWNCENTER and CORNFIELD malls, dominant restrictive land-use principles offered the opposite guidance.

Economic-GROWTH principles have also competed with citizen-involvement principles (DEMO) on six Lawrence issues. Opponents of the incumbent pro-growth city MANAGER and of projects to promote economic growth — such as upgrading the AIRPORT and developing the RAIL-served and RESEARCH parks — have tended to articulate and hold citizen-participation principles, probably because they thought that the absence of citizen involvement would ensure that the pro-growth orientations of representatives, bureaucrats, and notables would prevail.[6]

Dominant NEIGHborhood-protection principles compete not only with economic-GROWTH principles but also with the desire of citizens to have their governments apply ECONomic and AGGregative criteria to the resolution of community issues. On the EAST Lawrence downzoning issue, dominant principles about the priority of economic and utilitarian criteria weighed against neighborhood protection principles. On the CATHolic Center issue, neighborhood-protection concerns collided with concerns about the priority of economic criteria. Such competition among principles occurs because concerns about neighborhood protection may have economic costs and involve shielding particular interests from developments providing general community-wide benefits.

A final noteworthy clash of dominant principles that recurred in the sample of issues pitted AGGregative principles against citizen-involvement principles (DEMO). Some analysts have suggested that concerns about the overall public interest (i.e., the maximization of aggregate utility) and about citizen participation are compatible aspects of the cultural values of public-regarding and moralistic communities.[7] In contrast, this analysis suggests that opponents of policies that reflect dominant utilitarian principles frequently invoke citizen participation as a protest principle. Retaining the city MANAGER, closing the rural schools (CLOSE), and developing the RAIL-served industrial park were each justified in terms of utilitarian principles, and in each case protesters demanded broader citizen participation. Thus, demands for citizen participation may be the major weapon available to opponents of policies that are thought to serve the public interest.

Table 11.1  Complementary and Competing Dominant Principles on Lawrence Issues

| | GROW | NEIGH | SERV | WELF | ECON | AGG |
|---|---|---|---|---|---|---|
| NEIGH | IRB+ −<br>OREAD+ −<br>BLUFFS+ −¹<br>STORM+ −<br>CORNFIELD− +<br>PARK+ −<br>TOWNCENTER− + | | | | | |
| SERV | MANAGER+ −<br>N2ST+ +<br>STORM+ −<br>CORNFIELD− +<br>TOWNCENTER− − | SIGN+ +<br>STORM− −<br>CORNFIELD+ +<br>SIZELER+ −<br>TOWNCENTER+ − | | | | |
| WELF | MANAGER+ − | − − | MANAGER− − | | | |
| USETAX | − − | − − | − − | − − | VIDEO+ + | − − |
| LIB | − − | ENVIR+ − | | − − | INTANGIBLES+ + | |
| ECON | AIRPORT+ −<br>RESEARCH+ + | EAST+ −<br>CATH− + | | | | |

| | | | | | |
|---|---|---|---|---|---|
| **AGG** | MANAGER++<br>RAIL – –<br>IRB++ | IRB – +<br>SIGN++<br>EAST+ – | MANAGER – +<br>SIGN++<br>CLOSE+ – | MANAGER – +<br>LIFELINE – + | EAST – – |
| **DEMO** | MANAGER+ –<br>AIRPORT+ –<br>RAIL – +<br>RESEARCH+ –<br>STORM++<br>PARK+ –<br>TOWNCENTER – + | STORM – +<br>PARK – –<br>TOWNCENTER++ | MANAGER – –<br>STORM – +<br>CLOSE++<br>TOWNCENTER – + | MANAGER – – | WARDS+ –<br>AIRPORT – –<br>RESEARCH+ – | MANAGER+ –<br>RAIL – +<br>CLOSE – + |

*Note:* The dominant principles abbreviated in the row and column headings provided complementary guidance for those issues having similar signs. Such principles provided conflicting guidance for those issues having contrasting signs. The first sign after the name of an issue indicates whether the issue was resolved consistently (+) or inconsistently (−) with the column principle. The second sign indicates consistency or inconsistency with the row principle.

[1]Because the BLUFFS issue was resolved in "virtualities" that compromised competing principles, only the inconsistency of the guidance or principles is relevant.

In summary, it is not easy for representatives to resolve issues in ways consistent with the dominant principles of citizens. Most issues — 62 percent of those in the Lawrence sample — embody a variety of competing dominant principles, and usually policymakers are confronted with the dilemma of which dominant principle(s) in the community they must violate. An understanding of which principles are most potent is therefore essential.


## A REVISED CULTURAL PERSPECTIVE

Perhaps policies reflect — and should reflect — those principles that are *most relevant* to issues and/or that are *most dominant* in political cultures. Consider first the AIRPORT improvement issue. The data in Table 6.1 showed that both ECONOMIC criteria and DEMOCRATIC-process principles are relevant to the AIRPORT issue, but economic-GROWth principles seem more relevant because they are most strongly related to the positions of participants on the issue. Perhaps the greater relevance of economic-growth principles explains why airport policies reflect them over concerns about economic criteria and citizen involvement. Consider, too, the LIFELINE issue. The data in Table 9.1 showed that supporters of LIFELINE had liberal public-WELFare principles on their side, and opponents had more conservative AGGregative principles on their side. While both public-welfare and aggregative principles are dominant in Lawrence, aggregative principles are much more dominant among the public than are welfare principles. Perhaps the greater dominance of aggregative principles explains why the outcome of LIFELINE reflected aggregative concerns rather than welfare concerns.

To test the hypothesis that more relevant principles are most reflected in issue outcomes, the index of cultural support was modified to weigh principles by their relevance, by the degree to which various principles have affected people's positions on issues.[8] However, policy changes were not significantly related to the resulting index of cultural support weighted by the relevance of principles ($r = .18$). In short, the extent to which participants and citizens link their principles to policy proposals does not seem to influence which principles are reflected in policy decisions.

To test the hypothesis that policy outcomes are most likely to reflect the most dominant principles in the political culture, the index of cultural support was also modified to weigh relevant principles by their degree of public support.[9] This modification did enhance the relationship between principles and policy outcomes ($r = .29$, which is significant at the .06 level), indicating that principles that are most widely shared by citizens are most reflected in policy decisions. Conversely, those dominant principles that have only slightly more public support than do their counterparts are seldom reflected in policy

Table 11.2  The Extent to Which Various Dominant Principles Were Reflected in Policy Outcomes in Twenty-nine Lawrence Issues

| Dominant Principles | Relevant Cases in Which Principles Were Articulated and Linked | Problematic Cases in Which Principles Were Articulated but Unlinked |
|---|---|---|
| Subsidize growth | $8.5/12^a = .75$ | $3/6 = .50$ |
| Restrict land use | $7.5/13 = .62$ | $1/4 = .25$ |
| Increase public services | $4/8 = .50$ | $1/4 = .25$ |
| Increase public welfare | $.5/3 = .17$ | $0/0 = -$ |
| Tax by benefits received | $2/2 = 1.00$ | $2/2 = 1.00$ |
| Allow social liberty | $0/3 = .00$ | $1/2 = .50$ |
| Stress economic criteria | $5/7 = .71$ | $2/2 = 1.00$ |
| Stress utilitarian criteria | $5/8 = .63$ | $2/3 = .67$ |
| Provide for public involvement | $4/10 = .40$ | $0/1 = .00$ |

[a]The numerator is the number of issues in which the indicated dominant principle was reflected in the policy outcomes. When issues were resolved in ties — as happened with the BLUFFS and SOCIAL services issues — a half case of principle-policy congruence is recorded. The denominator is the number of issues in which the principle was relevant (the number of issues having principle/policy congruence *and* the number of issues having principle-policy incongruence).

decisions. Table 11.2 clarifies this relationship by showing the potency of various dominant principles.

As shown in the center column of the table, the least potent dominant principles were those to permit individual choices and increase public welfare. With the possible exception of the SOCIAL service issue, cases having either of these liberal principles at stake had policy outcomes that reflected their conservative counterparts, and (as shown earlier in Table 4.1) these principles were less consensually held among citizens than were most other dominant principles. The rather slim dominance that these liberal principles enjoy over their counterparts is easily threatened in concrete cases because of the slippage between principles and policy preferences. Some people who say that, in principle, they support the public provision of welfare may be reluctant (for a variety of issue-specific reasons) to support concrete proposals calling for increased taxes. Furthermore, some people who say that, in principle, they support individual liberty may see the desirability of specific social controls. Thus, slim majorities on behalf of liberal principles can easily be transformed into majority opposition to the specific policy goals of liberals.

Another relatively impotent dominant principle concerns public involvement. On only four of ten relevant cases were issues resolved in ways consistent with citizen-participation principles. Though such principles are the most consensually held among citizens, they are not dominant among participants. This suggests that when participants do not hold the values of citizens, another type of disharmony occurs that diminishes the potency of dominant cultural principles.

Principles most dominant in the culture seem most potent. For example, pro-growth and neighborhood-protection principles, which Table 4.1 revealed to be among the most widely held principles in the community, tend to get reflected in policy decisions. On eight of twelve issues that invoked growth principles, pro-growth outcomes clearly prevailed, and on one additional issue (BLUFFS), pro-growth principles were substantially accommodated. On seven of thirteen land-use issues, neighborhood-protection principles clearly prevailed, and such principles were partially accommodated on the BLUFFS issues. Both of these principles might have been more potent except for their tendency to compete with each other.

In summary, the attainment of principle-policy congruence is hindered because several dominant cultural principles can be relevant to specific issues. The Lawrence study provides some evidence that policymakers resolve this policymaking predicament by taking guidance from those principles most widely held by both citizens and participants.[10] Because it seeems appropriate that more widely accepted principles should be more potent than less widely accepted ones, this finding is, perhaps, reassuring for those who evaluate the resolution of community issues. This finding also suggests that cultural explanations of public policies should stress the most widely held principles in the culture—not simply dominant cultural principles.

## THE IMPORTANCE AND LIMITS OF THE ECONOMISTIC PARADIGM

In recent years, urban analysts have increasingly turned away from a cultural perspective to embrace an economistic perspective for understanding the policy directions of local governments.[11] According to Paul Peterson, competition with other cities for productive labor and capital encourages local policymakers to resolve issues in ways that reflect certain economic imperatives. To pursue the economic interests of the city, policies must reflect principles supporting economic growth, minimal public welfare, taxes based on benefits received, economic and aggregative decision-making criteria, and limited citizen participation.[12] To test this economistic paradigm, an "index of economic imperatives" was developed by determining the extent to which each proposed policy change in the sample was consistent with those relevant principles that Peterson claims are conducive to the pursuit of the city's economic interest.[13] The importance of the economistic perspective is indicated by the finding that this index is significantly related to policy outcomes (r = .41). Indeed, policy outcomes are more closely linked to the economic interests of the city than to the distribution of support for these principles in the political culture.

By reviewing the potency of various principles from an economistic perspective, it is possible to suggest the strengths and weaknesses of both the cultural and economistic perspectives and to assess their (in)compatibilities. First, the finding that policy outcomes usually reflect pro-growth prinicples is, of course, consistent with the economistic perspective as well as with the cultural perspective. The dominance of pro-growth principles in the political culture may well be due to the requirements of a capitalist economy, but the effects of pro-growth principles are not as deterministic as suggested by the economistic perspective. The last column of Table 11.2 shows that Lawrence policymakers rejected pro-growth policies in three of six cases when pro-growth principles were articulated but when there was no significant link between economic-growth principles and policy preferences. Arguments that the BUNKER and SIZELER malls would provide growth and that SIGN regulations would inhibit growth were not sufficient to convince participants that their pro-growth principles were in fact at stake on these issues. These cases suggest that pro-growth principles are unlikely to determine outcomes unless most participants are convinced that their pro-growth principles are threatened. If participants significantly link their pro-growth principles to policy proposals, pro-growth outcomes are more likely. Nevertheless, on three of the twelve issues that involved growth principles, pro-growth outcomes were clearly rejected. In short, while pro-growth principles do tend to get reflected in policy outcomes, there are deviant cases. Furthermore, as the link between pro-growth principles and particular policy proposals becomes more problematic, the potency of pro-growth principles decreases.

According to Peterson, the finding that policy outcomes also tend to reflect neighborhood-protection principles is compatible with the economistic perspective, because neighborhood protection can be important for attracting the higher-status citizens who constitute productive labor.[14] Although this observation may be correct, it suggests that the economistic perspective has the same sort of contradictions among principles that plague the cultural perspective. If the economic interests of the city are served both by economic development and by neighborhood protection, the economistic perspective offers no greater understanding than does the cultural perspective of whether pro-growth principles or neighborhood-protection principles will prevail when they provide competing guidance on concrete issues.

By emphasizing that policies will reflect aggregative concerns about the overall economic interests of the community and that community leaders rather than citizens are best able to determine the interests of the community, Peterson may underestimate the role of protest principles regarding distributive justice and citizen participation in the resolution of community issues. Despite the dominance of aggregative (or utilitarian) principles in Lawrence, distributive concerns prevailed on three of eight issues. Concerns about citizen participation were at stake on ten issues, and they prevailed on four occasions. While the principles of distributive justice and citizen participation are not especially powerful in the resolution of community issues, both of these protest principles are sometimes successfully invoked, especially to resist the normal tendencies of local governments to pursue growth. Thus, although the structural bias toward growth is evident in Lawrence, this bias can be diminished by effectively raising other cultural principles regarding neighborhood protection, distributive justice, and citizen involvement.

Indeed, the bias toward pro-growth principles may be no stronger than that in favor of the use of economic criteria over political ones. As suggested by Table 11.2, policymakers seldom disregard relevant economic criteria. Proponents of the economistic perspective can explain this result by pointing out that economic criteria are often used to sustain growth policies, but the potency of economic criteria can also be explained by cultural considerations. According to the ethos theory, the progressive movement brought major changes to the political cultures of American cities by emphasizing the businesslike nature of local government.[15] Thus, both the economistic and cultural perspectives succeed in accounting for the potency of economic criteria.

The usefulness of the economistic perspective is most evident on public-welfare issues. According to Peterson, "The pursuit of a city's economic interests . . . makes no allowance for the case of the needy and unfortunate members of the society. Indeed, the competition among local communities all but precludes a concern for redistribution."[16] As a confirmation of Peterson's argument, public-welfare principles have seldom been at stake on Lawrence issues. When welfare issues arose, they were defeated, despite the dominance of liberal welfare principles in the political culture.

Peterson also argues that economic considerations preclude serious consideration of progressive tax principles because taxing the rich — like providing welfare for the poor — discourages those who contribute most to the economy from locating in the community.[17] As predicted by Peterson, progressive tax principles were seldom raised on the Lawrence issues, and on the one case where such principles were most clearly involved — the proposal to eliminate an INTANGIBLES tax on interest and dividend income — the progressive tax was defeated. In Lawrence this structural bias against progressive taxes was reinforced in the political culture by dominant benefits-received tax principles.

The economistic perspective thus helps to explain why policy decisions tend to reflect certain conservative principles. The economic interests of cities prompt them to pursue economic-development policies, emphasize economic criteria in decision making, minimize public welfare, reject progressive taxation, and limit citizen participation. Although the cultural perspective can also explain the pursuit of economic development, the emphasis on economic criteria, and the rejection of progressive taxes on the basis of dominant principles in the culture, proponents of the cultural perspective must concede the possibility that the dominance of these principles is due to the systemic power of economic concerns. Furthermore, the economistic perspective can explain the resistance to public welfare and citizen participation, while the cultural perspective can account for the impotence of these principles only by a revision that asserts that principles must be strongly held by both citizens and participants (rather than simply dominant among citizens).

The economistic perspective does not help to explain other conservative tendencies in the policymaking process. Peterson admits that economic imperatives provide no guidance to issues involving the provision of public services.[18] Because there is no clear economic gain or loss to the city as a whole from increases (or decreases) in public services, issues involving public-service principles are unaffected by economic imperatives. Similarly, there seem to be no clear economic imperatives on issues involving individual-choice versus social-control principles. In short, the economistic perspective does not explain why the resolution of public-service and social-control issues tends to have more conservative outcomes than warranted by the dominance in Lawrence of liberal principles relevant to such issues.

## CONCLUSIONS

The first ideal of pluralist democracies — that policy outcomes ought to reflect the dominant principles in a local political culture — is not very well attained on the twenty-nine Lawrence issues studied here. In large part, this is due to the contradictions within the political culture; Lawrence citizens and participants hold a mixture of liberal and conservative principles that offer competing guidance to the resolution of concrete issues.

Although the political culture of Lawrence gives about equal emphasis to liberal and conservative principles, policy decisions are tilted toward conservative ones. The one possible exception to this generalization is the potency of neighborhood-protection principles. Because of the widespread acceptance of the notion that property rights should be limited to protect neighborhoods and the larger community from disruptive developments, liberal neighborhood-protection principles compete with pro-growth principles on a nearly equal basis. The potency of neighborhood-protection principles suggests that political culture cannot be ignored in explaining the resolution of community issues.

The structural context of American cities — their need to compete with other cities for capital and productive labor — may help to explain the potency of a variety of conservative principles in Lawrence. The economic interests of the city as a whole may prompt most citizens to adopt principles emphasizing the desirability of economic growth, the need to emphasize economic criteria in decision making, and benefits-received tax principles. Such principles are usually reflected in issue outcomes, as predicted both by their dominance in the political culture and by structural considerations. In addition, the economic interests of the city may help explain the impotence of public-welfare and citizen-participation principles.[19]

Although the cultural and economistic perspectives are helpful in explaining the policy directions of local communities, they are limited because they do not consider the situational preferences and power of particular people involved in local issues.[20] When issues involve contradictory principles — exemplified by the conflict between economic growth and neighborhood protection — issue-specific considerations greatly affect the positions people take and thus the distribution of power on issues. When issues involve principles that are only somewhat more widely held than their counterparts — as is the case in Lawrence on issues involving public-service and individual-choice principles — issue-specific considerations can result in significant slippage from dominant liberal principles to dominant conservative issue-specific preferences. On most of the issues involving public-service and individual-choice principles, enough people adopted more conservative policy preferences than predicted by their principles, so responding to the dominant preferences of participants and citizens often resulted in conservative policy outcomes. Thus, explanations of the resolution of community issues must consider not only the systemic power of capitalism and the dominant principles in a political culture, but also the concrete preferences of people and the power that they wield to achieve their preferred policy outcomes.

# 12

# Political Power: Participants, Citizens, and Democracy

A second criterion of pluralist democracies for effective government is responsible representation, which requires that predominant power reside with elected representatives. Though pluralists assert that representatives should normally exercise their independent judgments when resolving community issues, they also assert that representatives should normally be responsive to citizen preferences and open to the views of bureaucrats, notables, mobilizers, and individual activists. In this chapter, the extent to which responsible representation has been achieved in Lawrence is assessed in two ways. First, we will summarize and analyze the congruence of specific policy decisions with the dominant preferences of representatives, citizens, bureaucrats, notables, mobilizers, and activists. Second, we will discuss the power of each of these types of people over the entire sample of Lawrence issues.

## RESPONSIBLE REPRESENTATION

In Chapter 2, a scale of responsible representation, based on whether policy decisions are congruent with the dominant preferences of various kinds of actors, was presented. In Chapters 5 through 10, the extent to which responsible representation was achieved on each of the twenty-nine issues was usually indicated. Table 12.1 summarizes these findings. The first seven columns of the table report whether each policy issue was resolved in a way that was congruent (+) or incongruent (−) with the dominant preferences of representatives, citizens (as measured by public opinion polls and as perceived by representatives), notables, bureaucrats, mobilizers, and individual activists. The last column indicates the level of responsible representation attained on each issue.

Overall, the data in Table 12.1 suggest that responsible representation in

Table 12.1   Analyzing Responsible Representation: Congruence of Dominant Preferences of Various Actors with Policy Outcomes

| Issues | Elected Representatives | Citizens Actual | Citizens Perceived | Notables | Bureaucrats | Mobilizers | Individual Activists | Level of Responsible Representation |
|---|---|---|---|---|---|---|---|---|
| WARDS | + | + | + | + | + | + | + | 10 |
| MAYOR | + | + | + | + | + | − | + | 8 |
| MANAGER | S | + | + | + | + | + | + | 10 |
| AIRPORT | + | + | S | + | + | + | + | 10 |
| N2ST | + | + | + | + | + | + | + | 10 |
| RAIL | + | − | − | − | − | − | − | 5 |
| RESEARCH | + | + | + | + | + | + | + | 10 |
| IRB | − | + | + | S | + | + | − | 4 |
| SIGNS | + | + | + | + | + | + | + | 10 |
| OREAD | + | − | S | + | S | − | S | 6 |
| EAST | + | + | S | − | − | + | − | 8 |
| BLUFFS | [S] | [−] | [−] | [+] | [+] | [−] | [−] | − |
| CATH | + | + | + | + | + | S | + | 10 |
| ENVIR | + | + | + | + | + | S | − | 8 |
| DRUG | + | + | S | + | S | NA | + | 10 |
| TRIBES | + | − | S | − | − | + | S | 7 |
| BIRTH | + | + | + | + | + | − | − | 6 |
| STORM | − | − | − | − | − | − | + | 5 |
| CLOSE | + | + | + | − | − | + | + | 7 |
| LIFELINE | + | − | − | − | + | − | + | 7 |
| SOCIAL | [−] | [+] | [−] | [+] | [−] | [+] | [−] | − |
| VIDEO | + | S | S | + | + | + | + | 7+ |
| INTANGIBLES | + | + | + | + | − | + | + | 9 |

| REAPPRAISE | (−/+) | (−/+) | (+/−) | (−/+) | (−/+) | (−/+) | (−/+) | (1/10) |
|---|---|---|---|---|---|---|---|---|
| CORNFIELD | + | + | + | + | + | + | + | 10 |
| BUNKER | + | − | + | − | S | + | + | 9 |
| PARK | + | + | S | + | + | + | − | 6 |
| SIZELER | − | + | + | − | − | − | − | 4 |
| TOWNCENTER | + | + | + | − | − | + | + | 9 |
| % consistent with domi-nant preferences[a] | 88 | 72 | 85 | 72 | 65 | 70 | 71 | $\bar{x}=7.8$ |

+ : Outcome consistent with dominant preferences in actor set.

− : Outcome inconsistent with dominant preferences in actor act.

S : Actors in set split on issue (47%–53%).

NA : No involvement by actors in this set.

[ ] : Issue resolved in virtual tie. Consistency indicated as if developers won BLUFFS issue and supporters of welfare won SOCIAL issue.

( ) : Issue was not resolved locally. Left-hand symbols and score reflect outcome prior to state legislative action; right-hand symbols and score reflect outcome after state action.

[a] Excludes BLUFFS, SOCIAL, REAPPRAISE, and cases with split opinions (S) and no involvements (NA).

Lawrence is quite high. REAPPRAISAL was the most problematic issue in terms of democratic performance. By awaiting legislative action for many years, local representatives permitted local preferences to be overridden by the inaction of external participants. When reappraisal occurred, the highest level of responsible representation was reached, illustrating that external participants can create democratic policies if they respond to the dominant preferences of local participants and citizens.

The remainder of the Lawrence issues were resolved in ways that ranged from instructed delegation (Level 4) to consensus (Level 10). In no issues in the sample did representatives set aside their independent judgments and ignore dominant citizen preferences in order to respond to the dominant wishes of notables, bureaucrats, mobilizers, or activists.

On eleven issues, the dominant preferences of representatives and citizens collided. Dominant citizen preferences prevailed on the SIZELER and IRB issues (where commissioners acted as instructed delegates) and on the STORMwater management issue (which was resolved by referendum). Dominant representative preferences prevailed on the RAIL-served industrial park issue (when county commissioners acted as unsupported trustees), on the BIRTHing room, OREAD downzoning, and PARKing lot issues (where representatives were persuaded to ignore citizen preferences by public administrators and/or notables), and on the TRIBES, school CLOSing, and LIFELINE issues (where representatives were persuaded by activists and/or mobilizers).[1]

Fifteen issues were resolved in ways consistent with the dominant preferences of both representatives and citizens. On three occasions (MAYORAL selection, EAST Lawrence downzoning, and the enforcement of the ENVIRONmental code), this required neglecting dominant group and/or activist preferences. On four occasions (EAST Lawrence downzoning, repeal of the INTANGIBLES tax, and the rejection of the BUNKER and TOWNCENTER mall proposals), this required acting contrary to dominant bureaucratic and/or notable preferences. Nine issues (e.g., WARDS, MANAGER, and AIRPORT) were resolved in a consensual manner, where consensus is understood not as the absence of conflict but as concurrence with the dominant preferences of various kinds of key actors in community politics.

What explains variations in the levels of responsible representation that are achieved on community issues? Adequate explanations must consider variations in the settings of political issues, as responsible representation may be influenced by the governmental structures, political cultures, and other differences among communities that are held constant in this study. For example, reformed governmental institutions (featuring a council-manager plan) are believed to depoliticize local governments, making them less responsive to constituency pressures,[2] and enhancing the roles in local decision making of bureaucrats,[3] notables,[4] and organized groups.[5] Although such research suggests that reformism reduces responsible representation, the findings in

Table 12.1 perhaps vindicate reformed institutions; fairly high levels of responsible representation appear to have been achieved through the council-manager system of Lawrence.[6] Within Lawrence, however, variations in responsible representation might be explained.[7] We will explore four types of explanations.

First, responsible representation may be affected by the composition of the policymaking body. For example, the 1981–83 city commission – the commission whose members were most committed to the ideas of public input and responsiveness – appears to have achieved higher levels of responsible representation than have other commissions and boards.[8] This suggests that voters can enhance the responsible representation of their governments by electing their representatives on the basis of their commitment to democratic ideals.

Second, responsible representation may be affected by the level of citizen participation on issues. Some democratic theorists have asserted that more extensive citizen participation is the key to ending the maladies of low democratic performance, especially elite and bureaucratic domination,[9] but others have asserted that too much participation leads to extensive community conflict, thwarting representative discretion, and undermining more centralized methods of achieving consensus.[10] In Lawrence there is no significant relationship between the number of people who participate on issues[11] and the level of responsible representation achieved on these issues ($r = .02$), suggesting that participation may be overemphasized.

Third, democratic performance may be affected by citizen oversight. In Lawrence, responsible representation was directly, positively, and significantly related to the level of citizen awareness of issues ($r = 40$).[12] Perhaps relatively diffuse citizen pressures on representatives – supplied by a context where representatives understand that citizens are watching and evaluating them – provide incentives for representatives to be responsive to public concerns. At the same time, mere citizen awareness – awareness unaccompanied by the more direct and extensive pressure exerted by direct participants – may provide representatives with the latitude they need to achieve higher levels of community-wide consensus.[13]

Finally, democratic performance may be affected when the imperatives of economic growth are at stake on policy issues. It has been suggested that there are trade-offs between economic imperatives and constituency pressures; the need to respond to economic imperatives may enhance elite power, diminish responsiveness to group demands and public opinion, and thus reduce responsible representation.[14] Nevertheless, in the Lawrence sample, the index of economic imperatives[15] was unrelated to responsible representation ($r = .03$). At least in political cultures where there is a strong commitment to economic growth, democratic consensus may be as likely to emerge as elite domination when issues involve economic-growth principles.

No doubt there are other explanations of responsible representation. The present analysis can only suggest that responsible representation varies across

issues and across communities, and that it is possible that responsible representation is affected by the composition of the policymaking body, the involvements of citizens, and the principles at stake.

## RESPONSIVENESS AND DIRECT POWER

In addition to bearing directly on democratic performance, the data in Table
12.1 address the power of representatives, bureaucrats, notables, mobilizers,
individual activists, and citizens at large. The bottom row of Table 12.1 summarizes the percentage of issues in which the dominant preferences of particular types of people prevailed. Thus, the prominence of representatives is
suggested by the finding that on all but three issues (88 percent of the time),
policy outcomes reflected dominant representative preferences. The dominant
preferences of citizens, notables, bureaucrats, group leaders, and individual
activists were also usually reflected in policy outcomes, suggesting that each
kind of actor plays a significant role in the resolution of community issues.

To assess further the prominence of various kinds of actors in the resolution of community issues, summary measures of responsiveness and direct
power are provided in Table 12.2. The extent to which policy outcomes have
been responsive to the preferences of representatives, notables, bureaucrats,
mobilizers, activists, and citizens is indicated by zero-order correlations relating the preferences of these actors to policy outcomes across twenty-eight
of the twenty-nine issues in the sample.[16] The more positive the correlation
between the preferences of a type of people and policy outcomes, the more
such people have achieved what they wanted in the resolution of policy issues. As shown in Table 12.2, the preferences of representatives and citizens
are most strongly related to policy outcomes, and the preferences of bureaucrats, notables, mobilizers, and activists and also positively related to outcomes at a .05 level of statistical significance.[17]

Such measures do not show whether these people have achieved what they
want as a result of their direct influence over policy decisions. To have power,
people must not only have preferences congruent with the outcome, but their
preferences must also affect the outcome.[18] For example, because the analysis
of responsible representation revealed no instances where bureaucrats or
notables obtained policies that they wanted without having the support of
representatives, it is possible that these actors do not have direct influence
but only get what they want when they prefer the same policies preferred by
those actors having direct influence. Regression coefficients indicate the direct
power of various types of people by relating their preferences to policy outcomes while controlling for the preferences of other people.

Regression analysis suggests that representatives are the only participants
that wield significant direct power in Lawrence (B = .62).[19] Notables and citizens

Table 12.2    Power in Lawrence: The Extent to Which the Outcomes of Twenty-eight
Policy Issues[1] Have Reflected the Preferences of Various Types of People

| Various Types of Actors | Responsiveness (Zero-order Correlations) | Direct Power (Beta-Weights) |
|---|---|---|
| Representatives | .72* | .62* |
| Bureaucrats | .33* | − .24 |
| Notables | .48* | .31 |
| Mobilizers | .48* | .01 |
| Individual Activists | .43* | − .19 |
| Citizens at large | .58* | .26 |
| | | Adjusted $R^2$ = .44 |

*S.L. < .05

[1]The REAPPRAISAL issue is omitted from this analysis because of the widespread perception that it was a state-level issue and because proponents of reappraisal suffered many losses before finally succeeding in 1986.

have positive beta coefficients, suggesting some direct influence as well, but these relationships are relatively weak (and not statistically significant). These data suggest that the direct power of both notables and citizens is confined to a small number of issues and is not instrumental in the resolution of community issues generally. There are no direct relationships between policy outcomes and the preferences of bureaucrats, mobilizers, or activists. Thus, the correlations between the preferences of these participants and policy outcomes occur because these relationships are either indirect or spurious.[20] In the remaining sections of this chapter, the power of these types of people is further described and interpreted.

REPRESENTATIVES:
THE POWER OF INDEPENDENT JUDGMENT

The power of representatives begins with their ability to set the agenda by formulating policy proposals.[21] To be sure, this is not a power that resides exclusively among representatives, nor is it a power that representatives often employ. On only eight issues in the Lawrence sample did any representative play a role as either the principal or contributing agenda setter. Overall, representatives viewed themselves as initiators of policy proposals on only 5 percent of the issues in which they were involved.[22] Even when representatives initiate proposals, their power can, of course, be limited by their failure to achieve their policy objectives, as illustrated by the failure of Tom Gleason to attain city MANAGER Watson's resignation.

The power of representatives is clearly greater in the issues-resolution stage than in the agenda-setting stage of the policy process. Most Lawrence issues were initiated by other actors, and representatives aligned themselves as proponents or opponents of these initiatives; 25 percent of the time representatives claimed to be "weak" supporters or opponents of such initiatives, and 51 percent of the time they claimed to be "strong" supporters or opponents. In such roles, the power of commissioners is rooted in their persuasive abilities and in their vote. Often commissioners argued vigorously for their positions, occasionally influencing their fellow commissioners. By casting their votes with the majority, commissioners attained policy successes, but when they voted with the minority, they sustained policy losses, and their power was, of course, limited.[23]

Representatives indicated that they were "referees" on 19 percent of the issues in which they participated; they neither supported nor opposed the initiatives of others, but had to judge among the alternatives. Such was the role of Marci Francisco at the executive session on the City MANAGER issue. Because Barkley Clark and Don Binns were strong supporters of Watson and because Tom Gleason and Nancy Shontz were opponents, Francisco held the decisive vote. Nevertheless, Francisco might or might not have exercised power on the issue. To exercise power, representatives must have their independent judgments reflected in policy outcomes. When representatives see themselves as referees, they might have no clear personal perferences or judgments about issues and become mere agents of those who apply pressure on them. Alternatively, representatives might weigh the substantive pros and cons of policy proposals and arrive at their own independent judgment about the issue; if they vote on the basis of such judgments, they exercise personal power.[24]

When representatives are referees, it is not always clear — even to the representatives themselves — whether they have responded to external pressures or exercised independent judgments. On the one hand, it could be argued that Francisco responded to community pressures on the MANAGER issue; she had a variety of complaints about Watson's performance, but she understood that these complaints were not well understood by the rest of the community and that voting for his dismissal would have subjected her to intense public hostility. On the other hand, it could be argued that Francisco used her own independent judgment; despite her reservations about Watson's performance, she understood (and perhaps accepted) the arguments that the community was best served by his retention, and she thought the issue was resolved successfully because a written review policy was adopted. This example illustrates the fragility of the concept of "independent judgment" and thus the ambiguity of the political power of representatives acting as referees.

The failure of representatives to act on the basis of their preferences and judgments can limit their individual and collective power. If representatives who hold the swing vote(s) on issues abandon their preferences or judgments and respond to external pressures, the power of a commission as a collective entity is reduced. None of the twenty-nine issues illustrates such a delegation of power by the commission, but the City MANAGER issue illustrates a case where such delegation was approximated. If Francisco abandoned her independent judgment and simply deferred to external pressures, the retention of Watson would have been inconsistent with dominant commissioner preferences. However, there is no basis for rejecting Francisco's own assessment that she responded neither to Watson's supporters nor to his opponents, but sought a "middle way" — subjecting Watson to a systematic evaluation and subseqent vote on his retention — that reflected her own assessment of the community interest.[25] By exercising such judgment, she empowered representatives.

Another related limitation on the power of representative bodies is their willingness to make specific policy decisions that contradict their general policy orientations. For example, the majority of city commissioners expressed independent judgments, regarding matters of general policy, that it was a mistake to give IRBs to businesses that compete with existing firms in the community. Nevertheless, majorities could usually be constructed to support specific IRB requests; thus, when the Holidome sought IRBs, commissioners thought that the community's need for a convention center outweighed their general concerns about providing competitive advantages. When representatives make specific policy decisions that undermine their overall judgments about appropriate policy directions, responsible representation is impaired.

A third limitation on the power of representative bodies involves their failure to maintain majority support within these bodies for projects that take an extensive period of time to adopt. The 1981–83 city commission — which unanimously supported the SIZELER project — was disempowered when the project could not sustain majority support in the 1983–85 commission. Similarly, the 1983–85 and 1985–87 commissions that supported TOWNCENTER were disempowered by the actions of the 1987–89 commission.

A fourth way in which the collective power of representatives can be limited is when citizens override their decisions through referenda. For example, the city commission was disempowered when the surcharge on water bills to finance a STORMwater management study was defeated by voters.

A final limitation on the power of representatives is their reluctance to pursue policies that they prefer because they believe that the issue should be resolved by another policymaking body. Thus, despite a widespread preference to REAPPRAISE property, commissioners were powerless on the issue. Indeed, a number of potential issues were not pursued in Lawrence during the period of this study because of the limited home rule powers of local governing bodies.

Despite such limits on the power of representatives, their dominance in the resolution of local community is clearly indicated by the facts that most policies reflect the dominant preferences and judgments of commissioners and that commissioner preferences have the greatest direct effect on policy outcomes.

In pluralist communities, however, representatives do not arrive at their conclusions in a manner insulated from the views of others. When exercising direct power, representatives may respond to the views of bureaucrats, notables, mobilizers, activists, and citizens.

## BUREAUCRATS: THE POWER OF ADMINISTRATIVE OFFICE

Public administrators can play important roles in the initiation as well as the implementation of policy. In addition to introducing municipal budgets, Buford Watson and his city hall staff were viewed by commissioners as contributing to the initiation of five issues in the Lawrence sample (e.g., the PARKing lot and AIRPORT improvement proposals were developed by the city staff in conjunction with specific commissioners and citizens having strong interests in these projects). Only one issue in the sample was primarily a bureaucratic proposal; Superintendent of Schools Carl Knox and his staff initiated the proposal to CLOSE various rural schools, and this initiative was rejected by the school board.

Although the image of bureaucrats as powerful initiators of policy appears unwarranted, the opposite image of bureaucrats as neutral bystanders in the resolution of community issues is equally unwarranted. Some administrators had clear positions on each issue in our sample. The planning department made recommendations on land-use issues. The public works department supported the PARKing lot, the improvements of N2ST, and the STORMwater management fee. In general, department heads and employees limited their involvement to the issues effecting their departments. Only Buford Watson and Assistant City Manager Mike Wildgen were involved in a variety of issues.[26]

Overall, Watson and his staff were generally successful in achieving policies that reflected their positions; however, there is little evidence that their success is rooted in their direct power rather than in their persuasiveness. Only the IRB issue had an outcome that was more consistent with bureaucratic preferences than the preferences of representatives, and on this issue, commissioners cited the project applicants rather than the administration as being persuasive.

Watson and the staff did lose on several issues. They failed to persuade the city commission to drop the EAST Lawrence downzoning proposal; they failed to persuade the county commission to permit the RAIL-served industrial park; and they failed to generate support for various downtown mall proposals. In addition, voters ended the INTANGIBLES tax and rejected the STORMwater fee, despite restrained bureaucratic support for these taxes. In general, these were issues in which administrative preferences were less strong and in which administrative involvement was more limited.

In short, the power of administrators appears to be considerable but not unbounded. If the Lawrence data are representative, administrators tend to respond to the proposals of others rather than develop bureaucratic initiatives. When administrators *do* take policy initiatives or become advocates for various outcomes, they do not succeed when opposed by representatives or citizens. On a number of occasions, bureaucratic recommendations are set aside, as representatives act on the basis of their own preferences or other pressures.

## NOTABLES:
## THE POWER OF ECONOMIC AND SOCIAL RESOURCES[27]

As in all communities, some citizens have disproportionate control over economic resources and/or social status in Lawrence. Table 12.3 presents a rank-ordering of the thirty-five leading notables in the Lawrence community, their occupations, and the extent to which their reputations as notables is based on their possession of economic and/or social resources.[28]

As elite theorists have consistently demonstrated, notables are not very representative of the rest of the community. All Lawrence notables are white, and only six are women. Notables, of course, are usually members of the upper class, and their class standing is indicated not only by their reputations but also by objective indicators. None of the notables live in neighborhoods having low property values. Social notables, as well as economic notables, have above-average incomes. All have college educations, and many have postgraduate degrees. The average age of these notables was fifty years, and they have, on average, lived in Lawrence for twenty-eight years.

In Table 4.1 the political principles of comunity notables were presented. These data indicated that notables support economic growth, even more strongly than did citizens. Relative to citizens, notables also oppose public welfare, prefer regressive taxes, view Lawrence government as a business, have aggregative principles, and are skeptical of widespread citizen involvement.

Despite these general tendencies and orientations, viewing Lawrence notables as a cohesive force on local issues would be a mistake. The data in Table 4.1 show that notables are as heterogeneous in their principles as citizens and other actors. Moreover, while these notables tend to be familiar with one another, the communications network among them can be described as sporadic, indirect, and fragmented.[29] These differences in principles and the lack of an integrated communications network explain why there were few issues in which notable participation was widespread, unified, and successful.

Commmunity notables seldom initiated policy changes. Duane Schwada, a local developer and economic notable, did initiate the BLUFFS controversy by proposing a development on that site, and he was the central figure in the TOWNCENTER proposal. Lynn Anderson was a member of the partnership proposing the RAIL-served industrial park. Lawrence's top-ranked notable, Bob

Table 12.3  Lawrence Notables, 1983–1985: A Reputational Ranking

| Rank | Name | Occupation | Economic[1] | Social[2] | Total |
|---|---|---|---|---|---|
| 1 | Bob Billings | Developer | 272 | 28 | 300 |
| 2 | Petey Cerf | Volunteer | 81 | 15 | 96 |
| 3 | Joel Jacobs | Corporate manager | 65 | 7 | 72 |
| 4 | Dolph Simons, Jr. | Newspaper editor | 29 | 30 | 59 |
| 5 | Sherry Schaub | Corporate manager | 40 | 6 | 46 |
| 6 | Lynn Anderson | Banker | 38 | 6 | 44 |
| 7 | Gene Budig | KU chancellor | 7 | 37 | 44 |
| 8 | Dolph Simons, Sr. | Chairman of newspaper board | 29 | 12 | 41 |
| 9 | Tom Maupin | Owner of business | 32 | 6 | 38 |
| 10 | Roger Hill | Corporate manager | 36 | 2 | 38 |
| 11 | Charles Oldfather | Law professor, school board member | 26 | 10 | 36 |
| 12 | Duane Schwada | Developer | 31 | 0 | 31 |
| 13 | John McGrew | Realtor | 27 | 2 | 29 |
| 14 | Homer "Butch" Henderson | Minister | 0 | 28 | 28 |
| 15 | Glenn Kappelman | Realtor | 17 | 8 | 25 |
| 16 | Tensie Oldfather | Volunteer | 19 | 5 | 24 |
| 17 | Olin Petefish | Lawyer | 16 | 8 | 24 |
| 18 | Jessie Branson | State representative | 12 | 11 | 23 |
| 19 | Ned Cushing | Banker | 15 | 6 | 21 |
| 20 | Bob Moore | Developer | 18 | 2 | 20 |
| 21 | Riley Burcham | Banker | 13 | 4 | 17 |
| 22 | Dick Raney | Downtown businessman | 7 | 8 | 15 |
| 23 | Warren Rhodes | Banker | 11 | 3 | 14 |
| 24 | Bob Stephens | Realtor | 13 | 0 | 13 |
| 25 | Hank Booth | Owner of radio station | 2 | 10 | 12 |
| 26 | Ann Evans | Arts center director | 0 | 11 | 11 |
| 27 | Jim Schwartsburg | Owner of business | 9 | 0 | 9 |
| 28 | Jackie Davis | Volunteer | 0 | 9 | 9 |

| | | | | |
|---|---|---|---|---|
| 29 | Jack Arensberg | Downtown businessman | 6 | 2 | 8 |
| 30 | Carl Knox | School superintendent | 0 | 7 | 7 |
| 31 | Barkley Clark | Law professor, commissioner | 0 | 7 | 7 |
| 32 | Martin Dickinson | Law professor | 0 | 6 | 6 |
| 33 | Barbara Waggoner | Writer, volunteer | 0 | 6 | 6 |
| 34 | Ralph Reed | Physician | 0 | 6 | 6 |
| 35 | Pete Whitenight | Downtown businessman | 0 | 6 | 6 |

[1] Number of times cited for controlling capital investment decisions or for contributing money to community projects by participants in 1983 and 1985 reputational studies.

[2] Number of times cited for having social status in the community or for having the respect of the community in 1983 and 1985 reputational studies.

Billings, proposed the RESEARCH park. Additionally, a variety of notables were members of Action 80, the group that proposed the BUNKER Mall. Such elite initiatives did not fare particularly well; the RAIL-served industrial park, the BUNKER Mall, and the TOWNCENTER Mall proposals failed.

For the most part, Lawrence notables reacted to the initiatives of others. For example, when Politicos urged a change in Lawrence's form of government and when Tom Gleason sought Buford Watson's resignation, many notables became active in opposing the WARDS proposal and in supporting the city MANAGER. Although the AIRPORT improvements and SIZELER Mall were initiated by nonelites, these issues attracted the active support of about a dozen notables. The only other issue in which more than ten notables were involved was SOCIAL services. Here, the predominant pattern was for notables to be involved as volunteers, often as chairpersons, of fund-raising drives for charitable organizations such as the United Fund.

As shown in Table 12.1, the predominant position of those notables involved in specific issues prevailed 72 percent of the time. A significant number of notables failed to achieve their objectives on the various downtown mall proposals and the RAIL-served park, and a few notables were on the losing side of the EAST Lawrence downzoning, school CLOSING, and TRIBES issues.

There were no instances when notable preferences prevailed against the predominant preferences of formal decision makers.[30] When notables succeeded, their power appeared to be either indirect or coincidental. On issues such as the PARKing lot, AIRPORT improvements, and the CATHolic Center, a number of notables actively pursued the outcomes achieved and were cited by some commissioners as important supporters of these projects. In the case of LIFELINE, notables won — not by actively opposing the ordinance — but by organizing a charitable alternative to Lifeline called Warm Hearts that helped convince wavering commissioners that the Lifeline program was unnecessary. On still other issues where notables "won," there is little evidence that any notable played an influential role. For example, dominant notable preferences were consistent with the outcomes of the ENVIRonmental code, DRUG paraphernalia, INTANGIBLES tax, and CORNFIELD Mall issues, but in none of these cases is there any evidence of notable participation being extensive, visible, decisive, or in any way distinguishable from other community-based pressures.

Thus, the evidence suggests that community notables do not dominate the resolution of Lawrence issues. This does not mean that they are no more powerful than other Lawrence citizens. Economic notables have initiated a number of economic-development issues, and their support of economic development has contributed to the success of a variety of developmental policies. Notables successfully defended the city manager form of government and Buford Watson, thus assuring their continued access to the policy process. Nevertheless, there is little evidence that policymakers have simply deferred to the economic resources or social status of community notables by resolving issues in ways that respond to elite preferences rather than to their independent assessments of community needs.

## MOBILIZERS: THE POWER
## OF GROUP LEADERSHIP AND ORGANIZATION

If disproportionate control of economic resources and/or social status distinguish community notables, disproportionate control of organizational resources distinguish mobilizers (group leaders) and group members from other players in the game of community politics. When mobilizers participate, they utilize their personal resources just as they would if they were individuals acting independently of any group, but mobilizers also draw upon organizational resources that are unavailable to individual activists. Most obviously, mobilizers claim to represent the members of their organization; because they speak on behalf of many people and not just for themselves, their views may be given more weight than may the views of single individuals. In addition, mobilizers may coordinate the efforts of group members, enhancing the effective application of their individual resources. Finally, mobilizers may draw on emergent group properties — resources beyond those of group leaders and group members — that arise from ongoing activities of those in the organization. For example, mobilizers can enhance their effectiveness by drawing upon the reputations of their organizations for contributing to the welfare of the community or for wielding clout in local elections. Such organizational resources should give mobilizers (and their group constituents) significant power in local issues.

Critics of pluralism argue that the heavenly chorus of the group system sings with an upper-class accent,[31] "an Anglo/Honky accent,"[32] or a deep male voice;[33] in short, such critics contend that political groups enhance the power of the people who already have disproportionate economic and political resources. To assess the power and bias of the group system, we must address three questions. First, Are organizational resources disproportionately held by upper-class white men? Second, Is organization a very potent political resource? Third, Are policymakers more responsive to certain types of groups than to others?

In order to address these questions, the permanent and ad hoc organizations involved in the twenty-nine issues in the sample were identified.[34] Table 12.4 lists the major political groups in Lawrence, the number of issues in which they have been involved and their success rates on these issues. In addition to the *Lawrence Journal-World*,[35] fifty-four different groups were observed. In general, 60 percent of these groups were active on only one issue,

Table 12.4  The Involvement and Success of Political Groups in Twenty-nine Lawrence Issues

| Type and Name of Group | Number of Issues | | Winning Percentage |
| --- | --- | --- | --- |
| | Initiated | Addressed | |
| *Lawrence Journal-World* | 0 | 26 | 77 |
| Standing citizen advisory committees | | | |
| Lawrence-Douglas County Planning Commission | 0 | 6 | 40 |
| Community Development Block Grant Board | 0 | 2 | 50 |
| Other (e.g., the Aviation Board) | 1 | 2 | 100 |
| Business-oriented organizations | | | |
| Chamber of Commerce | 5 | 16 | 67 |
| Lawrence Building and Construction Trades Council | 0 | 3 | 33 |
| Downtown Lawrence Association | 0 | 4 | 75 |
| Development corporations | 5 | 7 | 28 |
| Other businesses | 1 | 1 | 100 |
| Permanent neighborhood groups | | | |
| East Lawrence Improvement Association | 2 | 8 | 25 |
| Oread Neighborhood Association | 1 | 5 | 40 |
| Others | 0 | 3 | 100 |
| Civic groups (e.g., League of Women Voters) | 0 | 5 | 40 |
| Environmental groups (e.g., Douglas County Environmental Improvement Council) | 1 | 3 | 67 |
| Social service organizations (e.g., Public Assistance Coalition) | 1 | 3 | 0 |
| Civil rights organizations (e.g., NAACP) | 0 | 1 | 100 |
| Professional organizations (e.g., OB/GYN Group) | 0 | 1 | 100 |
| Religious organizations (e.g., St. Lawrence Catholic Church) | 1 | 2 | 100 |

| | | | |
|---|---|---|---|
| University-related groups (e.g., Endowment Association) | 0 | 2 | 100 |
| Governmentally appointed task forces (e.g., Downtown Improvement Committee) | 0 | 2 | 0 |
| Privately initiated task forces (e.g., Action 80) | 4 | 6 | 50 |
| Neighborhood protest groups (e.g., Crescent-Engel Neighborhood Association) | 0 | 3 | 50 |
| Other protest groups (e.g., Citizens for Better Downtown) | 1 | 9 | 67 |

but one group (the Chamber of Commerce) was involved in over half (sixteen) of the issues. On only one issue (DRUG) was there no discernible group involvement. Only four issues (RESEARCH, VIDEO, INTANGIBLES, and TRIBES) failed to produce countervailing group pressures. A typical issue aroused the interest of 3.25 groups; there were ninety-four group involvements on the twenty-nine issues.

To assess the participation of various types of people in the Lawrence group system, a series of representation ratios are presented in Table 12.5. These ratios were calculated by dividing the percentage of a particular type of citizen (for example, the lower class) who participated in a particular way (for example, as group leaders) in any of the twenty-nine issues, by the percentage of that citizen type in the Lawrence population. As representation ratios approach one, the percentage of a citizen type involved in a particular activity is about the same as the percentage of the citizen type in the community; for example, the ratio of 1.07 regarding lower-class involvement among mobilizers means that the lower class is proportionately represented among group leaders. Representation ratios greater than 1.0 indicate overrepresentation; for example, the ratio of 2.90 regarding upper-class involvement among mobilizers means that members of the upper class are almost three times as prevalent among group leaders as they are in the community as a whole. Representation ratios of less than 1.0 indicate underrepresentation; for example, the ration of 0.11 regarding the involvement of the middle class among mobilizers is based on the findings that only 5.6 percent of all mobilizers are middle class, while members of the middle class comprise 50 percent of the community.

In general, the data in Table 12.5 show that the group system in Lawrence is indeed unrepresentative demographically. Members of groups tend to be disproportionately upper class, white, and male. Country Clubbers, Hometowners, and Seniors also tend to be significantly overrepresented among group members. However, the data in Table 12.5 suggest that groups contribute very little to the underrepresentation of the lower class, minorities, women, Visitors, and Rookies. As shown in the first column of the table, these people are less involved as participants on community issues, but, once members of various underrepresented segments of the community become active on policy issues, they are as likely to become associated with groups as are their overrepresented counterparts. Indeed, the data on mobilizers in the last column of the table suggest that groups may seek out women and, perhaps, members of the lower class for leadership roles, perhaps to symbolize their commitment to being as representative as possible. Nevertheless, the tendency of political groups to recruit their members and leaders from the unrepresentative ranks of participants results in organizational resources being disproportionately possessed by those relatively powerful in other political resources.

One reason for concern about such demographic biases in the group system

Table 12.5    Representation Ratios of Various Types of Citizens in the Lawrence Group System

| Citizen Type | Participants | Nongroup Members | Group Members | Mobilizers |
|---|---|---|---|---|
| Lower Class | .96 | 1.23 | .85 | 1.07 |
| Middle Class | .57 | .60 | .56 | .11 |
| Upper Class | 1.98 | 1.62 | 2.13 | 2.90 |
| Cellar Dwellers | 1.05 | 1.14 | 1.02 | .67 |
| Split Levellers | .60 | .66 | .56 | .39 |
| Country Clubbers | 1.81 | 1.50 | 1.94 | 2.94 |
| Women | .54 | .45 | .58 | .92 |
| Men | 1.42 | 1.51 | 1.38 | 1.07 |
| Minorities | .54 | .67 | .49 | .56 |
| Whites | 1.05 | 1.04 | 1.06 | 1.05 |
| Hometowners | 2.94 | 2.98 | 2.91 | 3.17 |
| Newcomers | 1.01 | .83 | 1.08 | 1.21 |
| Visitors | .49 | .59 | .45 | .31 |
| Rookies | .73 | .75 | .73 | .55 |
| Veterans | 1.19 | 1.18 | 1.19 | 1.17 |
| Seniors | 1.62 | 1.58 | 1.64 | 2.45 |
| Conservatives | .88 | .76 | .93 | .69 |
| Liberals | 1.31 | 1.29 | 1.32 | 1.61 |

Representation ratio: Percentage of citizen type among participants
Percentage of citizen type in Lawrence

is that upper-class white males may have distinctive – presumably conservative – policy orientations and principles that become amplified in the policy process. However, the data in Tables 12.5 and 4.1 suggest that the Lawrence group system is quite representative attitudinally. Table 12.5 shows that liberals are somewhat overrepresented, not underrepresented, among group members and leaders. Table 4.1 shows that the policy principles of mobilizers are, for the most part, quite similiar to those of citizens. Overall, group leaders display the diversity of political attitudes that exists in the broader community, perhaps diminishing the importance of the demographic biases that exist in the group system.

Data regarding the overall effectiveness of organizational resources were previously presented in Tables 12.1 and 12.2. Table 12.1 shows that 70 percent of the issues in the Lawrence sample were resolved in ways consistent with dominant mobilizer preferences (and group pressures);[36] however, Table 12.2 shows that the direct effect of mobilizer pressure on policy outcomes is negligible (B = .01). When dominant group pressures prevailed on the resolution of community issues, policy outcomes almost always reflected the preferences of representatives and citizens. The preferences of these people seem to have influenced outcomes directly. The dominant direction of group pressures may indirectly affect policy outcomes by influencing the judgments of representatives and the preferences of the public (the zero-order correlations between net group pressure and the preferences of representatives and citizens are .65 and .49 respectively), but these actors do not set aside their own judgments and preferences and simply adopt the policies sought by most group leaders.

This does not mean, of course, that groups are powerless in the resolution of community issues. In addition to exercising indirect power by influencing the preferences of others, groups may exercise differential power that is masked by the very broad analyses presented in Tables 12.1 and 12.2. It is possible, for example, that the Chamber of Commerce is very powerful and various neighborhood groups are relatively powerless. Thus, net group pressure may affect policy outcomes on those issues where the chamber is a major actor, but net group pressure may have little policy impact on issues where neighborhood groups are active and the chamber is not. Such possibilities suggest the need to examine the ninety-four group involvements on the issues in order to determine which kinds of groups were most successful. Table 12.6 presents the characteristics that are associated with group success.[37]

Table 12.6 shows that not only does the heavenly chorus of the group system sing with upper-class, Anglo, male voices, but policymakers appear to be relatively responsive to such voices. The more that groups were composed of members of the upper class, whites, and men, the more successful they were in the resolution of community issues. Although these correlations are not strong, they are (with the possible exception of the correlation involving the gender variable) statistically significant. However, there is insufficient evidence that such biases involve direct discrimination.[38] When the zero-order relationships between demographic characteristics of groups and policy outcomes are controlled for other factors that affect outcomes, it is possible to account for the apparent biases. In general, groups comprised largely of the lower class, minorities, and women tend to be oriented toward policies offering separable goods and against economic growth policies; such groups are usually opposed by other groups.

The factor that best predicts group success on an issue is whether it seeks a special benefit (or a separable good) at public expense.[39] As shown by the beta-weights in Table 12.6, there is a strong negative direct relationship between the extent to which a group seeks a separable good and attains its goal ($B = -.55$). This finding is particularly noteworthy because it directly contradicts the conventional wisdom that group politics is the politics of special interests—that typically groups are most effectively organized around narrow special interests.[40] In Lawrence, at least, this bias is clearly against groups seeking separable goods.

Table 12.6    Relationships between Group Characteristics and Success

| Group Characteristics | Relationships with Group Success | |
| --- | --- | --- |
| | Zero-Order Correlations | Beta-Weights |
| Demographic Characteristics | | |
| Percentage upper class | .19** | .11 |
| Percentage women | − .13* | .04 |
| Percentage minority | − .16** | − .00 |
| Other problematic bases of bias | | |
| Concern for separable goods | − .33** | − .55** |
| Orientation toward growth | .17** | .14 |
| Longevity | .05 | |
| Mobilization | .05 | |
| Legitimate bases of bias | | |
| Net support | .29** | .30** |
| Size | .05 | |
| Number of active participants | .07 | |
| Cohesion | .17* | .23** |
| Persuasive participation | .18** | .06 |
| Time expended on issue | − .02 | |
| Adjusted coefficient of determination | | .34 |

*SL < .10
**SL < .05

Groups supporting economic development policies are also more successful than groups opposing such policies or supporting allocative and redistributive policies that undermine developmental policies; as shown in Table 12.6, the correlation between the extent to which a group seeks growth-oriented policies and attains success is .17.[41] This finding is consistent with the emerging consensus in the urban politics literature that there are systemic or structural biases toward growth.[42] Nevertheless, the bias toward growth-oriented groups is weak — indeed, it becomes insignificant when other factors are considered. The factor that explains the bias toward growth-oriented groups is the distribution of support from other groups, Net Support in Table 12.6.[43] The more groups pursue economic growth, the greater is their support among other groups; and the greater is their support among other groups, the greater is their policy success (B = .30).[44]

Some critics of pluralist group processes have argued that permanent groups having continuous access to policymakers are much more successful than ad hoc groups,[45] but there is no significant association between group longevity and success in Lawrence. Other critics of group processes have argued that the group system is characterized by hyperpluralism (i.e., groups that mobilize for militant political action become the squeeky wheels that get the grease).[46] Despite such predictions, there is no significant correlation between mobilization and success in Lawrence.

Critics of interest groups have identified a number of problematic biases in the group system, arguing that the group system is stacked in favor of the upper class, whites, men, permanent groups, aggressive groups, and groups seeking separable goods and economic growth; the discussion thus far indicates that such biases are either weak or nonexistent in Lawrence. Defenders of interest groups have suggested that policymakers are most likely to be influenced by legitimate factors, suggesting that policymakers usually are most responsive to larger, more cohesive, more active, and more persuasive groups.[47] The Lawrence data also provide only weak support for such notions. More cohesive groups that engaged in higher levels of participation aimed at persuading policymakers (for example, by speaking at commission meetings) were relatively successful, but there is little evidence that other group characteristics that might legitimately be related to success—factors such as group size— make much difference for group effectiveness.[48]

In summary, group leaders emerge on most community issues, mobilizing others to become involved in their organizations and asserting that they speak for group members. As has been observed in other communities, the group system in Lawrence is unrepresentative of the broader public. Rather than contributing to unrepresentative participation in politics, groups reflect the unrepresentative nature of participants. Groups in Lawrence are generally effective; policy decisions usually reflect dominant group pressures. However, there is little evidence that group leaders exercise direct power; their success is limited to their ability to persuade others. Some groups are more powerful than others, but the demographic characteristics of groups are not strong determinants of group success. What matters most are the policy positions of groups, as there are strong biases against groups that seek special benefits.

## INDIVIDUAL ACTIVISTS:
## THE POWER OF PARTICIPATION

Local politics provide an arena where individual activists can readily participate in the resolution of issues. Indeed, most citizens who participated in the twenty-nine issues in the Lawrence sample were such activists; they held no office, lacked elite resources, and claimed no group involvement.[49] The typical issue in our sample stimulated forty-two individual activists to do such things as contact commissioners, speak at public hearings, or write letters to the editor. This is, of course, a minuscule proportion of the community. However, from a pluralist perspective, it is not the level of such participation that is important,[50] but rather the representativeness and effectiveness of such participation.

The data from the Lawrence study indicate that individual activists are not representative demographically of the inactive citizenry. The upper class, men, Hometowners, and Seniors are among the kinds of citizens who are disproportionately active as individuals.[51] In Lawrence, however, these demographic biases do not translate into significant attitudinal biases. Individual activists have political principles that are remarkably consistent with those of inactive citizens, as shown in Table 4.1.[52] On only six of the twenty-nine issues did dominant activist preferences misrepresent dominant citizen preferences.

In general, the dominant preferences of individual activists were reflected in the resolution of Lawrence issues. The correlation between activist preferences and policy outcomes across the twenty-nine issues is .43. In 71 percent of the cases, outcomes were consistent with dominant activist preferences. Thus, activism seems to be rewarded, perhaps reinforcing the belief in citizen competence (the belief by individuals that they can influence governmental decisions through political action) that is frequently cited as an important condition for pluralist politics.[53] Nevertheless, such responsiveness to activist preferences is usually achieved without activists exercising direct influence in the policymaking process. As shown in Table 12.2, the dominant preferences of individual activists have no direct causal impact on policy outcomes. For the most part, individual activists succeed in the resolution of community issues because their preferences coincide with those of representatives and/or the public.[54]

Mancur Olson has argued that there is a "collective action problem." Because policy outcomes often benefit nonparticipants as well as participants and because the impact that individuals can have on policy outcomes is "imperceptibly small," it is not rational for individuals to invest time and energy on political participation.[55] Perhaps Buzz Zook made a perceptible difference on the STORMwater management issue, but it is difficult to point to many instances where specific individuals or the aggregation of individual activists had a significant impact on the resolution of issues. Although it may be only rational in a strict economic sense to participate if one can make a decisive difference, many Lawrence citizens chose to participate in community issues. The fact that policy outcomes are normally responsive to the dominant preferences of individual activists — that most activists turn out to be on the winning side even if they do not directly influence the outcome — may provide part of the solution to the collective action problem. Individuals may participate simply because they hope to become winners on issues regardless of their (indeterminant) individual impact on outcomes.

## CITIZENS: THE POWER OF THE PEOPLE

Representatives, bureaucrats, notables, mobilizers, and individual activists participate in the resolution of community issues, but citizens are only occasionally aware of these issues. Most citizens (about 80 percent) were aware of highly controversial issues — such as the various mall proposals in Lawrence — but citizen awareness of issues can be much lower. For example, only 25 percent of Lawrence citizens were aware of the BLUFFS controversy, despite widespread coverage of the issue in the local press; and less than half of Lawrence citizens were aware of the REAPPRAISAL issue despite its significance for their property taxes.

If the "attentive public" is defined as those who have both some awareness of issues and unambiguous preferences about their outcomes,[56] the size of this public varied across issues from about 60 percent of all citizens on the controversial downtown redevelopment issues to about 20 percent on the BLUFFS issue. Such attentive publics stand for the broader public both theoretically and methodologically. Theoretically, representatives can be faulted on grounds of responsible representation only if they fail to respond to the dominant preferences of the attentive public. Given the diversity of public views on policy issues — encompassing not only support and opposition but also unawareness, indifference, mixed feelings, and preferences for other alternatives than the "pro" and "con" options — representatives cannot be faulted simply because a majority of all citizens do not support their decisions. Methodologically, attentive publics stand for the broader public because the inclusion of the "preferences" of those outside the attentive public would introduce extensive "nonattitudes" into analysis.[57]

Overall, policy outcomes in Lawrence reflect the preferences of the attentive public ($r = .58$, as shown in Table 12.2). In 72 percent of the cases, issues were resolved in ways congruent with dominant citizen preferences. In the remainder of this chapter we will consider first the processes by which such responsiveness is achieved and then some explanations for the cases of unresponsiveness.

### A Variety of Processes for Achieving Responsiveness

Democratic theorists have provided several interpretations of the processes by which responsiveness occurs.[58] Although the Lawrence data permit neither precise estimates of the relative importance of these various processes nor an examination of the conditions when various processes occur, the eighteen cases where dominant citizen preferences were clearly congruent with policy outcomes illustrate seven ways in which responsiveness seems to be achieved. Figure 12.1 diagrams these seven processes.

First, by placing issues on public ballots, referenda (Route A in Figure 12.1)

**Figure 12-1**

**Processes for Achieving Policy Responsiveness
to Dominant Citizen Preferences**

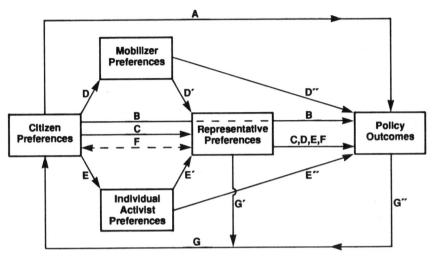

**Processes of Responsiveness**

| | |
|---|---|
| A: Referenda | E: Activist Participation |
| B: Instructed Delegation | F: Shared Preferences |
| C: Election of Representatives | G: Governmental Manipulation |
| D: Group Participation |     or Citizen Reaction |

provide opportunities for citizens to influence policy outcomes directly. Four issues in the Lawrence sample—those concerning WARDS, STORMwater management, the INTANGIBLES tax, and the TOWNCENTER Mall proposal—were subjects of referenda. Dominant citizen preferences prevailed on each of these issues, even though the referendum on TOWNCENTER was merely advisory.

Although common sense suggests that referenda provide an assured method for achieving responsiveness, the WARDS and STORMwater management issues illustrate that such responsiveness can be limited. During the decade following the defeat of the WARDS proposal in the 1977 referendum, public opinion surveys showed greater support than opposition for both the creation of wards and the direct election of a full-time mayor.[59] Similarly, the surveys taken in 1984 and 1986 revealed twice as much support as opposition for STORMwater management, despite the rejection in the referendum of the monthly fee on water bills (to finance a study of the problem). Although the nonrepresentativeness of the voters in referenda[60] may help explain such differences between the results of referenda and those of subsequent polls, the more likely explanation of these differences focuses on the multidimensionality of issues. In the 1977 referendum, voters were presented with a single question involving several changes. If they wanted to retain the manager (as most did), they had to reject wards (and a directly elected mayor). The referendum results were widely interpreted as a public mandate against wards, discouraging efforts to resurrect the issue and provide the public with a more limited reorganization proposal responding to dominant but latent preferences among the attentive public. The STORMwater management issue was also multidimensional, as most citizens supported governmental provision of stormwater management but opposed the fee on water bills as a means to that end. Nevertheless, the results of the referendum were interpreted by subsequent commissioners as a public mandate against stormwater management generally, and they refused to pursue the issue using other revenue sources. Thus, referenda can ensure responsiveness on some dimensions of complex issues while discouraging consideration of other dimensions of those issues where dominant citizen preferences remain unsatisfied.

A second process for achieving responsiveness to citizen preferences is "instructed delegation." Like referenda, the process of instructed delegation—depicted by Route B in Figure 12.1—provides citizens direct influence over policy outcomes. Instructed delegation occurs when representatives set aside their own judgments and decide issues on the basis of their accurate perceptions of dominant citizen preferences. The rejection of the SIZELER Mall proposal illustrates the process of instructed delegation, as representatives cited their (accurate) perceptions of citizen opposition to the project as a primary basis for their decision.

The general importance of instructed delegation as a method of achieving responsiveness is suggested by two findings. First, as shown in Table 12.1, representatives resolved 85 percent of the issues in ways that were consistent with their perceptions of dominant citizen preferences. Second, representative perceptions of citizen preferences were strongly related to citizen preferences as measured by public opinion polls ($r = .69$ across the twenty-nine issues). However, most Lawrence commissioners rejected the notion that they should normally act as instructed delegates. When providing reasons for their votes on most issues, commissioners argued that substantive concerns formed the basis of their policy decisions and that public opinion simply squared with their independent judgments. Thus, concluding that citizen preferences directly influenced these decisions, as required by the process of instructed delegation, is problematic.

The process by which the public elects representatives (Route C in Figure 12.1) provides a third method for achieving responsiveness. If candidates for a commission take distinct policy stands (offering citizens clear choices on issues), if citizens vote for candidates who best approximate their own preferences, and if the winning candidates implement their stands on issues, citizens may be able to control policy decisions through the electoral process.[61] Perhaps Lawrence citizens used commission elections to control the CORNFIELD and TOWNCENTER mall issues. By rejecting all candidates who campaigned for a suburban mall, voters ensured that their dominant preferences to avert such a development have been respected by the commission. By replacing three commissioners who supported Towncenter with three persons who campaigned against the project, voters were also able to ensure responsiveness on that issue.

The election of representatives is unlikely to account for responsiveness on other Lawrence issues. Many of the other cases arose and were resolved in short time periods in which there were no elections and thus no opportunities for voters to elect representatives on the basis of their preferences on the issues. Even if the timing of elections provided voters with an opportunity to resolve issues by selecting persons holding their views, clear policy choices were seldom given to the electorate. For example, elections provided an opportunity for achieving responsiveness on the SIZELER issue, but none of the new commissioners took a clear stand against the project in their campaigns, and voters could not indicate their anti-Sizeler preferences through their votes. More generally, it is unlikely that many citizens vote for candidates on the basis of a positive match between their policy preferences and the stands of candidates. Such matching requires that voters place greater importance on issues than on other considerations (e.g., the perceived competence, honesty, and experience of candidates) when casting their votes, and matching is complicated by the presence of more than one relevant issue.[62] Because of the diversity of motivations available to citizens when they vote for candidates, it is not possible to discern dominant citizen preferences on an issue from the outcome of elections for representatives, thus making elections a limited mechanism for achieving responsiveness.[63]

Citizen participation in the resolution of issues provides the fourth and fifth routes for achieving responsiveness depicted in Figure 12.1.[64] If group leaders are representative of the broader public (Route D in Figure 12.1), and if representatives are persuaded (Route D') or coerced (Route D'') by dominant mobilizer demands, "group participation" can provide a means of achieving responsiveness. If individual activists are representative of the broader public (Route E), and if policymakers are persuaded (Route E') or coerced (Route E'') by the dominant preferences of individual activists, "activist participation" can provide a means of achieving responsiveness.

For the most part, net group preferences and dominant activist preferences reflected citizen preferences in Lawrence. (These correlations are .53 and .63 respectively across the twenty-nine issues.) Seventy percent of the time, representatives resolved issues in ways consistent with net group demands or dominant individual preferences. However, such findings are not sufficient to demonstrate that citizen participation accounts for reponsiveness on specific issues. Additionally, citizen participation must directly influence policy decisions or change the preferences of representatives. Only on the IRB issue did such a process occur. Despite a general reluctance to issue IRBs to firms that competed locally with other firms, commissioners were sometimes persuaded by applicants and spokespersons for the Chamber of Commerce to issue the IRBs, a position that was generally supported by the public. On other issues where citizen participation affected the judgments of representatives and thus policy outcomes (for example, on the school CLOSING, TRIBES, LIFELINE, and VIDEO tax issues) the preferences of most participants did not reflect dominant citizen preferences. On other issues where mobilizers and activists did represent citizen preferences, representatives already agreed with the participants, making their participation superfluous.

Another method for achieving responsiveness—depicted by Route F in Figure 12.1—involves citizens and representatives simply sharing the same preferences. If most citizens and most representatives have similar attitudes about the desirability of issue outcomes, representatives must only decide issues according to their own preferences in order to achieve responsiveness. A proposal to make the consumption of apple pie illegal would cause few problems for responsible representation because it would seem equally outrageous to citizens and representatives.[65]

Most Lawrence issues were characterized by citizens and representatives sharing the same dominant preferences; however, while shared preferences may be the "best-fitting" explanation that can be provided for the existence of responsiveness on most issues, it is the least adequate explanation theoretically. Indeed, the shared-preference interpretation is simply a description of the residual congruence between the preferences of citizens and representatives that cannot be explained by other processes. Like approving apple pie, most citizens and representatives supported the RESEARCH park, the ENVIRONmental code, and regulation of DRUG paraphernalia, among other issues, but the question remains: why did congruence occur on these issues?

Political socialization is usually offered as an explanation for such congruence.[66] For example, everyone is socialized to value clean economic growth and tidy neighborhoods, resulting in both representatives and citizens supporting the research park and the environmental code. However, the problem with the socialization explanation is that it requires that certain abstract values and goals become widely accepted and that these values be readily converted into the appropriate preferences on concrete issues. The earlier analysis of political principles suggests, to the contrary, that there is a good deal of disagreement about abstract values and that the conversion of values to policy preferences is problematic. The congruence between citizens and representatives on the DRUG paraphernalia issue cannot be explained by both citizens and representatives being socialized to accept the desirability of legislating morality. After all, such principles are not widely accepted by citizens and representatives, and neither citizens nor representatives grounded their preferences on the issue in such abstract values. Thus, the notion that responsiveness occurs because of socialization processes that inculcate similar values into citizens and representatives is not satisfying.

Perhaps chance is a better explanation than socialization for shared preferences. Even if citizen and representative preferences are formed in a completely random way, dominant citizen preferences should be consistent with dominant representative preferences half of the time.[67] While congruence may have occurred on many of the issues simply by chance, consideration of a final interpretation for responsiveness might be useful.

As depicted by Route G in Figure 12.1, responsiveness can also occur through a process of "governmental manipulation"[68] or citizen reaction. If representatives influence citizen preferences (Route G') or the policies adopted by representatives influence citizen preferences (Route G") making them consistent with policy outcomes, responsiveness is achieved by a process of positive citizen reaction to governmental initiatives. The lack of time-series data on citizen preferences precludes an adequate examination of this interpretation, but the Lawrence data suggest its plausibility.

Consider, for example, the AIRPORT improvement issue. In 1973, Lawrence citizens rejected a bond issue for airport improvements, but governmental officials pursued the matter by using revenue sharing funds to leverage federal grants for the project. During the next decade, citizen support for the project increased as representatives found ways of pursuing their goals that were acceptable to the public while continually arguing for the project. Increased citizen support for airport improvements may have been due to the persuasive efforts and acceptable policies of governmental officials.

Existing policies probably generated supportive citizen preferences on several other issues. The perceived effectiveness of the city manager system and the accomplishments of incumbent Manager Watson perhaps created citizen support for their maintenance when threatened by the WARDS and MANAGER issues. Similarly, the existence of an ENVIRONmental code may have enhanced the perception among the public that local governments have a legitimate responsibility for ensuring the tidiness of yards, generating citizen support for stringent enforcement of the code.

On several other issues, representatives supported new policy initiatives and sought to convince citizens of the desirability of these initiatives. For example, most Lawrence commissioners wanted to develop the RESEARCH park, and they sought to create public acceptance of the project by suggesting that it could provide Lawrence with costless economic growth. Responsiveness on such issues as the research park does not occur because of processes involving "citizen action and governmental reaction" but is instead achieved by processes involving "governmental action and citizen reaction."

Although it seems more democratic if governmental officials respond to citizens rather than the reverse, it is unclear that the process of governmental action and citizen reaction should be considered a perversion of democratic processes. Although the term "manipulation" suggests that citizens are being brainwashed through propaganda, and rhetoric, and symbolic language,[69] the process may be more benign. First, citizen preferences do influence policymakers by serving as a constraint on arbitrary actions even while citizen preferences are being influenced by governmental officials. For example, Lawrence policymakers had to make small, incremental improvements to the AIRPORT so as to avoid increases in taxes and citizen opposition. Second, manipulation seldom occurs at the expense of open and free debate. Some commissioners did oppose the airport improvements, and their views were widely publicized. To say that government manipulates public opinion is a shorthand expression for a much more complicated process in which the arguments and actions of some governmental officials achieve greater public support than the counterarguments and actions of other governmental officials. Third, the process of manipulation does not mean that citizens are without critical judgment. Some arguments by policymakers will be unpersuasive, and some policies will seem ineffective to most citizens. For example, dominant citizen support for the airport improvements turned to dominant dissatisfaction when the community lost its commuter airline just as the project was being completed. In short, governmental manipulation is simply a process by which citizens form reactive judgments to the proposals and policies of governmental leaders.[70] If these proposals and policies are supported by most citizens, the policy process is not undemocratic merely because initiatives do not come from citizens.

In summary, policy outcomes in Lawrence usually reflected the dominant preferences of the attentive public. In part, such responsiveness occurs because citizens can exercise direct influence on policy decisions through referenda and through the process of instructed delegation, but responsiveness also occurs because citizens and policymakers simply share similar policy goals or because policymakers generate citizen support for their goals. Thus, the resolution of community issues will usually reflect dominant citizen preferences even though these preferences seldom determine policy decisions.

## Explanations for Unresponsiveness

More problematic for responsible representation than the limited direct influence of citizens is unresponsiveness to citizens. As shown in Table 12.1, most of the public opposed outcomes of nine cases in Lawrence. A further understanding of the limited power of citizens is attained by considering the reasons for these unresponsive outcomes.

First, representatives may consider citizen preferences irrelevant if representatives question their own jurisdiction on issues. Although polls indicated that 62 percent of the attentive public supported the REAPPRAISAL of property during the early 1980s, local officials (perhaps hoping to avoid responsibility for such controversial issues) maintained that this issue needed to be resolved at the state level.

Second, representatives may misperceive citizen preferences, as they did on the LIFELINE issue. Although public opinion polls showed that 60 percent of the attentive public supported Lifeline, commissioners estimated that there was much less support (about 30 percent). They observed that the overwhelming majority of activists on the issue were opposed to the program, and they mistakenly believed that these activists spoke for the public as a whole.

Third, representatives may conceptualize citizen preferences in terms other than the dominant preferences of the attentive public. Although polls showed that over 80 percent of the attentive public supported the BIRTHING-room concept, the trustees of Lawrence Memorial Hospital estimated that only one-third of the public supported the proposal. The reason for this discrepancy was that some trustees conceptualized citizen preferences as market demand (How many expectant mothers would use the facility?) rather than as political support. These trustees were the only representatives in the sample who were not elected. Perhaps elections do remind representatives that citizens are the voting public rather than the consuming public.

Fourth, representatives often view themselves as mediators of disputes between different interests rather than as guardians of broader public preferences. Representatives may consider dominant citizen preferences of little relevance when issues are viewed as affecting small segments of the public. On the OREAD, BLUFFS, and TRIBES issues, for example, representatives were more concerned with minimizing citizen unrest than with responding to dominant but latent preferences. The OREAD and BLUFFS issues were "neighborhood issues," and representatives were primarily concerned with reconciling the different interests of developers and local residents. Although they recognized that many citizens supported neighborhood interests because of the prevalence of neighborhood-protection principles, they viewed such citizen preferences as a minor consideration. Similarly, the TRIBES issue was regarded as an issue of interest to only a small number of parents and the immediate school staff. Believing that the broader public was unaware and unconcerned about the issue, school board members generally thought their role involved containing the issue. Representatives thus sought compromise solutions to those issues that satisfied opposing participants. Although these compromises may have been tilted slightly against dominant public preferences, there is no evidence of widespread public discontent with these decisions.[71]

Fifth, representatives may believe that dominant preferences of important participants outweigh dominant public preferences. This was the case on the school CLOsing issue. Sixty percent of Lawrence citizens favored closing the rural schools, and school board members accurately estimated citizen preferences. Regardless, since activist opposition was so strong, most representatives concluded that the concerns of the intense minority had to take priority over "majority rule." In this case, representatives reasoned that a failure to respond to the intense preferences of parents from the threatened schools would engender deep hostility toward the board and the school system among affected citizens. They also reasoned that a failure to respond to the dominant preferences of inactive citizens would result in only temporary dissatisfaction. Indeed, four years after the decision, surveys revealed that there was twice as much satisfaction as dissatisfaction with the outcome.

Sixth, representatives may believe that citizen opposition to a proposal was mobilized in an untimely fashion, after irreversible commitments have already been made. Fifty-eight percent of the attentive public opposed the decision to build a PARKing lot, and commissioners accurately perceived public preferences on the issue. Despite these perceptions, commissioners chose to ignore citizen preferences because they had already made legally binding financial commitments by authorizing parking revenue bonds prior to any protest about the project. Most commissioners attempted to ride out the storm of public discontent, but they could not escape democratic accountability; Nancy Shontz and Tom Gleason effectively campaigned on the issue and replaced two "unresponsive" commissioners in the subsequent election. Thus, bad timing does not make citizen preferences irrelevant. Local elections give citizens an opportunity to make retrospective judgments, and citizens are likely to hold representatives rather than themselves responsible for failures in democratic performance.

Finally, citizen preferences may have limited influence simply because representatives believe that their judgments are a better guide to effective policy than is dominant public opinion.[72] This was the case on the RAIL-served industrial park issue, where commissioners understood that they were acting against dominant citizen preferences (as well as the dominant preferences of other participants). In the final analysis, the county commissioners who blocked that project simply believed that the site was inappropriate and that a better location for a similar project could be found. They were willing to act as trustees, explaining their opposition while promising their support for a better site. Although such unresponsiveness risked the same kind of electoral retaliation that occurred in the aftermath of the PARKing lot incident, the RAIL decision never became a significant campaign issue. Perhaps citizens are more likely to forgive inaction than action. Perhaps the greater passage of time between making an unpopular decision and running for reelection ensures that citizens will forget that their wishes were ignored.[73] Or perhaps commissioners were simply able to persuade people that they acted in the best interest of the community. In any event, representatives were able to act as trustees on the issue without provoking extensive citizen dissatisfaction.

## CONCLUSIONS

The ideals of representative democracy are reasonably well attained in Lawrence; the community has been able to resolve issues without the maladies of external, elite, bureaucratic, or minority domination. Representatives have resolved most issues on the basis of their independent judgments, and their decisions have usually been consistent with the dominant preferences of various other participants and citizens. Bureaucrats, notables, mobilizers, and individual activists have had influence, but such influence appears to be limited to their ability to persuade representatives of the merits of their positions. Policy decisions normally reflect citizen preferences, but citizens exercise direct power on only those issues resolved by referenda or where representatives act as instructed delegates. Usually responsiveness to public preferences is achieved because representatives and citizens share the same policy goals or because policymakers generate support for their goals among the broader public.

Although Lawrence has achieved a high level of responsible representation on the issues examined here, this does not mean that other communities are also governed democratically or that all issues in Lawrence are resolved democratically. Perhaps elite domination occurs on important decisions made by private organizations. Perhaps bureaucratic domination occurs on routine, street-level decisions. Perhaps interest-group domination occurs on noncontroversial allocational issues. Despite these possibilities, the power of notables, bureaucrats, and mobilizers is limited on controversial governmental issues in Lawrence. Power is simultaneously concentrated in the hands of representatives and dispersed to many others who can exert indirect influence by persuading representatives to adopt their policy goals.

# 13

# Political Justice: Divisions, Standings, and Complex Equality

A third criterion for effective democratic government is that there be legitimate explanations for inequalities of political power between competing interests within communities. In pluralist communities, different kinds of people often have conflicting preferences regarding the resolution of community issues. The lower class may compete with the upper class, whites may compete with minorities, the Growth Machine may compete with Preservationists, and other "teams" (defined in terms of other social characteristics and political orientations) may compete on various community issues. Such teams may not compete on equal terms. Parity (or simple political equality) among competing interests is not expected or required in pluralist politics. Nevertheless, critical pluralists are concerned with explaining the dominance of one side over its counterpart(s). In order to achieve complex political equality, there must be satisfactory explanations for dominance.[1]

The analysis of complex equality in Lawrence begins with a determination of the types of conflicts that exist on the twenty-nine issues in the sample and of the winners and losers in these conflicts. The first section of this chapter thus presents the overall standings in the game of politics in Lawrence and shows the presence of simple inequalities among teams within various divisions. In subsequent sections I shall consider four explanations of these inequalities.

1. Differences in Participation. Teams with more participants or whose participants are more deeply involved in acts of persuasive participation and mobilization should be relatively powerful.

2. Inequalities in Representation. Because of the extensive direct power of representatives, those teams that are overrepresented by officials who share their backgrounds and orientations should be higher than underrepresented teams in the divisional standings.

3. Differences in Popular Support. Because citizen preferences sometimes affect policy outcomes, those teams whose positions are most supported by the public should be division leaders.

4. Differences in Principles. Teams that seek outcomes consistent with the most dominant principles in the political culture or with structural economic imperatives should be relatively successful.

If political standings are explained by differences in participation, representation, public support, and political principles, the justice of political inequalities can be partially clarified but not fully resolved. On the one hand, unexplained inequalities are not necessarily unjustified. For example, if whites dominate minorities and if this dominance is not explained by differences in participation, representation, popular support, or political principles, then one would be tempted to view such dominance as unjust; white domination would seem to indicate unequal treatment of whites and minorities simply because of their race. Such a conclusion, however, must be held tentatively; perhaps some unconsidered factor would explain the apparent discrimination. On the other hand, explained inequalities may not be defensible inequalities. Suppose that the dominance of whites is rooted in their overrepresentation on the city commission. While such overrepresentation may explain the power of whites, it may not justify it. One might argue, for example, that overrepresentation is itself an injustice, the cause of which needs to be determined and reformed.[2] Or suppose the dominance of the Growth Machine is rooted in its favoring policies consistent with economic imperatives. While the "city interest" in economic growth and its attendant principles may explain this dominance, such an explanation would have little legitimacy for Preservationists, who question the need to respond to economic imperatives. Before considering the difficulties involved in the analysis of complex equality, the simple inequalities in the success of various "teams" must first be described.

## POLITICAL STANDINGS AND SIMPLE INEQUALITY

Table 13.1 shows the standings in the game of community politics, as played on twenty-nine issues.[3] The standings were determined on the basis of participant cleavages, citizen cleavages, and official perceptions about these cleavages. In order to understand the derivation of these standings, it is useful to refer to Table 13.2, which presents a more detailed description of outcomes in the Class Division, the first division listed in Table 13.1.

To determine the presence of (class) cleavages on specific issues among participants (P in Table 13.2), the (class) characteristics and positions of those representatives, bureaucrats, notables, mobilizers, and individual activists in-

Table 13.1 Political Standings: The Game of Community Politics in Lawrence

| | Participants | | | | Citizens | | | | Official Perceptions | | | |
|---|---|---|---|---|---|---|---|---|---|---|---|---|
| | W | L | T | % | W | L | T | % | W | L | T | % |
| **Class Division** | | | | | | | | | | | | |
| The Middle Class | 7 | 2 | 0 | .778 | 3 | 1 | 0 | .750 | 8 | 2 | 1 | .773 |
| The Upper Class | 3 | 5 | 1 | .389 | 4 | 1 | 0 | .800 | 7 | 4 | 2 | .615 |
| The Lower Class | 2 | 5 | 1 | .313 | 0 | 1 | 0 | .000 | 2 | 9 | 2 | .231 |
| **Neighborhood Division** | | | | | | | | | | | | |
| Country Clubbers | 12 | 5 | 1 | .694 | 1 | 0 | 0 | 1.000 | 7 | 2 | 0 | .778 |
| Split Levellers | 8 | 4 | 1 | .653 | 1 | 0 | 0 | 1.000 | 3 | 1 | 1 | .700 |
| Cellar Dwellers | 4 | 11 | 1 | .281 | 0 | 1 | 0 | .000 | 3 | 6 | 1 | .350 |
| **Race Division** | | | | | | | | | | | | |
| Whites | 1 | 0 | 1 | .750 | 0 | 0 | 0 | — | 0 | 1 | 1 | .250 |
| Minorities | 0 | 1 | 1 | .250 | 0 | 0 | 0 | — | 0 | 1 | 1 | .250 |
| **Gender Division** | | | | | | | | | | | | |
| Men | 8 | 6 | 2 | .563 | 0 | 1 | 0 | .000 | MD | MD | | |
| Women | 7 | 9 | 0 | .438 | 2 | 0 | 0 | 1.000 | MD | MD | | |
| **Age Division** | | | | | | | | | | | | |
| Veterans | 8 | 0 | 1 | .944 | 3 | 0 | 1 | .875 | MD | MD | | |
| Seniors | 8 | 1 | 1 | .850 | 5 | 1 | 1 | .786 | MD | MD | | |
| Rookies | 1 | 9 | 1 | .136 | 1 | 4 | 1 | .250 | MD | MD | | |
| **Town-Gown Division** | | | | | | | | | | | | |
| Towns | 3 | 1 | 0 | .750 | 3 | 0 | 0 | 1.000 | 0 | 2 | 0 | .000 |
| Gowns | 1 | 3 | 0 | .250 | 0 | 3 | 0 | .000 | 2 | 0 | 0 | 1.000 |
| **Sector Division** | | | | | | | | | | | | |
| Privates | 9 | 2 | 1 | .792 | 3 | 0 | 0 | 1.000 | MD | MD | | |
| Publics | 2 | 9 | 1 | .208 | 0 | 1 | 0 | .000 | MD | MD | | |

| | | | | | | | | | | | | |
|---|---|---|---|---|---|---|---|---|---|---|---|---|
| **Residency Division** | | | | | | | | | | | | |
| Hometowners | 5 | 1 | 0 | .833 | 1 | 0 | 0 | 1.000 | MD | MD | MD | |
| Newcomers | 2 | 2 | 0 | .500 | 0 | 1 | 1 | .000 | MD | MD | MD | |
| Visitors | 0 | 4 | 0 | .000 | 0 | 1 | 1 | .000 | MD | MD | MD | |
| **Ideological Division** | | | | | | | | | | | | |
| Conservatives | 12 | 1 | 2 | .867 | 1 | 2 | 0 | .333 | 11 | 1 | 2 | .857 |
| Liberals | 1 | 11 | 2 | .143 | 2 | 0 | 0 | 1.000 | 1 | 11 | 2 | .143 |
| **Partisan Division** | | | | | | | | | | | | |
| Republicans | 6 | 1 | 0 | .857 | 1 | 0 | 0 | 1.000 | 4 | 0 | 0 | 1.000 |
| Democrats | 1 | 6 | 0 | .143 | 1 | 1 | 0 | .500 | 0 | 4 | 0 | .000 |
| **Ethos Division** | | | | | | | | | | | | |
| Managerialists | 7 | 1 | 0 | .825 | 2 | 0 | 0 | 1.000 | 5 | 1 | 0 | .833 |
| Politicos | 1 | 7 | 0 | .125 | 0 | 2 | 0 | .000 | 1 | 5 | 0 | .167 |
| **Divisions of Special Interest** | | | | | | | | | | | | |
| Growth Machine | 7 | 4 | 1 | .625 | 3 | 2 | 0 | .600 | 10 | 4 | 1 | .700 |
| Preservationists | 4 | 7 | 1 | .375 | 1 | 2 | 0 | .333 | 5 | 8 | 1 | .393 |
| Market Providers | 10 | 1 | 1 | .875 | 2 | 0 | 1 | .750 | 6 | 1 | 1 | .813 |
| Public Providers | 1 | 10 | 1 | .125 | 0 | 2 | 1 | .167 | 1 | 5 | 1 | .214 |

MD = Missing data (official perceptions unavailable on these cleavages)

Table 13.2    Issues Classified by Type of Class Conflict and by Outcomes

|  |  | Strong Cleavages[1] | Weak Cleavages | Significant Differences |
|---|---|---|---|---|
| Upper Class | Wins | CORNFIELD *(P, C)* **WARDS** *LIFELINE* | **AIRPORT (P)** | **MANAGER (C)** N2ST *(P)* SIGNS *(C)* *EAST* **ENVIR (C)** |
|  | Losses | *SIZELER (P)* VIDEO *(P)* *TRIBES (P)* | CATH *(P)* PARK *(P)* | BIRTH *(C)* |
| Middle Class | Wins | CORNFIELD *(P, C)* VIDEO *(P)* **AIRPORT (P)** *LIFELINE* | CATH *(P)* IRB *(P)* PARK *(P)* | **WARDS** N2ST *(P)* SIGNS *(C)* **ENVIR (C)** |
|  | Losses | *SIZELER (P)* *TRIBES (P)* |  | BIRTH *(C)* |
| Lower Class | Wins | *SIZELER (P)* *TRIBES (P)* |  |  |
|  | Losses | CORNFIELD *(P, C)* **WARDS** VIDEO *(P)* **AIRPORT (P)** *LIFELINE* | IRB *(P)* PARK *(P)* | **MANAGER** *EAST* **ENVIR** |

P: Participants divided along class lines.
C: Citizens divided along class lines.
Issues in boldface: at least 50 percent of officials perceived class cleavage.
Issues in italic: 25 to 50 percent of officials perceived class cleavage.

[1]Most officials perceived a class conflict on the SOCIAL service issue. Some officials perceived a class conflict on the BLUFFS issues, and participants were weakly divided along class lines on the issue. These issues ended in ties and thus are excluded from the above matrix.

volved in each issue were analyzed. To determine the presence of (class) cleavages among citizens (C in Table 13.2), the (class) characteristics and preferences of citizens surveyed in public opinion polls were similarly analyzed. A class cleavage exists among participants when the majority of one class of participants is on one side of a specific issue, a majority of another class of participants is on the other side, and the difference between the preferences of these classes is significant. Similarly, a class cleavage exists among citizens when the majority of one class of citizens is on one side of an issue, a majority of another class of citizens is on the other side, and this difference is significant. A strong cleavage occurs if such differences are statistically significant at (or below) the .05 level, and a weak cleavage occurs if such differences are statistically significant at the .10 level. For example, most upper-class and middle-class participants and citizens opposed the CORNFIELD Mall, but most lower-class participants and citizens supported it. Because these class differences are statistically significant at the .05 level, there were strong class cleavages on the issue. In contrast, active opponents of the CATHolic Center tended to come from the upper class, while active supporters tended to come from the middle class, but because these class differences are only significant at the .10 level, there was only a weak cleavage on this issue. (Moreover, there was no clear lower-class position on the CATHolic Center issue, and there were no significant class differences among citizens on the issue. Accordingly there are no designations for these interests in Table 13.2.) If either a strong or weak cleavage is exhibited on an issue, at least one "team" will win, and at least one team will lose. For example, the defeat of the CORNFIELD Mall proposal was a victory for both the upper class and the middle class but a loss for the lower class.

No cleavage but a significant difference is exhibited on an issue when the preferences of members of different classes are different at the .05 level of statistical significance, but most members of each class have the same preference. For example, the majority of lower-class, middle-class, and upper-class participants supported the North Second Street Improvements (N2ST), but there was significantly more support for the project among the upper and middle classes than among the lower class. When there are significant differences — but no cleavages — on an issue, policy decisions yield victories or losses for the team(s) most favoring the proposal, but neither victories nor losses for other teams. Thus, as shown in Table 13.2, the N2ST improvements resulted in a victory for both upper- and middle-class participants who strongly supported the project. However, the outcome for the lower class is problematic. On the one hand, since 60 percent of the lower class supported the project, the outcome could be construed as a win for the lower class. On the other hand, since most of the opposition to the project came from the lower class, the outcome could be construed as a loss for the lower class. Thus, the issue is classified as neither a victory nor a loss for the lower class.

Official perceptions of political standings in Table 13.1 are based on interviews with representatives and bureaucrats, who were asked if they observed various cleavages on each of the issues in which they participated.[4] Follow-up questions determined the teams involved in the conflict and who prevailed. If more than 50 percent of these officials perceived a particular kind of cleavage and outcome on an issue, the issue was designated as having a strong perceived cleavage; such issues are indicated in bold type in Table 13.2. For example, the majority of public officials perceived class cleavages on the WARDS, AIRPORT, MANAGER, and ENVIRONmental code issues, and these officials perceived that the upper class won on each of these issues. (Although the analysis of preferences and class characteristics of participants and citizens revealed no class cleavage on the WARDS issue, such analyses revealed a weak class cleavage on the AIRPORT issue and significant differences among the classes on the MANAGER and ENVIROnmental code issues, as shown in Table 13.2). If 25 to 50 percent of the officials perceived a particular kind of cleavage and outcome on an issue, the issue was designated as having a weak perceived cleavage; such issues are italicized in Table 13.2. For example, some officials saw the CORNFIELD Mall issue as aligning the victorious upper and middle classes against the defeated lower class.[5] In summary, Table 13.2 indicates class conflict and the winners and losers of such conflict on the twenty-nine issues. If a "P" and/or "C" follows an issue, a strong or weak cleavage or a significant difference was exhibited on the issue among participants (P) and/or citizens (C). If an issue is bold-faced or italicized, officials perceived class cleavages on it. Of course, analysis could reveal a class conflict on an issue that was not perceived by officials (as is the case on the VIDEO tax issue), and officials could perceive class conflicts that were not apparent in the analysis of class differences in the preferences of participants and citizens (as is the case on the WARDS issue). However, the perceptions of officials usually reflected actual class cleavages or differences among participants or citizens.

The Class Division standings in Table 13.1 summarize these descriptions of class conflict from Table 13.2. For example, Table 13.2 shows that upper-class participants were victorious on the CORNFIELD Mall, AIRPORT improvements, and N2ST issues, but suffered defeats on the SIZELER Mall, VIDEO tax, TRIBES, CATHolic Center, and PARKing lot issues; their record of three wins and five losses is duly recorded in Table 13.1 and puts them in second place in the Class Division. The outcome of one issue characterized by class conflict among participants (the rezoning of the BLUFFS) was deemed a tie. Issues that ended in such ties are omitted from Table 13.2 (and subsequent tables describing the outcomes of various cleavages), but ties are included in the political standings in Table 13.1. Thus, the record of upper-class participants includes one tie (which was considered to be a half victory and a half loss when calculating the team's winning percentage).

The political standings in Table 13.1 indicate that conflict among participants is considerably more structured than conflict among citizens. In most divisions, cleavages among participants occur on two or three times as many issues as do cleavages among citizens.[6] Thus, cleavages among participants — and the simple inequalities of treatment that derive from these cleavages — only occasionally extend into the broader population, perhaps enhancing community stability.[7]

The political standings also show that some kinds of cleavages are more frequent than others. On the one hand, among participants, issues frequently involved neighborhood, gender, sector, and various kinds of attitudinal cleavages. On the other hand, there is almost no racial conflict in Lawrence. Only four issues resulted in Town-Gown conflict among participants, despite the centrality of the University of Kansas to Lawrence. Partisan conflict is also relatively muted, reflecting the nonpartisan aspect of the city's reformed institutions.

Simple political inequality is evident in the political standings of Lawrence, since division leaders frequently dominate their adversaries. For example, in the Sector Division, where teams are defined on the basis of whether participants are employed in the public or private sectors of the economy, the Privates have an impressive 9-2-1 record, while their adversaries, the Publics, have a dismal 2-9-1 mark. In similar manners, conservatives dominate liberals, Republicans dominate Democrats, Managerialists dominate Politicos, the Growth Machine dominates Preservationists, and Market Providers dominate Public Providers. Seniors and Veterans usually form an alliance against Rookies, leading to their dual dominance in the age division. Similarly, Country Clubbers and Split Levellers usually align on issues to dominate the Cellar Dwellers in the Neighborhood Division. Only in the Gender Division, where men participants (8–6–2) hold a two-issue edge over women participants (7–9–0), is there much parity (at least in those divisions having a greater number of cleavages).[8]

Unlike sports, participants (and citizens) are not members of a single team within a single division; instead, they have a variety of social characteristics and political orientations which make them simultaneously members of particular teams within a variety of divisions. For example, conservatives are usually (though not always) Republicans, Managerialists, Market Providers, and members of the Growth Machine. To the extent that there are strong relationships among the social characteristics and political orientations of individuals, the cleavages and inequalities that occur within one division can simply be reproduced as cleavages and inequalities within related divisions.[9] Table 13.3 examines these interrelationships among cleavages.

The left-hand side of Table 13.3 presents the results of a factor analysis of the extent to which various cleavages were present on each of the twenty-nine issues.[10] The results suggest a high degree of overlap among various cleavages. Loading strongly on Factor 1 are five cleavages: those involving the Growth Machine against Preservationists, and those involving gender, neighborhood, partisan, and ideological conflicts. The columns to the right of these factor scores provide simple Pearson correlation coefficients among these cleavages. Because all of these correlations are strong, positive, and significant at the .01 level, they provide additional evidence of overlap among these cleavages. In short, these results suggest that issues having cleavages pitting the Growth Machine against Preservationists also tend to have cleavages pitting men against women, Country Clubbers and Split Levellers against Cellar Dwellers, Republicans against Democrats, and conservatives against liberals.

The second factor (and the corresponding Pearson correlation coefficients)

Table 13.3  Rotated Factor Matrix and Intercorrelations within Factors for Thirteen Community Cleavages

| Community conflict | Factor 1 | Factor 2 | Factor 3 | Intercorrelations with Other Cleavages within Factor | | | |
|---|---|---|---|---|---|---|---|
| | | | | Grow | Gender | Neigh | Party |
| Grow vs. Preserve | .91 | .08 | -.10 | 1.00 | | | |
| Gender | .84 | -.02 | .33 | .76 | 1.00 | | |
| Neighborhood | .76 | .41 | .16 | .69 | .61 | 1.00 | |
| Partisan | .72 | .44 | .27 | .56 | .66 | .74 | 1.00 |
| Ideological | .64 | .27 | .59 | .52 | .66 | .72 | .72 |
| | | | | Residency | Age | Town-Gown | |
| Residency | .08 | .87 | .26 | 1.00 | | | |
| Age | -.03 | .81 | .37 | .78 | 1.00 | | |
| Town-Gown | .34 | .81 | .13 | .74 | .63 | 1.00 | |
| Ethos | .57 | .61 | .09 | .61 | .45 | .68 | |
| | | | | Market/Public | Race | | |
| Market vs. Public Providers | .06 | .15 | .89 | 1.00 | | | |
| Race | .05 | .14 | .83 | .65 | 1.00 | | |
| Sector | .39 | .11 | .83 | .73 | .69 | | |
| Class | .26 | .47 | -.25 | | | | |

indicates substantial overlap among cleavages defined on the basis of residency (i.e., how long people have lived in Lawrence), age, affiliation with the university, and ethos. Issues having cleavages pitting Hometowners against Visitors also tend to align Seniors and Veterans against Rookies, Towns against Gowns, and Managerialists against Politicos.

The third factor indicates substantial overlap among three additional cleavages. Issues having cleavages pitting Market Providers against Public Providers tend also to pit Privates against Publics, and whites against minorities.

Finally, class conflict is relatively independent of other cleavages, since it does not load strongly on any of these three factors and because class cleavages are only weakly related to other cleavages.

The overlap between various cleavages suggests that there would be a good deal of redundancy in undertaking and reporting separate analyses of the inequalities within each of the thirteen divisions. Consequently, in the remainder of this chapter we will focus on four cleavages: class conflict and one cleavage from within each of the three clusters of cleavages derived from the factor analysis: neighborhood, age, and the cleavage between Market Providers and Public Providers. These choices are based on the frequency of such conflicts and on the extensive inequalities of success that competing teams in these divisions have enjoyed on the twenty-nine issues.


## CLASS CONFLICT AND MIDDLE-CLASS BIAS

The middle class dominates the upper and lower classes in the resolution of issues in Lawrence. Such dominance is indicated both in the political standings in Table 13.1 and through more complex analyses summarized in Table 13.4. Although there are significant class differences in participation, representation, public support, and political principles, these differences do not explain the dominance of the middle class, especially over the upper class.

In addition to calculating win-loss records, the success of various classes can be assessed by determining the overall levels of responsiveness to the preferences of members of each class.[11] Such responsiveness is shown in the first two rows of Table 13.4 by the zero-order correlations across the twenty-nine issues between policy changes and the preferences of the lower class, the middle class, and the upper class among citizens and participants. Among citizens, policy outcomes are weakly but positively related to the preferences of the middle and upper classes and weakly but negatively related to the preferences of the lower class. Such measures of responsiveness are consistent with the winning percentages of these classes on the few issues having class cleavages among citizens. Among participants, policy outcomes are most strongly and significantly related to the positions of the middle class ($r = .54$). Outcomes are unrelated to upper-class positions. Perhaps surprisingly, out-

Table 13.4   Middle-Class Bias: Uncontrolled and Controlled Relationships between Policy Outcomes and the Preferences and Participation of the Lower, Middle, and Upper Classes

| | Lower Class | Middle Class | Upper Class | Control Variable | Adj. $R^2$ |
|---|---|---|---|---|---|
| Citizen preferences | | | | | |
|   Uncontrolled correlations | − .07 | .22 | .22 | | |
| Participant preferences | | | | | |
|   Uncontrolled correlations | .26* | .54** | − .01 | | |
|   Beta coefficients controlling for preferences of | | | | | |
|     other classes | .18 | .56** | − .17 | | .28 |
| Net participation | | | | | |
|   Uncontrolled correlations | .34** | .33** | .07 | | |
|   Beta coefficients controlling for net participation | | | | | |
|     of other classes | .34* | .55** | − .41* | | .18 |
|     and | | | | | |
|   Middle-class representation | .39** | .50** | − .45* | − .23 | .20 |
|   Popular support | .30 | .36 | − .36 | .29 | .21 |
|   Cultural support | .33* | .51* | − .41 | .07 | .15 |
|   Economic imperatives | .33* | .40 | − .34 | .33* | .23 |
| Uncontrolled correlates for | | | | | |
|   Cases with class conflict | − .29 | .40 | − .20 | | |
| Cases without class | | | | | |
|   conflict | .64** | .30 | .21 | | |

*S.L. < .10
**S.L. < .05

comes are weakly but positively related to lower-class preferences ($r = .26$). The difference between this positive responsiveness to lower-class preferences and the low winning percentage of lower-class participants (.313) highlights the differences between responsiveness and win-loss records as measures of success. When issues lack significant class cleavages, the dominant preferences of the lower class are normally reflected in policy outcomes. Thus, despite usually losing on a limited number of issues having class cleavages, the overall pattern is to resolve many issues in ways that reflect the positions of lower-class participants.

There are several possible explanations for unequal responsiveness to the various classes; these explanations can be explored using multiple regression analysis. To establish a baseline for such analyses, the impact on policy outcomes of the preferences of each class, independent of the impact of other classes, were estimated and are reported in the third row of Table 13.4.[12] Controlling for the preferences of other classes slightly alters the estimated impact on policy of the preferences of various classes, but the basic findings remain the same. The preferences of middle-class participants are most reflected in policy outcomes, and those of the upper class are least reflected in policies.

To explore whether these simple inequalities in responsiveness to various classes mask an underlying complex equality, it is important first to consider whether the dominance of the middle class and the apparent impotence of the upper class is rooted in differences in political participation. Table 13.5 shows that 23 percent of the participants were lower class, 29 percent were middle class, and 48 percent were upper class.[13] Thus, participation among the upper class is relatively high, since only 25 percent of the community as a whole is upper class. In contrast, the middle class is underrepresented among participants, at least relative to its 50 percent composition of the community. In addition, Table 13.5 shows that there are class differences in the depth of participation among members of each class. Members of the upper class report that they engage in more acts of persuasive participation than do their counterparts in the middle and lower classes; they contact representatives and bureaucrats and speak at public hearings more frequently.[14] (There are no significant class differences in extensiveness of mobilization, as participants from each class are equally likely to circulate petitions, publicize issues in the media, and organize group meetings while being equally unlikely to engage in demonstrations and boycotts.[15])

Differences in participation seem to explain the dominance of the middle class over the lower class, but these differences add to the puzzle of the dominance of the middle class over the upper class. As shown in the fourth row of Table 13.4, policy outcomes are significantly and equally related to the net participation of the lower and middle classes but unrelated to the net participation of the upper class.[16] Indeed, the multivariate analysis reported in the fifth row of Table 13.4 — which estimates the effects of the participation of each class on outcomes when controlling for the effects of other classes — suggests that middle-class participation and (to a lesser extent) lower-class participation have significantly positive effects on outcomes, while upper-class participation has a significantly negative direct effect on outcomes.[17]

In short, there is only a limited amount of responsiveness to the preferences of the lower class, in part because of the relatively small number of lower-class participants, but when the members of the lower class participate, they have a significant positive influence. There is little responsiveness to members of the upper classs, despite their extensive participation, because such participation seems to be discounted. There is extensive responsiveness to the middle class, not because members of the middle class are especially participatory, but because their participation is more positively received than that of other classes.

Do differences in representation among policymakers explain the differences

Table 13.5   Class Differences in Participation, Representation, Popular Support, and Political Principles

|  | Lower Class | Middle Class | Upper Class |
|---|---|---|---|
| Percentage of Citizens | 25 | 50 | 25 |
| **Participation** | | | |
| Percentage of participants | 23 | 29 | 48 |
| Extent of persuasive participation | 2.05* | 1.86* | 2.39* |
| Extent of mobilization | .34 | .37 | .41 |
| **Representation** | | | |
| Percentage of policymakers | 5 | 46 | 49 |
| Representation/citizenship ratio | .20 | .92 | 1.96 |
| Representation/participation ratio | .22 | 1.58 | 1.02 |
| **Popular Support** | | | |
| Correlations between support of participants and citizen preferences | .25* | .55** | .24 |
| Percentage of issues in which dominant preferences of participants coincided with dominant citizen preferences | 64 | 76 | 59 |
| **Principles (with significant differences)** | | | |
| Percentage of participants preferring | | | |
| Subsidizing economic growth | 49 | 76 | 69 |
| More public services | 55 | 39 | 61 |
| Regulating morality | 40 | 57 | 28 |

*S.L. < .10
**S.L. < .05

in the impact of the participation of various classes? Table 13.5 shows that the different classes are unequally represented. Representatives are drawn equally from the middle and upper classes, and they are rarely drawn from the lower class. The middle class does not seem to be overrepresented, as it holds political office in approximate proportion to the size of the middle class in the community.[18] The upper class is almost 100 percent overrepresented relative to its part in the composition of the community, and the lower class is vastly underrepresented relative to both its part in the composition of the community and its participation on community issues.

Nevertheless, these differences in class representation do not seem to account for inequalities in responsiveness to the various classes. Perhaps the underrepresentation of the lower class contributes to its losing on issues having class cleavages, as members of the lower class had no more than one representative on any of the issues in which they lost. However, the representation of the lower class does not explain why it was successful on some issues and unsuccessful on others; the lower class was consistently underrepresented on all issues and never comprised a majority of any decision-making body that could win through class voting.

Although governing bodies were usually composed of either a majority of middle-class representatives or a majority of upper-class representatives, there was little class cohesion among these representatives. Thus, the extent to which members of the middle class were represented does not explain their dominance.[19] As shown in the sixth row of Table 13.4, controlling for the level of middle-class representation does not significantly affect the extent of responsiveness to various classes. The middle class tended to be successful regardless of whether the governing body was controlled by middle-class or upper-class representatives.

Perhaps the dominance of the middle class is due to the popularity of its positions among the public. Table 13.5 shows that the dominant preferences of middle-class participants were strongly and significantly related to public opinion (r = .55); in general, middle-class participants better represented overall public preferences than did lower- and upper-class participants. Nevertheless, as shown in the seventh row of Table 13.4, controlling for public opinion only slightly reduces the estimated impact of middle-class participants on policy outcomes.

Perhaps the principles of the middle class better conform to dominant cultural values or to structural economic imperatives than do the principles of the lower or upper classes. Table 13.5 shows that middle-class participants are significantly more conservative than their lower-class and upper-class counterparts; they prefer more subsidization of economic growth, less public services (and lower taxes), and more regulation of morality. However, as shown previously in Table 4.1, dominant cultural values in Lawrence call for more public services and less regulation of morality. Thus, controlling for cultural support — the extent to which proposed policy changes are consistent with dominant cultural values[20] — does not explain the disproportionate power of middle-class participants.

Perhaps the dominance of middle-class participants is due to their being most strongly committed to subsidizing economic growth and thus benefiting from the structural tendency of cities to pursue the "city interest" in developmental policies. However, as shown in the ninth row of Table 13.4, controlling for economic imperatives[21] only slightly reduces estimates of responsiveness to the middle class. As illustrated by the defeat of the CORNFIELD Mall proposal, middle-class preferences and participation can prevail over structural tendencies.

Thus, the participation of the middle class seems to be more influential than the participation of the upper class, and such influence is not explained by the overrepresentation of the middle class on governing bodies, by the popularity of middle-class positions, or by middle-class principles being consistent with dominant cultural values or economic imperatives. Because there is no apparent explanation for such unequal influence, one might suppose that policymakers are simply more sympathetic to the demands of middle-class participants than to those of upper-class participants, at least in Lawrence.

The participation of the lower class seems to be as influential as that of the middle class, perhaps because policymakers are also sympathetic toward such participants, but in the lower class such sympathy seems to be limited to issues without class conflict. On issues where the lower class and the middle class are at odds, policymakers are much more responsive to the participation of the middle class ($r = .40$ in the tenth row of Table 13.4) than to the participation of the lower class ($r = -.29$).[22] It is primarily on issues without class conflict that lower-class participants seem effective ($r = .64$ in the last row of Table 13.4), perhaps because such participation signifies to officials the existence of a broad community-wide consensus.

## NEIGHBORHOOD CONFLICT AND THE IMPOTENCE OF THE CELLAR DWELLERS

Eighteen of the twenty-nine issues exhibited strong cleavages, weak cleavages, or significant differences among participants from various neighborhoods, as shown in Table 13.6; thus, local issues appear to be more structured by neighborhood divisions than by class divisions. Moreover, outcomes within the neighborhood division are patterned differently than in the class division. Although the participation of the upper class has not been especially effective, Country Clubbers (those living in the most affluent neighborhoods) have had an impressive 12-5-1 record when they participated in community issues. Normally, Country Clubbers prevailed over Cellar Dwellers (those living in the poorest areas), and they often did so in alliance with Split Levellers (those living in middle-income neighborhoods).

Although there is some overlap between class cleavages and neighborhood cleavages on various Lawrence issues ($r = .34$),[23] the distinctiveness of neighborhood cleavages arises from the territorial nature of many local issues. The proposals to downzone the OREAD and EAST Lawrence neighborhoods, to develop STORMwater disposal systems, to REAPPRAISE property, and to develop TOWNCENTER are examples of issues that directly affected residents of specific neighborhoods and thus mobilized people across various classes within neighborhoods. Neighborhood interests in maximizing representation were also at stake in the WARDS, MAYOR, and MANAGER issues. Thus, neighborhood cleavages were more frequent than class cleavages and often distinct from them.

Neighborhood conflict is much more evident among participants than among citizens. Only on the highly controversial issue of whether to fire the City MANAGER did neighborhood cleavages among participants extend into

Table 13.6    Issues Classified by Type of Neighborhood Conflict and Outcomes

|  |  | Strong Cleavages[1] | Weak Cleavages[1] | Significant Differences |
|---|---|---|---|---|
| Country Clubbers | Wins | **WARDS (P)** <br> *MAYOR (P)* <br> **MANAGER (P, C)** <br> **AIRPORT (P)** <br> SIGNS (P) <br> *OREAD (P)* <br> DRUG (P) <br> **PARK (P)** | LIFELINE (P) <br> *REAPPRAISE (P)* | N2ST (P) <br> **ENVIR (P)** |
|  | Losses | SIZELER (P) <br> *TOWNCENTER (P)* | **EAST (P)** <br> STORM (P) | RAIL (P) |
| Split Levellers | Wins | **WARDS (P)** <br> **MANAGER (P, C)** <br> SIGNS (P) | STORM (P) <br> LIFELINE (P) <br> REAPPRAISE (P) | N2ST (P) <br> ENVIR (P) <br> *BUNKER* |
|  | Losses | SIZELER (P) | **EAST (P)** <br> PARK (P) | RAIL (P) |
| Cellar Dwellers | Wins | SIZELER (P) <br> *TOWNCENTER (P)* | **EAST (P)** <br> STORM (P) | *BUNKER* |
|  | Losses | **WARDS (P)** <br> *MAYOR (P)* <br> **MANAGER (P, C)** <br> AIRPORT (P) <br> SIGNS (P) <br> *OREAD (P)* <br> DRUG (P) <br> **PARK (P)** | N2ST (P) <br> LIFELINE (P) <br> *REAPPRAISE (P)* |  |

P: Participants divided along neighborhood lines.
C: Citizens divided along neighborhood lines.
Issues in boldface: at least 50 percent of officials perceived neighborhood cleavages.
Issues in italic: 25 to 50 percent of officials perceived neighborhood cleavages.

[1]Some officials perceived a neighborhood cleavage on the SOCIAL service issue. Participants were strongly divided along neighborhood lines on the BLUFFS issues. These issues ended in ties and thus are excluded from the above matrix.

broader neighborhood cleavages among citizens. For the most part, citizens from various neighborhoods did not exhibit statistically significant differences in policy preferences. Among citizens, policy outcomes were weakly but positively related to the preferences of Cellar Dwellers, Split Levellers, and Country Clubbers (see the first row of Table 13.7).

The win-loss records of participants from various neighborhoods are reflected in the levels of responsiveness to them, as shown in the second and third rows of Table 13.7. Overall, policy outcomes are highly responsive to

Table 13.7   Complex Equality among Actors from Various Neighborhoods: Uncontrolled and Controlled Relationships between Policy Outcomes and the Preferences and Participation of Cellar Dwellers, Split Levellers, and Country Clubbers

| | Cellar Dwellers | Split Levellers | Country Clubbers | Control Variable | Adj. $R^2$ |
|---|---|---|---|---|---|
| Citizen preferences | | | | | |
| Uncontrolled correlations | .16 | .24 | .24 | | |
| Participant preferences | | | | | |
| Uncontrolled correlations | −.21 | .14 | .50** | | |
| Beta coefficients controlling for preferences of other neighborhoods | −.18 | .06 | .44** | | .18 |
| Net participation | | | | | |
| Uncontrolled correlations | .03 | .29* | .24* | | |
| Beta coefficients controlling for net participation of other neighborhoods | −.19 | .38 | .04 | | .01 |
| and | | | | | |
| Cellar-Dweller representation | −.19 | .38 | .04 | −.02 | .00 |
| Popular support | −.22 | .19 | .02 | .42** | .11 |
| Cultural support | −.27 | .36 | −.02 | .23 | .01 |
| Economic imperatives | −.14 | .41 | −.05 | .34* | .11 |
| Uncontrolled correlates for | | | | | |
| Cases with neighborhood conflict | −.29* | .20 | .09 | − | − |
| Cases without neighborhood conflict | .44* | .42* | .60** | − | − |

*S.L. <.10
**S.L. <.05

the preferences of Country Clubbers, weakly responsive to Split Levellers, and unresponsive to Cellar Dwellers. Are these simple inequalities due to neighborhood differences in participation, representation, popular support, and political principles?

Table 13.8 shows that 45 percent of all Lawrence residents are Split Levellers, 35 percent are Cellar Dwellers, and 20 percent are Country Clubbers. Only 23 percent of the participants on the twenty-nine issues were Split Levellers, despite their large proportion of the citizen base. Comprising 39 percent of the participants on local issues, the Cellar Dwellers participated at levels that slightly exceeded their composition in the community; the extensiveness of such participation can be attributed to the presence of active neighborhood organizations (and to CDBG funds, which sustain such organizations in low-income neighborhoods). Comprising 38 percent of the participants, Country

Clubbers participated at levels that greatly exceeded their composition in the community, due largely to the greater political involvement of the upper class that tends to reside in wealthier neighborhoods.

The participation of Cellar Dwellers, Split Levellers, and Country Clubbers may not be equally effective. As shown in the fifth row of Table 13.7, increases in participation by Split Levellers seem to affect policy outcomes positively (B=.38), those by Country Clubbers are ineffective (B=.04), and those by Cellar Dwellers are, perhaps, counterproductive (B= −.19). Thus, Country Clubbers have been relatively successful on Lawrence issues because policy-makers seem to respond to their preferences regardless of their level of participation. Split Levellers have been successful because policymakers respond to increases in their participation, but Cellar Dwellers have usually been unsuccessful because policymakers discount both their preferences and their participation.

What accounts for such an unequal pattern of responsiveness to the participants from various neighborhoods? First, Country Clubbers are over-represented on decision-making bodies, as shown in the fifth row of Table 13.8. The preponderance of Country Clubbers on governing bodies provides a context where Country Clubber preferences normally receive a positive response.[24] Second, Split-Leveller participants usually articulate positions that coincide with public opinion in the community (see the sixth and seventh rows of Table 13.8). Thus, by responding to public opinion, policymakers also respond to Split-Leveller participation. Third, relative to other participants, Cellar Dwellers hold principles that compete with economic imperatives. Although the economic interests of the city preclude redistribution, Cellar Dwellers tend to hold public welfare principles, as illustrated by their support of the LIFELINE proposal. Although the economic interests of the city require emphasizing economic criteria, Cellar Dwellers tend to emphasize political criteria, as illustrated by their support of downzoning in the OREAD and EAST Lawrence neighborhoods. Although the pursuit of economic interests leads to a devaluation of citizen involvement, Cellar Dwellers emphasize voter participation, as illustrated by their support of WARDS and their opposition to the City MANAGER.

In summary, the inequalities in power of participants from various neighborhoods seems to be derived from a variety of sources. The power of Country Clubbers seems rooted in their overrepresentation on governing bodies. The power of Split Levellers seems to derive from their taking positions that reflect public opinion, and the impotence of Cellar Dwellers seems rooted in the structural tendencies of city governments to resist redistribution, politicization, and extensive participation.

Table 13.8   Neighborhood Differences in Participation, Representation, Popular Support, and Political Principles

|  | Cellar Dwellers | Split Levellers | Country Clubbers |
|---|---|---|---|
| Percentage of citizens | 35 | 45 | 20 |
| **Participation** |  |  |  |
| Percentage of participants | 39 | 23 | 38 |
| Extent of persuasive participation | 2.11 | 2.25 | 2.40 |
| Extent of mobilization | .41 | .30 | .42 |
| **Representation** |  |  |  |
| Percentage of policymakers | 19 | 29 | 52 |
| Representation/citizenship ratio | .54 | .64 | 2.60 |
| Representation/participation ratio | .49 | 1.26 | 1.37 |
| **Popular support** |  |  |  |
| Correlations between support of participants from various neighborhoods and citizen preferences | .24* | .54* | .24* |
| Percentage of issues in which dominant preferences of participants from various neighborhoods coincide with dominant citizen preferences | 36 | 81 | 70 |
| **Principles (with significant differences)** |  |  |  |
| Percentage of participants preferring: |  |  |  |
| More public services | 68 | 50 | 42 |
| Public welfare | 60 | 63 | 28 |
| Emphasizing economic criteria | 31 | 42 | 55 |
| More democratic participation | 56 | 28 | 31 |

*S.L. < .05

## AGE DIFFERENCES AND THE IMPOTENCE OF ROOKIES

Although neighborhoods provide an obvious basis for the organization of conflict in local politics, the different ages of people seem an unlikely source of substantial political cleavages.[25] However, Table 13.9 reveals a surprising number of issues (twelve) having age cleavages or differences. Less surprising are the standings in the Age Division. As shown in Table 13.1, Rookie participants (those less than thirty years old) suffered nine losses before handing Seniors (those over fifty-five years old) their only defeat (on the CATHOLIC Center issue). Meanwhile, Veteran participants (those between thirty and fifty-five) have remained undefeated. In general, policy outcomes were much more responsive to the preferences of Veterans ($r=.47$ in the second row of Table 13.10) and Seniors ($r=.50$) than to those of Rookies ($r=-.10$).

Nevertheless, these age cleavages and inequalities are more prominent among participants than among citizens. Examination of public opinion polls re-

Table 13.9   Issues Classified by Type of Age Conflict and by Outcomes

|  |  | Strong Cleavages[1] | Weak Cleavages | Significant Differences |
|---|---|---|---|---|
| Seniors | Wins | WARDS (P, C)<br>MANAGER (P)<br>SIGNS (P)<br>LIFELINE (P, C)<br>PARK (P) | MAYOR (P)<br>IRB (P)<br>DRUG (P, C)<br>BIRTH (C) | SIZELER (C) |
|  | Losses | CATH (P, C) |  |  |
| Veterans | Wins | WARDS (P, C)<br>MANAGER (P, C)<br>SIGNS (P)<br>CATH (P)<br>LIFELINE (P) | MAYOR (P)<br>DRUG (P, C)<br>BIRTH (P) |  |
|  | Losses |  |  |  |
| Rookies | Wins | CATH (P, C) |  |  |
|  | Losses | WARDS (P, C)<br>MANAGER (P)<br>SIGNS (P)<br>LIFELINE (P, C)<br>PARK (P) | MAYOR (P)<br>IRB (P)<br>DRUG (P, C)<br>BIRTH (P, C) |  |

P : Participants divided along age lines
C : Citizens divided along age lines

[1]Citizens were strongly divided along age lines on the issue of SOCIAL service funding, which ended in a tie.

vealed that only six issues involved age cleavages or differences. Although the preferences of Veteran and Senior citizens tended to prevail over those of Rookie citizens on such issues, the pattern over all issues was for citizens of each age group to have their preferences weakly reflected in policy decisions (as shown in the first row of Table 13.10).

Thus, in analyzing inequalities in the Age Division, it is again useful to focus on differences among participants of various ages. An obvious explanation for the policy failures of Rookies is their lack of participation. As shown in Table 13.11, a majority of Lawrence citizens are young, reflecting the community's large student population; however, the young comprise only nine percent of all participants on policy issues. Though Rookies are vastly underrepresented among participants, Veterans are greatly overrepresented; almost three-fourths of all participants were between thirty and fifty-five years old. Seniors participate beyond their composition in the community but still comprise only 19 percent of the participants on the twenty-nine issues.

Not only do Rookies fail to participate, but their participation seems to

Table 13.10    Complex Equality among Participants of Various Ages: Uncontrolled and Controlled Relationships between Policy Outcomes and the Preferences and Participation of Rookies, Veterans, and Seniors

|  | Rookies | Veterans | Seniors | Control Variable | Adj. $R^2$ |
|---|---|---|---|---|---|
| Citizen preferences |  |  |  |  |  |
| Uncontrolled correlations | .12 | .21 | .24* |  |  |
| Participant preferences |  |  |  |  |  |
| Uncontrolled correlations | −.10 | .47** | .50** |  |  |
| Beta coefficients controlling for preference of other age groups | −.11 | .32 | .30 |  | .23 |
| Net participation |  |  |  |  |  |
| Uncontrolled correlations | −.03 | .21 | .33** |  |  |
| Beta coefficients controlling for net participation of other age groups | −.12 | .05 | .32 |  | .01 |
| and |  |  |  |  |  |
| Persuasive participation | −.11 | .31 | .05 |  | .00 |
| Veteran representation | −.12 | .05 | .33 | .02 | .00 |
| Popular support | −.29 | .18 | −.02 | .53** | .15 |
| Cultural support | −.17 | .09 | .20 | .19 | .00 |
| Economic imperatives | −.07 | −.06 | .31 | .34* | .09 |
| Uncontrolled correlates for |  |  |  |  |  |
| Cases with age conflict | −.65** | .31 | .33 |  |  |
| Cases without age conflict | .34 | .19 | .34 |  |  |

*S.L. <.10
**S.L. <.05

be less effective than that of Veterans and Seniors. The data in the fourth and fifth rows of Table 13.10 suggest that the participation of the young has no policy impact, but that of Seniors may have a positive impact. The participation of Veterans tends to get reinforced, not because Veteran participation is directly effective but because Veterans are usually aligned with Seniors. Thus, explanations of inequality in the Age Division must focus on the relative ineffectiveness of Rookie participation and the relative effectiveness of Senior participation.

One possible explanation focuses on the extensiveness of involvement by participants (see Table 13.11). Not only do relatively few Rookies participate, but those that do are less likely than persons in other age groups to engage in acts of persuasive participation; Rookies are less likely to contact representatives and bureaucrats and speak at public meetings than are older persons. Weighting participation by an index of extensiveness of such conventional involvements reduces the gap in the effectiveness of Rookie and Senior participation and thus helps to explain the bias toward older participants.[26]

Table 13.11   Age Differences in Participation, Representation, Popular Support, and Political Principles

|  | Rookies | Veterans | Seniors |
|---|---|---|---|
| Percentage of citizens | 53 | 35 | 12 |
| Participation | | | |
| Percentage of participants | 9 | 72 | 19 |
| Extent of persuasive participation | 1.77* | 2.23* | 2.34* |
| Extent of mobilization | .29 | .40 | .40 |
| Representation | | | |
| Percentage of policymakers | 0 | 68 | 32 |
| Representation/citizenship ratio | 0 | 1.94 | 2.67 |
| Representation/participation ratio | 0 | .94 | 1.68 |
| Popular support | | | |
| Correlations between support of participants and citizen preferences | .30* | .39** | .46** |
| Percentage of issues in which dominant preferences of participants coincided with dominant citizen preferences | 54 | 70 | 70 |
| Principles (with significant differences) | | | |
| Percentage of participants preferring | | | |
| Subsidizing economic growth | 60 | 74 | 45 |
| More public services | 80 | 52 | 49 |
| Regulating morality | 12 | 40 | 50 |

*S.L. < .10
**S.L. < .05

Another possible explanation focuses on the representativeness of policy-makers. As shown in Table 13.11, Rookies were excluded from the ranks of representatives.[27] About two-thirds of the representatives were Veterans and one-third were Seniors. Such domination of office by Veterans and Seniors probably provides a context of responsiveness to the preferences of older persons, but (as shown in the seventh row of Table 13.10) controlling for level of representation of Veterans (versus Seniors) does not alter inequalities in the effectiveness of participation by persons of various age groups.

Seniors and Veterans have also taken more popular positions on issues than have Rookie participants, as shown in the eighth and ninth rows of Table 13.11. For example, older participants have taken positions supported by most citizens on WARDS, the City MANAGER, the change in MAYORAL selection, IRBs, the SIGN ordinance, and regulation of DRUG paraphernalia. Seniors lost only on the CATHOLIC Center when they tended to oppose this widely supported development. Thus, controlling for public opinion (in the eighth row of Table 13.10) reduces estimates of the direct effectiveness of Senior participation. Seniors succeed because their positions are popular, and they can fail when the public is unsupportive.

Though the positions of Rookies have been less popular than those of their older counterparts, Rookies have, more often than not, taken positions consistent with public opinion. Nevertheless, they have lost on a number of issues (e.g., LIFELINE, the PARKing lot, and the BIRTHing room) where public opinion was on their side. Given public opinion, Rookies should have been somewhat more successful than they were. Thus, public opinion does not fully account for inequalities of responsiveness in the Age Division.

Finally, differences in political principles are relevant to standings in the Age Division and are thus presented in the last three rows of Table 13.11. Rookies tend to be liberal in supporting increased public spending for public services and in opposing the regulation of morality. Veterans are the strongest supporters of promoting economic growth.

As shown in the ninth row of Table 13.10, the cultural perspective — that division leaders should hold principles consistent with dominant community norms — does not explain the dominance of Seniors and Veterans or the impotence of Rookies. After all, the liberal principles of Rookies are consistent with the political culture in Lawrence. A more plausible argument might be that the contributions that Rookies make to defining the political culture of Lawrence tend to get discounted. The liberalism of Rookies on public spending and on social liberty is important in making these liberal principles dominant in the culture; yet these principles are relatively impotent. Thus, the participation of Rookies on behalf of liberal principles on such issues as LIFELIFE, DRUG regulation, and the BIRTHing room may be ineffective because older policymakers do not recognize these liberal principles as dominant in Lawrence; after all, their older and more active constituents stress more conservative alternative principles.

Finally, the success of Veterans seems enhanced by their principles, especially their endorsement of economic growth. When controls are introduced for the economic imperative to pursue the city's interest in growth, the positive impact of increases in Veteran participation vanishes (see the tenth row of Table 13.10). In general, Veterans seem to succeed because they dominate the entire context of local policymaking. Most participants are Veterans; most representatives are Veterans; Veterans represent public opinion; and Veterans seek policy goals consistent with the economic interests of the city. In this context, increases in Veteran participation are of little consequence; victory is practically assured.

## IDEOLOGICAL CONFLICT AND
## THE DOMINANCE OF MARKET PROVIDERS

Community conflict can be analyzed by focusing on ideological cleavages as well as on demographic ones. However, while analysis of cleavages between liberals and conservatives is commonplace in national and state-level politics, these terms are seldom employed in the analysis of local cleavages.[28] Urban analysts have nevertheless sought appropriate labels for describing ideological conflict at the local level. For example, ethos theorists suggested that the principle cleavage in city politics pitted "public-regarding, holists" against more "private-regarding, individualists";[29] conflict between Managerialists and Politicos involves such ideological differences,[30] and, as shown in Table 13.1, such ideological conflict occurred among participants on eight issues with Managerialists suffering only one defeat. Another example of ideological conflict — described in more recent literature dealing with the politics of urban development — pits supporters of rapid growth (The Growth Machine) against opponents of growth (Preservationists).[31] As shown in Table 13.1, twelve issues involved such ideological conflict, and the Growth Machine was usually victorious.

Despite the frequency and importance of these ideological cleavages, the most prominent ideological cleavage in Lawrence pits Market Providers — those who believe in minimal governmental services as a means of minimizing tax burdens — against Public Providers — those who believe in extending and improving governmental services, even if taxes must be raised.[32] As shown in Table 13.12, Market Provider participants have dominated Public Provider participants in their battles on twelve Lawrence issues. Market Providers have succeeded in opposing new public facilities and services (e.g., STORMwater management systems, a BIRTHing facility), public welfare (e.g., LIFELINE), and taxes (e.g., the VIDEO and INTANGIBLES taxes). Market Providers have also succeeded in opposing governmental restrictions on market forces on the OREAD downzoning issue, and they have succeeded on those organizational issues when their dominance was threatened (e.g., WARDS, MAYOR, and MANAGER). Although Market Providers have (thus far) failed to develop a CORNFIELD Mall, they have been instrumental in thwarting public improvements to accommodate downtown redevelopment (e.g., the BUNKER, SIZELER, and TOWN-CENTER malls). Although the AIRPORT improvements were widely perceived by policymakers as a victory for Public Providers, the data fail to indicate significant cleavages between Market Providers and Public Providers on the issue, perhaps because Airport supporters included people who thought that the project would generate the kind of economic growth that would reduce taxes and because Airport opponents included people who thought that the improvements would simply divert funds from other public expenditures that they supported.

What explains the dominance of Market Providers? As shown in Table 13.14, Market Providers outnumber Public Providers among citizens.[33] Over one-fourth of the citizens of Lawrence are committed to minimal government and low taxes. Lawrence has a smaller minority — less than a fifth of its citizens — who are enthusiastic about expansive government and willing to bear the tax burdens of better public services. Most citizens, however, are not firmly committed to either Market Provider or Public Provider values. Such citizens

Table 13.12    Issues Classified by Type of Conflict between Market Providers and Public Providers and by Outcomes

|  |  | Strong Cleavages[1] | Weak Cleavages | Significant Differences |
|---|---|---|---|---|
| Market Providers | Wins | OREAD (P)<br>BIRTH (P)<br>**LIFELINE (P, C)**<br>VIDEO (P)<br>**SIZELER (P)** | **MANAGER (P)**<br>INTANGIBLES (P)<br>**STORM (P, C)**<br>MAYOR (P) | **TOWNCENTER (P)**<br>**BUNKER** |
|  | Losses | CORNFIELD (P)<br>**AIRPORT** |  |  |
| Public Providers | Wins | CORNFIELD (P)<br>**AIRPORT** |  |  |
|  | Losses | OREAD (P)<br>BIRTH (P)<br>**LIFELINE (P, C)**<br>VIDEO (P)<br>**SIZELER (P)** | **MANAGER (P)**<br>INTANGIBLES (P)<br>**STORM (P, C)**<br>MAYOR (P) | **WARDS**<br>TRIBES (P) |

P: Participants divided along attitudinal lines.
C: Citizens divided along attitudinal lines.
Issues in boldface: at least 50 percent of officials perceived cleavage between Market Providers and Public Providers.

[1]Participants and citizens were strongly divided along attitudinal lines on the issue of funding SOCIAL services and officials strongly perceived this cleavage on the SOCIAL issue, which was resolved in a tie.

may, in principle, support more extensive services (as suggested previously in Table 4.1) but their limited enthusiasm for higher taxes make them skeptical of specific proposals.

Although Market Providers outnumber Public Providers among the general public, their dominance is not explained by their greater participation on local issues. On the contrary, as shown in the second row of Table 13.14, Public Providers outnumber Market Providers among participants, and Public Providers are at least as involved in acts of persuasive participation and mobilization as are Market Providers. Despite the greater participation of Public Providers, policy decisions are more responsive to the preferences and the participation of Market Providers, as shown in the first five rows of Table 13.13. Increases in participation by Public Providers have no significant impact on policy decisions, while increases in participation by Market Providers seem to be somewhat effective.

Such bias toward Market Provider participants cannot be explained by their overrepresentation on policymaking bodies. As shown in Table 13.14, Public Providers make up 62 percent of the policymakers, and Market Providers com-

Table 13.13   Accounting for Market Provider Bias: Uncontrolled and Controlled Relationships between Policy Outcomes and the Preferences and Participation of Market Providers and Public Providers

| | Market Providers | Public Providers | Control Variable | Adj. $R^2$ |
|---|---|---|---|---|
| Popular support | | | | |
| Uncontrolled correlations | .20 | .13 | | |
| Participant preferences | | | | |
| Uncontrolled correlations | .23 | − .02 | | |
| Beta coefficients controlling for | | | | |
| preferences of counterparts | .29 | .12 | | .00 |
| Net participation | | | | |
| Uncontrolled correlations | .29* | .00 | | |
| Beta coefficients controlling for net | | | | |
| participation of counterparts | .34* | .13 | | .03 |
| and: | | | | |
| Market Provider representation | .27 | − .10 | .41* | .13 |
| Popular support | .14 | − .05 | .41 | .13 |
| Cultural support | .26 | .05 | .19 | .02 |
| Economic imperatives | .22 | .16 | .36* | .14 |
| Uncontrolled correlates for: | | | | |
| Cases with attitudinal conflict | .48* | − .25 | | |
| Cases without attitudinal conflict | .26 | .12 | | |

*S.L. < .10

prise only 12 percent. Thus, Public Providers — not Market Providers — are vastly overrepresented as commissioners. Moreover, controlling for the number of Market Providers who served as policymakers on specific issues does not explain the gap in effectiveness between Market Providers and Public Providers (see the sixth row of Table 13.13).

Public opinion provides a limited explanation for the bias toward Market Providers. As shown in the eighth and ninth rows of Table 13.14, the positions of Market Providers on specific issues were somewhat closer than those of Public Providers to dominant public opinion. For example, the public tended to agree with Market Provider objections to downtown redevelopment and, through public referenda, they upheld Market Provider positions when they eliminated the INTANGIBLES tax and overturned the fee for STORMwater management. Thus, controlling for public opinion reduces the gap in the effectiveness of Market Provider and Public Provider participation, but it does not fully eliminate it (see the seventh row of Table 13.13). This is because there are issues like the LIFELINE program and the BIRTHing room that representatives perceive as being more unpopular than they are. On such issues, representatives bow to the demands of Market Providers because they believe that their widespread and intense opposition is a measure of public opinion.

Table 13.14   Differences between Market Providers and Public Providers in Participation, Representation, Popular Support, and Political Principles

| | Market Providers | Public Providers |
|---|---|---|
| Percentage of citizens | 28 | 16 |
| Participation | | |
| Percentage of participants | 16 | 33 |
| Extent of persuasive participation | 2.00 | 2.14 |
| Extent of mobilization | .31 | .44 |
| Representation | | |
| Percentage of policymakers | 12 | 62 |
| Representation/citizenship ratio | .43 | 3.88 |
| Representation/participation ratio | .75 | 2.21 |
| Popular support | | |
| Correlations between support of participants and citizen preferences | .31** | .25* |
| Percentage of cases in which dominant preferences of participants coincide with dominant citizen preferences | 68 | 58 |
| Principles (with significant differences) | | |
| Percentage of participants preferring | | |
| More public service | 23 | 74 |
| Public welfare | 22 | 80 |
| Progressive taxes | 14 | 45 |
| Regulating morality | 53 | 27 |
| Using economic criteria | 67 | 24 |
| Using utilitarian criteria | 72 | 51 |

*S.L.<.10
**S.L.<.05

As shown at the bottom of Table 13.14, Market Providers and Public Providers have many differences in political principles, but they both support more economic growth. Nevertheless, the economistic perspective rather than the cultural perspective helps to explain the dominance of Market Providers over Public Providers (as shown in rows 8 and 9 of Table 13.13). In Lawrence, cultural support for liberal public-service and public-welfare principles should empower Public Providers. The failure of Public Providers to be more successful in this culture is best explained by structural economic incentives that prompt policymakers to respond to Market Provider principles calling for minimal public welfare and regressive taxes, and giving priority to economic and utilitarian criteria.

## CONCLUSIONS

The domination that occurs when responsiveness to the opposing sides of community cleavages is unequal is generally more evident among participants than among citizens in Lawrence. Among citizens, there are few structured cleavages, and the outcomes of issues having class, neighborhood, age, and ideological cleavages among citizens do not persistently favor the upper class, the Country Clubbers, men, or other relatively advantaged people. Nevertheless, there are many structured cleavages among participants, and issues are usually resolved in ways that do favor relatively advantaged participants — especially the middle class, Country Clubbers, Seniors and Veterans, Hometowners, conservatives, Republicans, Market Providers, Managerialists, members of the Growth Machine.

The extensive successes of these advantaged participants on community issues and the extensive failures of their disadvantaged counterparts have a variety of explanations. The number of people who participate in community issues as members of competing teams partially explains, for example, the dominance of Veterans and Seniors over Rookies in the Age Division. The extent to which competing participants engage in various acts of persuasive participation can also help to explain unequal responsiveness, as part of the ineffectiveness of Rookie participants seems to be due to their reluctance to contact officials and make public presentations. Such differences in participation do not explain all forms of domination in Lawrence. Cellar Dwellers in the Neighborhood Division fail despite their extensive participation, and Public Providers are more participatory than Market Providers but are dominated by them. Simply increasing participation does not ensure that subordinate interests will achieve increased levels of power.

Inequalities in representation can help to explain the inequalities in responsiveness that are unexplained by participatory differences. The lower class and Rookies have had almost no representation on policymaking bodies, and Cellar Dwellers have been significantly underrepresented. Not surprisingly, these interests achieved few policy successes. Nevertheless, increased representation may not be the key to equal responsiveness. For example, when Cellar Dweller representation increased on a few issues, there were only marginal increases in responsiveness to the preferences and participation of Cellar Dwellers. This suggests that marginal increases in representation by relatively powerless interests — increases that leave counterparts in control of the commission — are insufficient for promoting equality of political standing.[34]

The public is not equally supportive of the policy positions taken by various interests, and differences in public support can explain inequalities in responsiveness. The positions of the middle class were usually consistent with dominant public opinion, partially explaining the dominance of the middle class. Seniors tended to take more popular positions than Rookies, leading to their more frequent successes, and the dominance of Market Providers over Public Providers is partly explained by their actual and perceived public support.

The different principles of competing interests also help to explain inequalities of success on policy issues. For example, the failures of Cellar Dwellers seem to be partly explained by their seeking public welfare and wanting issues resolved through more politicized and participatory procedures. Because such orientations are at odds with structural economic imperatives, they are resisted. The failures of Rookies seem rooted in their seeking policies involving increased public services and reduced regulation of morality. Because these orientations are resisted by older participants, their dominance in the culture is tenuous, and their potency in the policymaking process is limited. Thus, there seem to be "mobilizations of bias"[35] against certain interests. There is some unresponsiveness to certain interests because the local culture provides only weak support for their principles. There is considerable unresponsiveness to other interests because the city interest in economic growth undermines their principles.

Differences in participation, representation, popular support, and principles do not explain all forms of unequal responsiveness. In Lawrence, for example, these factors do not explain the dominance of the middle class. The bias toward the participation of the middle class — or the absence of complex equality in the Class Division — may not indicate any severe problems in the governance of Lawrence; after all, Lawrence is primarily a middle-class community. However, if the compartative-issues method can demonstrate middle-class biases in Lawrence, it can demonstrate other unexplained inequalities in other communities and thus reveal the presence of racial, gender, and other forms of political discrimination whenever they occur.

# 14
# Critical Pluralism and the Rules of the Game

Because pluralists deny that issues such as whether to build new parking facilities, fire the city manager, or downzone property can be resolved by appeals to "the truth" (i.e., "certain knowledge," "true science," or "absolute right"),[1] pluralist theory is procedural rather than substantive. Because pluralists are uncertain about the correctness of substantive policy alternatives, they judge policy outcomes by the processes that lead to them. People can argue endlessly about the best policy alternative for resolving a community issue, but pluralists believe that if an issue is resolved according to democratic rules and under fair conditions, the outcome is legitimate no matter which alternative prevailed. Three types of democratic rules might be identified:

1. The Rules of Polyarchy—Policymakers should be determined through contested elections.
2. The Rules of Pluralism—Participants should adhere to the informal norms of dealing fairly with others, tolerating the participation of opponents, and recognizing the legitimate claims of others.
3. The Rules of Law—Policymakers must respect those statutes, ordinances, and court rulings relevant to community issues.

Because pluralists have asserted that players in community politics "adhere (broadly) to the democratic rules of the game,"[2] pluralists are often regarded as apologists for those players and interests that prevail in the game of community politics.[3] To overcome this charge and attain the capacity for making critical judgments about the resolution of community issues, pluralists must develop a better understanding about the rules of the game and better methods of detecting violations of these rules. The criteria of responsible representation, complex equality, and principle-policy congruence were developed for such purposes. In this chapter we will consider how these criteria clarify and extend the meaning (both conceptually and operationally) of the rules of polyarchy, the rules of pluralism, and the rules of law.

For policy outcomes to be fair, they must be resolved under fair conditions, as well as according to democratic rules. Just as the home court can be an advantage in sports, so can various community settings bias policy outcomes in ways that undermine their legitimacy. Thus, we will end this chapter with a discussion of how extended applications of the conceptual framework and comparative-issues methodology employed to examine the resolution of policy issues in Lawrence can facilitate future investigations into the biases of various political settings.

## RESPONSIBLE REPRESENTATION
## AND THE RULES OF POLYARCHY

The criterion of responsible representation is an extension of the rules of polyarchy. According to Dahl and Lindblom, the rules of polyarchy provide for regular, open, and contested elections for office.[4] The polyarchical rule that policymaking authority is conferred on the winners of competitive elections enhances democratic performance in two ways. First, electoral victory gives representatives the authority to control nonelected power wielders such as bureaucrats, private elites, and special-interest groups. Second, elections make representatives accountable to citizens. Nevertheless, the formality of contested elections neither ensures that elected representatives will appropriately exercise the authority vested in them or that citizens will succeed in controlling representatives. On specific issues, representatives may capitulate to bureaucrats, notables, or special interests, and on too many issues, representatives may pursue policies at odds with dominant citizen preferences. When such outcomes occur, they belie the goals of contested elections: to empower representatives and to ensure that their decisions are normally consistent with citizen wishes.

Although the rules of polyarchy are satisfied by the mere existence of genuinely contested elections, the concept of responsible representation facilitates consideration of the extent to which the goals of contested elections are achieved in the resolution of community issues. The scale of responsible representation presented in Chapter 2 specifies the conditions when the goals of polyarchy are unrealized: when representatives fail to exercise their authority, when citizen preferences are ignored, and when policy processes are consequently dominated by (for example) private elites, bureaucrats, or special-interest groups. The scale of responsible representation also specifies the conditions where the goals of polyarchy are partially realized: when representatives are empowered but citizen preferences are ignored (e.g., when representatives act as trustees) or when representatives fail to use their authority but where citizen preferences are satisfied (e.g., when representatives act as instructed delegates). Finally, the scale of democratic performance specifies the conditions when the goals of polyarchy are fully realized: when representatives exercise their independent judgments and make decisions that reflect the will of their constituents.

The comparative-issues methodology permits investigation of the levels of responsible representation that are achieved on specific issues. By measuring the policy preferences of citizens and various kinds of participants and by relating these preferences to policy outcomes on various Lawrence issues, this method showed that responsible representation was sometimes partially and sometimes fully realized in Lawrence. The goals of polyarchical rules were normally upheld in Lawrence because representatives did exercise their authority over bureaucrats, notables, and special interests and resolved issues on the basis of their independent judgments. The additional goal of polyarchical rules — that citizens agree with the judgments of their representatives — was less well realized, as the dominant preferences of representatives and citizens collided on eleven issues (almost 40 percent of the time).

Pluralists recognize that some conflict will occur between the judgments of representatives and the preferences of citizens and have avoided providing assertions about how much conflict is too much conflict. Nevertheless, because policy disagreements between representatives and most citizens block the attainment of the highest levels of responsible respresentation, their frequent recurrence in Lawrence is disconcerting. A populist approach to the problem — more referenda — is insufficient from a pluralist perspective, for referenda simply enable citizen preferences to prevail over representative judgments and thus may fail to bring about policy agreements between representatives and citizens. Instead, pluralists usually focus on the process by which representatives are elected and question whether electoral structures encourage the kind of issue voting that enhances the selection of representatives who hold policy positions similar with those of most citizens.[5] For example, issue voting may be facilitated by political parties that provide voters with distinct policy choices.[6] If so, nonpartisanship in Lawrence and most other communities may inhibit issue voting, hinder policy agreement between representatives and citizens, and thus, reduce responsible representation.

In summary, the concept of responsible representation extends the rules of polyarchy by suggesting that the mere presence of contested elections is not sufficient to achieve the goals of empowering representatives and achieving policy agreement between representatives and citizens. The comparative-issues methodology permits assessment of the achievement of polyarchical goals. The application of this method in Lawrence showed that representatives were able to control bureaucrats, private elites, and special interests but that representatives often made decisions that were at odds with citizen wishes.

## COMPLEX EQUALITY AND THE RULES OF PLURALISM

The criterion of complex equality is an extension of the rules of pluralism — those informal and often unspecified understandings of "fair dealings" among various interests in the community. The rules of pluralism seem to provide broad norms, suggesting that specific policy outcomes are fair if the views of all interests have been given a fair hearing.[7] While the concept of fair dealing focuses on providing an equal opportunity to participate for all types of people whose interests are at stake on community issues, the concept of complex equality focuses on the equality of treatment that is provided for those who do participate. Discriminatory treatment of various types — based on class, race, gender, age, or other characteristics that are not germane to the validity of their positions on issues — clearly violates fair dealing among interests. However, political defeat on specific issues is not necessarily evidence of discriminatory treatment, since some interests will win and others will lose, even if processes are characterized by fair dealing.

In order to determine if complex equality has been violated, and discriminatory treatment has occurred, the outcomes of a variety of issues must be observed. If one interest (or grouping of people posited to have some common interests or preferences) tends to dominate competing interests in a variety of policy battles and if such dominance lacks a legitimate explanation, there is prima facie evidence of discrimination and, consequently, evidence that the fair-dealing rule of pluralism has been violated.

The comparative-issues methodology facilitates analysis of complex equality because it detects the presence of various kinds of cleavages on specific issues, permits calculation of the success rates of competing interests that define these cleavages, and probes various explanations of unequal responsiveness to competing interests. When applied to the twenty-nine issues in Lawrence, the comparative-issues methodology uncovered numerous cleavages among participants. It showed that those interests representing more liberal values (e.g., Politicos, Public Providers, and Preservationists) and having fewer resources (e.g., the lower class, Cellar Dwellers, women, and the young) tend to be less successful than their counterparts. It showed that, for the most part, these simple inequalities had legitimate explanations; dominant interests usually won because they were better represented, they participated at higher levels, or their positions were more consistent with public preferences and dominant cultural principles.

The comparative-issues methodology can also support charges of political discrimination by uncovering inequalities having explanations of problematic legitimacy or having no apparent explanation. For example, we can explain the dominance of Country Clubbers over Cellar Dwellers by structural economic incentives that provide strong biases against the preferences of residents of lower-income neighborhoods and others who oppose economic development. However, such an explanation may not legitimize this inequality. The high success rate of the middle class on issues in Lawrence was described but unexplained by the comparative-issues methodology; such unexplained inequalities suggest strong biases in favor of middle-class preferences. These examples indicate that the comparative-issues methodology can support critical evaluations about the ability of local communities to deal fairly with the diverse interests within them.

In sum, the second rule of the game in pluralist politics is that of fair dealing, more precisely defined as complex equality. This means that unequal treatment of various interests in the resolution of community issues must have legitimate explanations and not be merely discriminatory. Violations of this rule of complex equality can be uncovered by a comparative-issues methodology that shows the persistence of unequal responsiveness to competing interests, even when legitimate reasons for these inequalities are considered.[8]

## PRINCIPLE-POLICY CONGRUENCE AND THE RULES OF LAW

The criterion of principle-policy congruence complements the rules of law, serving some of the same functions that laws provide in regulating conflict on community issues while extending the mechanisms of conflict regulation from specific statutes and legal precedents to broad community norms. Rules of law can be important in transforming battles on community issues from mere power struggles into principled discussions about the desired destinations of the community. Rules of law often contain policy decisions, reached in previous contexts that were relatively deliberative and free of the pressure of immediate interests and power applications, about the general principles that should guide the resolution of future issues. Rules of law can thus serve as a constraint on the most powerful interests whose preferences may conflict with established laws. Zoning laws generally, and the Comprehensive Plan of Lawrence (Plan 95) specifically, illustrate these features of the rule of law. The Growth Machine may wish to build more intensive developments than permitted by existing zoning laws; such laws (and rules that make the revision of these laws difficult)[9] serve to constrain the power of the Growth Machine and give Preservationists a better chance to compete on developmental issues. Plan 95 was written to guide the development of Lawrence, and it provides for the widespread community goal of retaining the downtown as the center of retail development in the community. Plan 95 has helped to ensure that the Cornfield Mall issue would be resolved in a way consistent with this community goal rather than simply on the basis of the balance of power between promall and antimall forces.

Although rules of law can domesticate political power and bring principles to bear on the resolution of community issues, there is no assurance that laws embody appropriate principles or that laws are authoritative enough to provide clear guidance for policymakers in their deliberations.[10] The criterion of principle-policy congruence provides a second, more direct, way of bringing appropriate principles to bear on community decision making. Though the rule of law brings policy precedents to bear on community issues, the criterion of principle-policy congruence brings the most widely accepted cultural values to bear. If participants understand that policymakers act on the basis of those principles dominant in the political culture and relevant to the issue at hand, issues can be debated in terms of competing principles. The criterion of principle-policy congruence thus shares with rules of law the function of making the game of community politics more than a mere power struggle. The criterion of principle-policy congruence helps to frame issues in terms of their relationships to the general goals that people have for their communities.

The comparative-issues methodology facilitates investigation of principle-policy congruence by mapping the distribution of support within a community for various political principles, determining the extent to which these principles are relevant to particular issues, and suggesting the extent to which policy decisions are constrained by dominant principles in the community. The application of this methodology to Lawrence suggests that dominant community principles do not strongly shape the resolution of community issues.

The goal of having community politics regulated by dominant cultural principles seems undermined in several ways. First, the citizens of pluralist communities often fail to acquire shared understanding about important principles; when they are fairly evenly divided in their support of competing principles—as they are in Lawrence regarding the provision of public welfare and the regulation of morality—no principle may command the respect of policymakers. Second, neither citizens nor participants may succeed in relating their principles to their policy positions; when policy preferences are only weakly linked to people's principles, the relevance of articulated principles becomes problematic. Third, even when particular principles are clearly dominant in the culture and clearly relevant to a concrete issue, they may fail to provide clear guidance about the resolution of that issue because of the presence of other dominant and relevant principles that provide precisely the opposite guidance. On many developmental issues, for example, dominant economic-growth principles and neighborhood-protection principles provide conflicting guidance. Finally, the potency of dominant cultural principles may be undermined by structural economic imperatives. For example, even though most Lawrence citizens hold public-welfare and citizen-involvement principles, policymakers may recognize such principles as threats to the economic interests of the city and thus fail to allow these principles to regulate policy issues. Although these problems limit the regulative role of dominant principles in the resolution of community issues, the comparative-issues methodology shows that there was some tendency to resolve issues in ways that reflected the most dominant principles in the local political culture.

In summary, the concept of principle-policy congruence provides an additional mechanism beyond the rule of law for managing the power struggles of participants in the game of community politics. If principle-policy congruence is accepted as an important criterion that should be satisfied, policymakers are encouraged to understand the broad policy orientations prevalent in their local political cultures and to make decisions accordingly. The comparative-issues methodology permits an assessment of the extent to which policy decisions are consistent with dominant cultural principles and helps to identify some of the obstacles to higher levels of principle-policy congruence.

## BEYOND LAWRENCE:
## THE STUDY OF COMMUNITY SETTINGS

This study provides a conceptual framework for investigating the extent to which policy issues are resolved in particular communities in ways that correspond to three democratic ideals: responsible representation, complex equality, and principle-policy congruence.[11] An application of the comparative-issues methodology showed that Lawrence had certain deficiencies with respect to each of these ideals: responsible representation was limited by a number of cases of disagreement between representatives and citizens; complex equality was undermined by discrimination in favor of the middle class; and principle-policy congruence was more widespread for dominant conservative principles than for dominant liberal principles. Nevertheless, the overall assessment of the political process in Lawrence would seem generally positive. Lawrence has escaped the maladies of domination by external participants, bureaucrats, the private elite, and special interests. Most simple inequalities in the success of competing interests have legitimate explanations. Policy outcomes have been somewhat constrained by the most dominant principles in Lawrence's political culture.

Because the comparative-issues methodology that led to these conclusions has been applied to only a sample of Lawrence issues, there is no way of knowing whether other communities have fared more or less satisfactorily in terms of these three ideals. The mere fact that other cities provide different settings for resolving community issues suggests that cities differ in their attainment of pluralist goals.[12] Communities differ in their governmental institutions, social structures, economic bases, and political cultures. These differences may be systematically related to community differences in the achievement of responsible representation, complex equality, and principle-policy congruence. For example, unreformed governmental institutions may enhance the achievement of responsible representation, because partisan elections may reduce the frequency of policy disagreements between representatives and citizens. Economic diversity may enhance the achievement of complex equality, for the concentration of economic resources in the hands of a few businesses may greatly threaten that equality. Perhaps Lawrence has achieved relatively high levels of complex equality because discrimination in favor of the Growth Machine is minimal in university communities where economic well-being is less dependent on the prosperity of local businesses than on state appropriations for higher education. Moralistic political cultures may enhance the level of principle-policy congruence; participants and citizens in moralistic cultures may understand politics as involving political principles and linking their principles to concrete issues. The moralistic aspects of Lawrence's political culture may enhance — just as the individualistic aspects of its political culture may reduce — the level of principle-policy congruence achieved in Lawrence.[13] However, it is only possible to speculate about how diverse settings affect the attainment of pluralist goals; political scientists have yet to examine the relationships between political settings and the achievement of responsible representation, complex equality, and principle-policy congruence — at least as conceptualized and measured in this study. Thus, a broader application of the comparative-issues method to a variety of communities is necessary in order to understand the effects on democratic performance of various aspects of community settings.

# Appendix
## Determining the Principles
## at Stake on Concrete Issues

Investigations into the relationships between principles and policy preferences permit scientific assessments of the principles most relevant to particular issues (and thus whether the outcomes of these issues are congruent with dominant, relevant cultural principles). For example, because supporters of the proposal to create wards tended to hold public-involvement principles, and opponents of that proposal tended to hold representative-discretion principles, these contrasting democratic-process principles were apparently at stake (leading to the conclusion that the rejection of the wards proposal was inconsistent with the public-involvement principles dominant in Lawrence's political culture). In contrast, evidence that both supporters and opponents of wards were equally committed to pro-growth principles undermines the contention that competing principles regarding growth were also relevant to the issue (and that the wards proposal needed to be rejected in order to achieve an outcome consistent with dominant pro-growth principles). Thus, competing political principles are relevant to an issue to the extent that such principles divide participants and citizens into opposing sides.

In order to determine the alternative principles that were at stake on the issues in the Lawrence sample, the principles and policy positions of both participants and citizens have been analyzed. The data for these analyses were obtained from the same participant interviews and citizen surveys used to measure the distribution of support for the nine pairs of alternative principles in the political culture of Lawrence, as reported in Table 4.1. Participants were asked about their positions on those issues in which they had been involved, while citizens were asked to indicate their preferences on those recent Lawrence issues with which they were familiar. Only those participants and citizens with unambiguous policy preferences on an issue (i.e., those who clearly supported or opposed a proposed policy change) were included in these analyses.

Table A presents those relationships between principles and policy preferences that are statistically significant. The first column lists the twenty-ine concrete issues that are analyzed, and the second column indicates the number of participants ($N_p$) and citizens ($N_c$) whose policy preferences on these issues are included in each analysis. The sample sizes of participants and citizens varied substantially across issues. Of course, there was variance in the number of people involved in each issue, accounting for differences in $N_p$. Variance in the number of citizens analyzed ($N_c$) is due to two factors. First, the 1984 and 1986 citizen surveys — the only surveys containing questions about political principles — were combined for this portion of the analysis. Although citizen preferences on all issues except BUNKER and BLUFFS were investigated in the 1984 survey, only seventeen issues were included in the 1986 survey. Second, the number of citizens who were aware of particular issues and had unambiguous preferences about them varied across issues.

The next nine columns specify the principles dominant in Lawrence's political culture (as described in Chapter 4). The coefficients in the cells relating principles to preferences on concrete issues are zero-order Pearson correlation coefficients ($r_p$ for participants and $r_c$ for citizens) and standardized regression coefficients ($B_p$ for participants and $B_c$ for citizens).

The correlation coefficients indicate the degree and direction of relationships between principles and policy preferences. In order to facilitate interpretation of principle-policy congruence, measures of all principles have been coded or recoded, so higher scores indicate support for those principles dominant within Lawrence's political culture.[1] As a consequence, positive correlation coefficients indicate that the policy outcome specified in the row heading tended to be preferred by those holding principles dominant in Lawrence; negative coefficients indicate that the outcome specified in the heading tended to be preferred by those holding subordinate principles. For example, the positive coefficients in the cell relating DEMOCRATic-process principles to WARDS indicate that persons holding public-involvement principles (which are dominant in Lawrence) tended to support creating WARDS, and the negative coefficient ($r_p = -.30$) in the cell relating GROWth principles to preferences on WARDS indicates that support for WARDS was greater among those participants holding subordinate slow-growth principles than among those holding dominant pro-growth principles.

The usefulness of these correlation coefficients is limited because they may include spurious (or noncausal) associations. For example, the significant correlation shown in Table A between GROWth principles and preferences on the WARDS issue may be spurious because those who hold public-involvement principles may also tend to hold slow-growth principles; it could be that principles about public-involvement *influenced* participants' preferences regarding the wards proposal, and that the observed relationship between support for growth principles and WARDS is an artifact of the causal relationship.

Two-step forced-entry regression analyses were performed to obtain the beta coefficients (B) that control for such spuriousness. In the first step, measures of those principles articulated by participants were entered as independent variables predicting policy preferences for each of the twenty-nine issues. In the second step, measures of additional principles that were not articulated as relevant to the concrete issue but that nevertheless had significant zero-order correlations (at the .05 level) with preferences on the issue were added as independent variables in the regression model.[2] If the resulting regression coefficients were statistically insignificant,[3] they are not in the table. Thus, when only Pearson correlation coefficients are present in a cell, the relationship between the principles and preferences is spurious.

Finally, the last column of Table A provides measures of the extent to which those principles considered here explain the policy preferences of participants and citizens. When relating principles to preferences using multiple regression analysis, a best-fitting model was derived. The adjusted coefficients of determination (Adj. $R^2$) from such models indicate the percentages of variation in policy preferences accounted for by the principles of participants and citizens. For example, participants' principles explain 37 percent of their preferences on wards, while citizens' principles explain only 2 percent of their preferences on wards. Because such coefficients of determination are usually small, it is clear that principles — or at least the principles considered here — play only a limited role in determining how people align themselves on local policy issues.

Critical pluralist analyses do not require the assumptions that people are highly principled or that principles explain a great deal about the resolution of policy issues. Instead, such analyses assume that examinations of the relationships between principles and policy preferences facilitate an assessment of whether communities adopt policies congruent with those dominant cultural principles that are relevant to them. By providing an objective basis for assessing the principles that are relevant to the twenty-nine issues, the data in Table A are essential building blocks for evaluating the extent to which Lawrence policymakers have succeeded in achieving principle-policy congruence in the resolution of community issues.

Table A  The Relationships between Principles and Preferences on Twenty-nine Lawrence Issues for Participants and Citizens

| Issues | N | Principles | | | | | | | | | |
|---|---|---|---|---|---|---|---|---|---|---|---|
| | | GROW | NEIGH | SERV | WELF | USETAX | LIB | ECON | AGG | DEMO | Adj. $R^2$ |
| Create WARDS and strengthen the mayor | $N_p=37$ <br> $N_c=461$ | $r_p = -.30$ | | | $r_p = .44$ <br> $r_c = -.10$ | $r_p = -.31$ | $r_p = .27$ | $r_p = -.54$ <br> $B_p = -.35$ | | $r_p = .56$ <br> $B_p = .39$ <br> $r_c = .16$ <br> $B_c = .16$ | $P = .37$ <br> $C = .02$ |
| Open commission elections of the MAYOR | $N_p=14$ <br> $N_c=358$ | $r_p = .62$ | | $r_p = -.59$ | $r_p = -.70$ | | | $r_p = .46$ | $r_p = .49$ | $r_p = -.82$ <br> $B_p = -.83$ <br> $r_c = -.08$ | $P = .66$ <br> $C = .00$ |
| Fire the city MANAGER | $N_p=55$ <br> $N_c=468$ | $r_p = -.44$ <br> $r_c = -.16$ <br> $B_c = -.17$ | $r_p = .39$ | $r_p = .32$ <br> $r_c = .15$ <br> $B_c = .16$ | $r_p = .53$ <br> $B_p = .33$ <br> $r_c = .15$ | $r_p = -.33$ <br> $r_c = -.13$ | $r_p = .25$ <br> $r_c = .10$ | $r_p = -.33$ | $r_p = -.35$ <br> $r_c = -.13$ <br> $B_c = -.12$ | $r_p = .59$ <br> $B_p = .39$ <br> $r_c = .13$ <br> $B_c = .12$ | $P = .35$ <br> $C = .08$ |
| AIRPORT improvement | $N_p=31$ <br> $N_c=461$ | $r_p = .69$ <br> $B_p = .65$ <br> $r_c = .12$ <br> $B_c = .12$ | $r_p = -.42$ | | $r_p = -.46$ | $r_c = -.08$ | | $r_p = .35$ <br> $r_c = -.12$ <br> $B_c = -.16$ | $r_p = .53$ | $r_p = -.43$ <br> $r_c = -.15$ <br> $B_c = -.15$ | $P = .41$ <br> $C = .05$ |
| North Second Street Improvement (N2ST) | $N_p=23$ <br> $N_c=140$ | $r_p = .73$ <br> $B_p = .73$ | | $r_c = .25$ <br> $B_c = .25$ | | | | | | $r_p = -.35$ | $P = .52$ <br> $C = .05$ |
| Develop RAIL-served industrial park | $N_p=54$ <br> $N_c=266$ | $r_p = .50$ <br> $B_p = .44$ <br> $r_c = .13$ <br> $B_c = .14$ | | | $r_p = -.27$ <br> $r_c = -.10$ | | | | $r_p = .37$ <br> $B_p = .31$ | $r_c = -.23$ <br> $B_c = -.24$ | $P = .33$ <br> $C = .07$ |

| Issue | N | | | | | | | | | | P / C |
|---|---|---|---|---|---|---|---|---|---|---|---|
| Develop RESEARCH park | $N_p = 39$<br>$N_c = 325$ | $r_p = .67$<br>$B_p = .70$<br>$r_c = .10$ | | | $r_p = .28$ | | | $r_p = .32$<br>$B_p = .29$ | $r_p = .42$ | $r_c = -.15$<br>$B_c = -.15$ | $P = .57$<br>$C = .02$ |
| Nonrestrictive issuance of industrial revenue bonds (IRB) | $N_p = 40$<br>$N_c = 153$ | $r_c = .27$<br>$B_c = .22$ | $r_p = -.34$<br>$B_p = -.34$ | | | | | | $r_c = .36$<br>$B_c = .29$ | | $P = .09$<br>$C = .15$ |
| Regulation of billboards and SIGNS | $N_p = 20$<br>$N_c = 141$ | | $r_p = .52$<br>$B_p = .52$ | $r_c = .25$<br>$B_c = .25$ | | | $r_c = -.18$ | | $r_c = .21$<br>$B_c = .25$ | | $P = .23$<br>$C = .11$ |
| OREAD neighborhood downzoning | $N_p = 31$<br>$N_c = 114$ | $r_p = -.68$<br>$B_p = -.40$ | $r_p = .69$<br>$B_p = .43$ | $r_p = .41$ | $r_p = .39$ | | $r_p = .32$ | $r_p = -.66$ | | $r_p = .33$ | $P = .52$<br>$C = .03$ |
| EAST Lawrence downzoning | $N_p = 28$<br>$N_c = 285$ | $r_p = -.44$ | $r_p = .61$<br>$B_p = .36$ | $r_p = .49$ | $r_p = .55$ | $r_p = -.39$ | $r_p = .44$ | $r_p = -.44$<br>$r_c = -.17$<br>$B_c = -.17$ | $r_p = -.67$<br>$B_p = -.49$ | $r_p = .50$ | $P = .45$<br>$C = .02$ |
| BLUFFS development | $n_p = 21$<br>$N_c = 0$ | $r_p = .80$<br>$B_p = .43$ | $r_p = -.80$<br>$B_p = -.47$ | $r_p = -.61$ | $r_p = -.53$ | | $r_p = -.46$ | | $r_p = .47$ | $r_p = -.68$ | $P = .65$<br>$C = MD$ |
| CATHolic center expansion | $N_p = 23$<br>$N_c = 444$ | $r_c = .09$ | $r_p = -.55$<br>$B_p = -.43$<br>$r_c = -.18$<br>$B_c = -.18$ | | | | $r_c = -.10$ | $r_p = .55$<br>$B_p = .43$ | | | $P = .42$<br>$C = .03$ |

Table A   The Relationships between Principles and Preferences on Twenty-nine Lawrence Issues for Participants and Citizens (cont.)

| Issues | N | Principles | | | | | | | | | Adj. $R^2$ |
|---|---|---|---|---|---|---|---|---|---|---|---|
| | | GROW | NEIGH | SERV | WELF | USETAX | LIB | ECON | AGG | DEMO | |
| Enforcement of the ENVIRONMENT code | $N_p=28$ | | | $r_p=-.34$ | $r_p=-.36$ | | $r_p=-.44$ $B_p=-.44$ | | | | P=.16 |
| | $N_c=115$ | | | | | | | $r_c=-.16$ | | | C=.06 |
| Regulation of sales of DRUG paraphernalia | $N_p=6$ | | | | | | | | | | P=.00 |
| | $N_c=236$ | | | | | $r_c=.11$ | | | $r_c=.15$ $B_c=.13$ | | C=.01 |
| End TRIBES value clarification program | $N_p=12$ | $r_p=.59$ | | | $r_p=-.62$ | | $r_p=-.74$ $B_p=-.75$ | | | | P=.51 |
| | $N_c=87$ | | | | | | | | | | C=.00 |
| Create BIRTHing room at hospital | $N_p=19$ | | | | $r_p=.66$ | | $r_p=.61$ $B_p=.61$ | $r_p=-.70$ | | $r_p=.60$ | P=.33 |
| | $N_c=153$ | | | | | | | | | | C=.00 |
| STORMwater management | $N_p=21$ | $r_p=-.38$ $B_p=-.46$ | | | | | | | | | P=.10 |
| | $N_c=266$ | | $r_c=.14$ $B_c=.18$ | $r_c=.12$ $B_c=.13$ | | | | | | | C=.06 |
| CLOSE three elementary schools | $N_p=23$ | | | | | | | | $r_p=.18$ $B_p=.54$ | $r_p=-.35$ $B_p=-.63$ | P=.23 |
| | $N_c=401$ | | | $r_c=-.14$ $B_c=-.11$ | | | | | | $r_c=-.14$ $B_c=-.14$ | C=.03 |

| | N | (1) | (2) | (3) | (4) | (5) | (6) | (7) | (8) | (9) | (10) | P / C |
|---|---|---|---|---|---|---|---|---|---|---|---|---|
| Authorize LIFELINE gas rates | $N_p$ = 39<br>$N_c$ = 313 | | | $r_p$ = .40<br>$r_c$ = .19 | | | $r_p$ = -.30<br>$r_c$ = -.12 | | $r_c$ = -.12 | $r_p$ = -.40<br>$B_p$ = -.34 | | P = .40<br>C = .07 |
| Fund SOCIAL services | $N_p$ = 39<br>$N_c$ = 527 | $r_c$ = -.12 | $r_p$ = .28 | $r_p$ = .37<br>$r_c$ = .25 | $r_p$ = .60<br>$B_p$ = .45<br>$r_c$ = .24<br>$B_c$ = .26 | $r_p$ = .64<br>$B_p$ = .60<br>$r_c$ = .60<br>$B_c$ = .58 | $r_p$ = -.29<br>$r_c$ = -.11 | $r_c$ = .10 | $r_p$ = -.29<br>$r_c$ = -.11 | $r_p$ = -.35 | $r_p$ = .38 | P = .34<br>C = .34 |
| Tax VIDEOGAMES | $N_p$ = 11<br>$N_c$ = 175 | | $r_p$ = .68 | | | $r_p$ = .50 | $r_p$ = -.62<br>$B_p$ = -.48<br>$r_c$ = -.15<br>$B_c$ = -.18 | $r_p$ = .51 | $r_p$ = -.70<br>$B_p$ = -.59 | | $r_c$ = .15 | P = .64<br>C = .02 |
| End INTANGIBLES tax | $N_p$ = 30<br>$N_c$ = 106 | | | | | | $r_p$ = .49<br>$B_p$ = .48 | $r_c$ = -.24 | $r_c$ = .24<br>$B_c$ = .28 | | $r_c$ = .19 | P = .21<br>C = .07 |
| REAPPRAISE real estate | $N_p$ = 13<br>$N_c$ = 364 | | | $r_p$ = -.57<br>$B_p$ = -.42 | | | | | | | | P = .00<br>C = .00 |
| Build CORNFIELD mall | $N_p$ = 35<br>$N_c$ = 523 | | $r_p$ = .56[a]<br>$B_p$ = .40 | | | | | $r_p$ = .33 | | | | P = .43<br>C = .00 |
| Build BUNKER mall | $N_p$ = 48<br>$N_c$ = 0 | $r_p$ = .24 | $r_p$ = -.46<br>$B_p$ = -.45 | | | | | | | | $r_p$ = -.30 | P = .18<br>C = MD |

Table A   The Relationships between Principles and Preferences on Twenty-nine Lawrence Issues for Participants and Citizens (cont.)

| Issues | N | Principles | | | | | | | | | Adj. R² |
|---|---|---|---|---|---|---|---|---|---|---|---|
| | | GROW | NEIGH | SERV | WELF | USETAX | LIB | ECON | AGG | DEMO | |
| Build PARKING lot at 600 Mass. | $N_p = 31$ | $r_p = .62$ $B_p = .31$ | $r_p = -.41$ | | $r_p = -.43$ | | $r_p = -.55$ | $r_p = .35$ | | $r_p = -.70$ $B_p = -.56$ | P = .57 |
| | $N_c = 335$ | | $r_c = -.12$ $B_p = -.12$ | | | | | | | $r_c = -.11$ | C = .01 |
| Build SIZELER mall | $N_p = 39$ | | $r_p = -.37$ $B_p = -.46$ | $r_p = .29$ $B_p = .37$ | | | | | | $r_p = -.41$ | P = .25 |
| | $N_c = 482$ | | | | | | | | | | C = .00 |
| Build TOWNCENTER mall | $N_p = 36$ | $r_p = .42$ $B_p = .31$ | $r_p = -.56$ $B_p = -.34$ | | | | | | $r_p = .45$ | $r_p = -.56$ $B_p = -.32$ | P = .52 |
| | $N_c = 629$ | $r_c = .09$ | | $r_c = .08$ $B_c = .10$ | $r_c = .07$ | | | | $r_c = -.08$ | $r_c = -.18$ $B_c = -.17$ | C = .03 |

$N_p$ : Number of participants analyzed.

$r_p$ : Significant zero-order correlation (p<.05) between principles and policy preferences for $N_p$ participants on issue.

$B_p$ : Significant standardized regression coefficient (p<.10) between principles and preferences for $N_p$ participants on issue.

P : Adjusted coefficient of determination of best-fitting model predicting the policy preferences of participants on the basis of the principles they hold.

$N_c$ : Number of citizens analyzed from 1984 and/or 1986 surveys.

$r_c$ : Significant zero-order correlation (p<.05) between principles and policy preferences for $N_c$ citizens.

$B_c$ : Significant standardized regression coefficient (p<.05) between principles and preferences for $N_c$ citizens.

C : Adjusted coefficient of determination of best-fitting model predicting the policy preferences of citizens on the basis of the principles they hold.

MD : Missing data; no citizen preference data available for this issue.

[a] : For the cornfield mall issue only, the relevance of growth and neighborhood protection principles was determined by a single question asking respondents to indicate their priority between these concerns. The relationships between that measure and preferences regarding the cornfield mall are indicated in the GROW cell only.

# Notes

## CHAPTER 1. EVALUATING DEMOCRATIC
## PERFORMANCE IN COMMUNITY POLICYMAKING

1. This quotation is from one of 239 interviews conducted with the participants in recent policy issues in Lawrence. Because anonymity was promised to persons participating in interviews, the sources of these quotations are provided only if the remarks also appeared in public reports, such as stories in the *Lawrence Journal-World* (*LJW*), or if participants subsequently consented to the use of their quoted remarks. Quotations without attribution and without citation were provided by participants in the interviews.

2. Molotch, "The City as a Growth Machine."

3. The developers and realtors involved in this issue were not among the top economic and social notables in Lawrence, as revealed by the reputational analysis of community power presented below.

4. Elite theorists may concede that relatively unimportant allocational issues — those dealing with locational matters (e.g., where to build a new school) and housekeeping services (e.g., garbage collection) — are immune from elite control.

5. Hunter, *Community Power Structure*, 228–61.

6. Bachrach and Baratz, *Power and Poverty*, 39–51; Crenson, *The Un-Politics of Air Pollution*.

7. Gaventa, *Power and Powerlessness*.

8. Stone, "Systemic Power in Community Decision Making."

9. Polsby, *Community Power and Political Theory*, 96.

10. Dahl, *Who Governs?* 163–65.

11. Truman, *The Governmental Process*.

12. Lindblom, "The Science of 'Muddling Through.'"

13. Dahl, *Who Governs?* 85–86. Stone, "Paradigms, Power, and Urban Leadership," 136–38.

14. Dahl, *Who Governs?* 25–31.

15. Newton, "Feeble Governments and Private Power."

16. Lowi, *The End of Liberalism*.

17. Elazar, *American Federalism*, 93–102.

18. Prothro and Grigg, "Fundamental Principles of Democracy"; Sullivan et al., "The Sources of Political Tolerance."

19. Alford and Friedland, *Powers of Theory*, 61–82.

20. Ibid., 4, 36.

21. Walker, "A Critique of the Elitist Theory of Democracy."

22. Huntington, "The Democratic Distemper."

23. Wolfinger, "Reputation and Reality in the Study of Community Power."

24. Ricci, "Receiving Ideas in Political Analysis."

25. Ball, "From Paradigms to Research Programs."

26. Peterson, *City Limits*, 136–43.

27. Bachrach and Baratz, *Power and Poverty*, 3–16.

28. Dahl, *Who Governs?*; Wirt, *Power in the City*; Waste, *Power and Pluralism in American Cities*.

29. Morlock, "Business Interests, Countervailing Groups, and the Balance of Influence in 91 Cities"; Clark, "Community Structure, Decision-Making, Budget Expenditures, and Urban Renewal in 51 American Communities"; Schumaker and Getter, "Responsiveness Bias in 51 American Cities."

30. Clark, *Community Power and Policy Outputs*; Lineberry and Sharkansky, *Urban Politics and Public Policy*, 182–86.

31. Alford and Friedland, *Powers of Theory*, 161–268; Dye, *Who's Running America?* 4–13.

32. Jones, *Governing Urban America*, 90.

33. Waste, "Community Power and Pluralist Theory."

34. Manley, "Neopluralism: A Class Analysis of Pluralism I and Pluralism II"; Brand, "Three Generations of Pluralism."

35. Olson, *The Logic of Collective Action*.

36. Lindblom, *Politics and Markets*; Dahl, *Dilemmas of Pluralist Democracy*.

37. Aiken, "The Distribution of Community Power," 361.

38. Stone, *Economic Growth and Neighborhood Discontent*, 204–14.

39. Peterson, *City Limits*.

40. Ibid., 142.

41. Ibid., 132.

42. Peterson, "A Unitary Model of Local Taxation and Expenditure Policies."

43. According to Peterson, neither elitist nor pluralist models explain redistributive policies well — a third type of urban policy besides developmental and allocative policies. Proposals to develop services for the poor are usually banished from local political agendas; in a decentralized federal system their negative economic consequences are particularly acute at the local level. In order to compete with other communities that also want to pursue their economic interests and attract mobile capital and skilled labor, officials of all cities have incentives to minimize taxes that pay for welfare services.

44. Peterson, *City Limits*, 109–30.

45. Ibid., 38.

46. Ibid., 37.

47. Swanstrom, "Semisovereign Cities: The Politics of Urban Development; Stone, "The Study of the Politics of Urban Development."

48. Stone, *Regime Politics: Governing Atlanta, 1946–88*, and "Paradigms, Power, and Urban Leadership"; Elkin, *City and Regime in the American Republic*.

49. Stone, "Elite Theory and Democracy," 467.

50. Caro, *The Power Broker: Robert Moses and the Fall of New York*.

51. Held, *The Public Interest and Private Interests*.

52. Elkin, *City and Regime in the American Republic*, 148.

53. Ibid., 1–4.
54. Stone, "Paradigms, Power, and Urban Leadership," 149.
55. Stone, "Elite Theory and Democracy," 468.
56. Stone, "Paradigms, Power, and Urban Leadership," 149.
57. Stone, "Elite Theory and Democracy," 468.
58. Elkin, *City and Regime in the American Republic*, 83.
59. Stone, *Regime Politics*, 219–33.
60. Stone, "Elite Theory and Democracy," 468–69.
61. Elkin, *City and Regime in the American Republic*, 169.
62. Ricci, "Receiving Ideas in Political Analysis," 455–56.
63. These studies are reviewed in Hawley and Svara, *The Study of Community Power: A Bibliographical Review*.
64. Stone, "Elite Theory and Democracy," 470.

## CHAPTER 2. THREE IDEALS OF PLURALIST DEMOCRACY

1. See Lane, "Market Justice, Political Justice," and the literature cited there for a discussion of the skepticism about egalitarian goals that exists among the American public.

2. Crick, *In Defense of Politics*, 111–39; Macridis, *Contemporary Political Ideologies*, 18–104.

3. Many factors may affect variations in the achievement of the ideals of principle-policy congruence, responsible representation, and complex equality. Because of the limitations of the Lawrence data, only some hypotheses are explored here. Additionally, the analysis here focuses on explaining the inequalities of power among political interests—a task that is built into the analysis of complex equality. No attempt is made to explain the differences between Lawrence and other communities at achieving complex equality.

4. Dahl, *A Preface to Democratic Theory*; Kelso, *American Democratic Theory: Pluralism and Its Critics*.

5. Truman, *The Governmental Process*; Dahl, *Who Governs?*

6. Nivola and Rosenbloom, *Classic Readings in American Politics*, 5.

7. Kirk, *A Program for Conservatives*, 302–8. Nisbet, "Public Opinion versus Popular Opinion," 185.

8. Walzer, *Spheres of Justice*, 285–87.

9. Edelman, *Politics as Symbolic Action*, 1–11; Riker, *Liberalism against Populism*.

10. Because citizens in pluralist societies are subjected to alternative views about competing principles, they may view competing principles as equally valid.

11. Elazar, *American Federalism*, 84–126.

12. Riker, *The Art of Political Manipulation*.

13. This procedure is described in the "Policy Change" subsection of Chapter 3.

14. This hypothesis is drawn from the economistic paradigm developed in Peterson's *City Limits* and discussed in Chapter 1.

15. Pitkin's *Concept of Representation* remains the most important treatment of various perspectives on representation. The liberal position on representative government is perhaps best expressed by Mill in *Considerations on Representative Government*. The classic statement of the conservative position remains Burke's *Appeal to the Old Whigs from the New*. For a typical socialist position, see Durbin, *The Politics of Democratic Socialism*.

16. Congruence does not necessarily imply power; an outcome can be consistent

with the preferences of certain types of actors even though these actors have not had any impact on the outcome. For example, policymakers may be unaware of citizen's preferences on an issue and thus uninfluenced by them. Yet it may turn out that the decision is congruent with the preferences of the majority of citizens who are aware of the issue and who have an unambiguous preference about it. To have power, actors must not only have preferences congruent with the outcome, but their preferences must affect the outcome. The power of various types of actors—estimated by the *causal* relationships between the preferences of various actors and policy outcomes—is considered in Chapter 12.

17. Eulau and Karps, "The Puzzle of Representation," 69.

18. Taylor, *Public Opinion and Collective Action.*

19. Walzer, *Spheres of Justice.*

20. Caro, *The Power Broker*; Hunter, *Community Power Structure.*

21. Mobilizers are people who claim to represent an organized group on policy issues. They include those who organize others, hold positions in groups, and are active on behalf of the group. In the empirical analysis of group power in Chapter 12, the preferences of mobilizers are weighted by the size, cohesion, and activity of the groups they represent. This procedure enables summary measures of "dominant mobilizer preferences" to weigh the demands of mobilizers representing large, cohesive, and active groups more heavily than the demands of mobilizers representing small, divided, and passive groups.

22. Only one issue in the Lawrence sample was resolved by an appointed (hospital) board, and its responsible representation score was somewhat below the average of that for other issues.

23. Verba and Nie, *Participation in America,* 334-43.

24. Peterson, *City Limits.*

25. Pitkin, *Concept of Representation,* 144-67.

26. Walzer, *Spheres of Justice,* 304.

27. In *Spheres of Justice* (pp. 3-30), Walzer uses the concept of "monopoly" to describe simple inequalities of social goods (such as political power), and he uses the term "dominant" to describe those social goods that most often illegitimately invade distributions of other social goods (thus upsetting his conception of complex equality). In the present analysis, the term "dominance" corresponds to Walzer's concept of monopoly but conforms to conventional terminology.

28. In *Equalities,* Rae has shown that there are many forms of equality. Thus, providing "bloc-regarding" equality among these interests on a group basis may result in "individual-regarding" inequalities.

29. Dahl and Lindblom, *Politics, Economics, and Welfare.*

30. According to Walzer (*Spheres of Justice,* 304), complex equality is achieved in the sphere of political power when inequalities of power are explained by differences in people's persuasiveness. Because the persuasiveness of various interests defies objective measurement, no attempt is made here to account for simple inequalities in terms of persuasiveness. Nevertheless, Walzer's formulation points to violations of complex equality that can guide empirical research. Complex equality is violated if inequalities are rooted in factors that are not germane to persuasiveness. Arguments should not be more persuasive just because they are made by wealthy or socially prominent people. Other arguments should not be discounted merely because they are made by women, minorities, "radicals" or people having other characteristics irrelevant to an unbiased consideration of the merits of each case.

31. Hochschild, *What's Fair?* 60-75.

32. Walzer, *Spheres of Justice*, 20.

33. Hawley, *Nonpartisan Elections and the Case for Party Politics*; Welch and Bledsoe, *Urban Reforms and Its Consequences*.

34. Lukes, *Power: A Radical View*; Gaventa, *Power and Powerlessness*.

35. Castells, *City and the Grassroots*.

CHAPTER 3. A COMPARATIVE ANALYSIS
OF TWENTY-NINE LAWRENCE ISSUES

1. Although the methodology developed here may be applicable to larger political systems, such as the American states or various national governments, the principles at stake and the patterns of power within these larger systems may be very different than those in local American communities.

2. Data about the population of Lawrence and the United States generally are drawn from the *United States Census of the Population* for 1980.

3. According to the *Municipal Yearbook: 1978*, 48 percent of all American cities with populations over 100,000 have council-manager forms of government (41 percent have the next most prominent form, the mayor-council system), 69 percent elect council members at-large, 73 percent elect their mayors directly, and over 75 percent have nonpartisan ballots. The median size of city councils in the United States is five.

4. Dahl, "A Critique of the Ruling Elite Model."

5. The decisional method examines only the first face of power, the dimension of power that is exercised by participating in and achieving one's goals in the resolution of issues that already are on the agenda. According to Bachrach and Baratz (in *Power and Poverty*), a second face of power is exercised in setting the agenda. According to Gaventa (in *Power and Powerlessness*), a third face of power involves influencing the preferences of other participants.

6. In *Who Governs?* Dahl includes party nominations among his issues. In contrast, a comparative-issues approach focuses on policy issues only. Thus, inferences about democratic performance that are derived from the comparative-issues method are limited to the policy domain.

7. Inferences about whose preferences cause policy decisions are discussed in the section on "Responsiveness and Direct Power" in Chapter 12. See Note 18 of Chapter 12 for an explanation of why causal inferences about power require larger samples of issues.

8. Polsby, *Community Power and Political Theory*, 96.

9. Only the outcome of the 1977 referendum to change the form of government was known before the issue was selected. Because of the importance of this issue in understanding the political setting of Lawrence politics, and since many aspects of the issue (including the nature of the cleavages that formed on the issue and thus who won and lost on the issue) were unknown at the time, it was included in the sample.

10. Page and Shapiro, "Effects of Public Opinion on Policy," 181.

11. The numerous typologies in the urban and policy literatures for classifying issues — such as those by Williams and Adrian (in *Four Cities*) and Peterson (in *City Limits*) — do not claim to form a basis for sampling community issues.

12. Proponents of the positional approach to the study of power correctly insist that the incumbents of major institutions in the community must be examined. By analyzing the preferences of representatives and bureaucrats and relating these preferences to policy outcomes, the power of governmental officials can be estimated.

Thus, the comparative-issues approach directly examines the assumption of proponents of the positional method (e.g., Dye, *Who's Running America?* 59–112) that "great power" resides in those "who occupy the top positions in the institutional structure" of communities. By assuming that great power may be found only in institutional roles, the positional method neither offers a basis for assessing the limits on the power of officeholders nor permits an assessment of the power of public officials relative to that of other participants. In contrast, the comparative-issues approach permits some assessment of these matters by considering the notions that governmental officeholders may put aside their own preferences and act as agents of others and that they may be defeated, both individually and collectively, on policy issues.

13. This study is described in Bolland, "The Limits to Pluralism: Power and Leadership in a Nonparticipatory Society," 69–88. In "Reputation and Reality in the Study of Community Power," Wolfinger questions the validity of reputational studies because they mistake reputations for power with the actual wielding of power and because they fail to provide a basis for assessing the limits on the power of the top elite. Although such difficulties can limit the utility of the reputational method for providing an overall description of community power, this method does permit identification of the community elite. See Peterson, *City Limits*, 138–39.

14. Photocopies of the instruments used in these studies and of their results are available from John Bolland, Department of Political Science, the University of Alabama.

15. Such notables were identified by other community leaders as having the most economic and social resources in the community. In *Who Governs?* Dahl identified social notables on the basis of the invitation list to the annual assemblies of the New Haven Lawn Club, and he identified economic notables on the basis of positions in important economic organizations (banks, public utilities, and corporations with higher property assessments or employee payrolls) and on the basis of extensive property holdings. Such specific criteria for inclusion among the notables of a community lead to the possible exclusion of important persons. The more open-ended specification of notables using the reputational method allows for inclusion of persons affiliated with a variety of prestigious community organizations and holding diverse economic resources.

16. Measures of community support for alternative policy principles are most conveniently described in Chapter 4.

17. Occasionally representatives were involved in issues in a nonofficial capacity; only the preferences of representatives in office when major decisions were made on issues were included in measuring representative preferences. On a few occasions, elected officials expressed "mixed feelings," which were omitted in calculating the preferences of elected officials.

18. Notables sometimes claimed no involvement on issues, whereas others saw them as their most important supporters and opponents. Thus, the reputational method in combination with the comparative-issues approach permits measures of the less visible involvements of elites. It is precisely such "behind-the-scenes" involvements that the decisional method alone is said to miss.

19. Group leaders provided the estimates of ACTIVISTS, MEMBERS, and COHESION for their groups. When several group leaders were interviewed about a group's involvement on an issue, their estimates were averaged.

20. Other measures of group preferences were calculated to take into account the fact that groups differ in their possession of other resources, such as continuing access to policymakers and full-time professional staffs. However, none of these measures had greater predictive power than the measure described in the text; thus, these measures were not employed in the results reported below.

21. Except for the TOWNCENTER issue, the public referenda results were within three percentage points of those in the surveys. In April 1986, 57 percent of the survey respondents with unambiguous preferences said they supported TOWNCENTER, although only 45 percent approved of the $4 million in local public financing required for the project. In April 1987, the two advisory referenda questions dealing most directly with the TOWNCENTER project drew only 21 and 24 percent support. In the interim, the physical size and financial scope of the project expanded significantly, and an extensive campaign was waged against the project.

22. University students were omitted in determining class cleavages because their occupational status is unclear, and their parents' incomes are often more relevant to their class standing than are their own incomes.

23. The mean property values of neighborhoods are in 1984 prices as estimated by local realtors.

24. Eckstein, "Case Study and Theory in Political Science."

## CHAPTER 4. COMPETING PRINCIPLES AND URBAN IDEOLOGIES

1. Conservatives, liberals, and democratic socialists are friends of pluralism because they recognize that their ideological opponents have the right to criticize their principles, to propose alternatives, and to govern according to these alternative principles if elected to public office.

2. For a discussion of why the United States is exceptional among Western industrial democracies for the weakness of attachments to socialist principles, see Sombart, *Why There Is No Socialism in America*, and Hochschild, *What's Fair?* 1–26.

3. Peffley and Hurwitz, "A Hierarchical Model of Attitude Constraint."

4. Rawls, *A Theory of Justice*, 135. Philosophical inquiries that propose and justify such principles — exemplified by the work of Rawls — are nevertheless important in pluralist politics because they clarify the meaning of certain principles and because they provide arguments — often compelling arguments — for why these principles should be more widely adopted.

5. See, for example, Arkes, *The Philosopher in the City,* and Henig, *Federalism and Public Policy.*

6. The prevalence of liberal and conservative ideological labeling among Lawrence citizens is further evidence that Lawrence is characterized by pluralist politics. See Alford and Friedland, *Powers of Theory*, 412–15.

7. Set responses from respondents were discouraged by sometimes first preventing the more conservative viewpoint and by other times first presenting the more liberal viewpoint.

8. Though confidence levels are reported for both participants and citizens, they are most relevant to the interpretation of the principles of citizens, who were randomly sampled. Because interviews were conducted with most participants on the issues studied here, the sample statistics closely describe the various participant populations.

9. Regression analysis was conducted for all participants combined rather than for particular types of participants because the small numbers of representatives, bureaucrats, and notables (combined with the large number [nine] of independent variables) would make unstable the resulting beta coefficients for the subsamples.

For participants, two additional principles have weak independent impacts on ideological orientation, but their retention in the regression model continued to yield an adjusted $R^2$ of .42.

10. Walzer, *Spheres of Justice*, 32–62.

11. Peterson, *City Limits*, 3–29.

12. Ibid., 24.

13. In communities with high unemployment rates, economic growth may, of course, be of greatest economic benefit to the existing population. However, Lawrence had a low unemployment rate (between 4 and 5 percent of its labor force) throughout the period of this study, suggesting that the provision of more jobs through economic-development strategies requires new residents to fill these jobs.

14. The costs of growth are succinctly summarized by Henig, *Public Policy and Federalism*, 219–24.

15. The wording of principles may, of course, affect the distribution of support for them. While efforts have been made to minimize bias in the phrasing of principles, advocates of particular principles may prefer alternative phrasing. For example, growth advocates may object that the statements here point out some of the costs of growth without pointing out its benefits. Opponents of growth may object that other important costs are ignored.

16. Peterson, *City Limits*, 131–49.

17. Ibid., 149.

18. In general, principles regarding growth and land use are significantly related. The correlations between holding pro-growth principles and property-rights principles is .29 for participants and .14 for citizens. However, at least in Lawrence, 48 percent of the participants and 45 percent of citizens hold both economic-growth and neighborhood-protection principles.

19. Walzer, *Spheres of Justice*, 63–68.

20. Nozick, *Anarchy, State and Utopia*.

21. Walzer, *Spheres of Justice*, 83.

22. Peterson, *City Limits*, 150–66.

23. Ibid., 37–43.

24. Ibid., 43.

25. Rawls, *A Theory of Justice*.

26. Peterson, *City Limits*, 183.

27. Walzer, *Spheres of Justice*, 84.

28. Peterson, *City Limits*, 71.

29. Nisbit, *Twilight of Authority*.

30. Walzer, *Spheres of Justice*, 62.

31. Will, *Statecraft as Soulcraft*, 79–87.

32. Stone, Whelan, and Murin, *Urban Politics and Policy in a Bureaucratic Age*, 134–75.

33. Public administrators have traditionally been socialized to accept progressive values. However, the data in Table 4.1 show bureaucrats split between supporting economic and political criteria. One explanation for this finding may be that urban administrators have increasingly adopted the values of "the new public administration," centering on the political involvement of citizens; see Thomas, *Between Citizen and City*, 72–88. A second explanation for this finding may be the way the contrasting principles were formulated. By asking whether local government is primarily concerned with politics or economics, administrators may often have responded that government is political, not because they value political criteria but because they often perceive that their preferred economic criteria are compromised by political pressures.

34. Rawls, *A Theory of Justice*, 22–33.

35. Ibid., 29.

36. Levy, Meltsner, and Wildavsky, *Urban Outcomes*, 16.

37. Lineberry, *Equality and Urban Policy*.

38. Because most policies and public projects distribute some burdens, the notion of "significant burden" was stressed. If interviewees asked for clarification of this principle, they were told that our goal was to measure different degrees of concern for those who are disadvantaged by policy proposals. It was suggested that some people thought that the interest of the community as a whole should yield to concerns about the disadvantaged when a significant number of people are harmed by a policy proposal, when the harm to a small number of people is extensive, and/or when those harmed are already among the most economically and socially disadvantaged people in the community.

39. According to Barry (in *The Liberal Theory of Justice*), liberalism has embraced Rawls's theory of justice. If this is so, perhaps a Rawlsian formulation of the alternative to utilitarianism would link distributive principles more closely to liberal ideology.

40. Pitkin, *The Concept of Representation*, 144.

41. Peterson, *City Limits*, 109. See also Dahl, *Who Governs?* 276–81.

42. Elazar, *American Federalism*, 97.

43. For example, abstract evaluative issues dealing with public safety and crime — issues of great importance to urban public policy — are omitted here.

44. See Knoke, "Urban Political Cultures."

45. Clark and Ferguson, *City Money*, 175.

46. The positive, but weak, zero-order correlations between these principles and self-defined ideology (presented in Table 4.1) provide some justication for such labeling. Another justification is the large number of significant zero-order correlations among principles held by participants (P) and citizens (C) as specified in the following table:

Holding of Conservative Principles on Abstract Issues

|        |   | GROW   | NEIGH  | SERV   | WELF   | USETAX | LIB    | ECON   | AGG    |
|--------|---|--------|--------|--------|--------|--------|--------|--------|--------|
| NEIGH  | P | .29**  | 1.00   |        |        |        |        |        |        |
|        | C | .12**  | 1.00   |        |        |        |        |        |        |
| SERV   | P | .24**  | .40**  | 1.00   |        |        |        |        |        |
|        | C | .09**  | .03    | 1.00   |        |        |        |        |        |
| WELF   | P | .27**  | .37**  | .58**  | 1.00   |        |        |        |        |
|        | C | .08**  | .03    | .33**  | 1.00   |        |        |        |        |
| USETAX | P | .02    | .25**  | .18**  | .45**  | 1.00   |        |        |        |
|        | C | .15**  | .06*   | .14**  | .19**  | 1.00   |        |        |        |
| LIB    | P | .18**  | .41**  | .53**  | .40**  | .26**  | 1.00   |        |        |
|        | C | .07*   | .03    | .05*   | .12**  | .09**  | 1.00   |        |        |
| ECON   | P | .28**  | .38**  | .50**  | .44**  | .24**  | .28**  | 1.00   |        |
|        | C | .17**  | .11**  | -.02   | .06*   | .09**  | .11**  | 1.00   |        |
| AGG    | P | .21**  | .25**  | .17**  | .28**  | .15*   | .09    | .28**  | 1.00   |
|        | C | .11**  | .01    | .00    | .04    | .16**  | .09**  | .11**  | 1.00   |
| DEMO   | P | .13*   | .23**  | .10    | .21**  | .03    | .13*   | .17**  | .19**  |
|        | C | .08**  | .08**  | .09**  | .00    | .04    | .07*   | .06*   | .06*   |

*$P < .05$
**$P < .01$

Pro-growth principles are positively and significantly associated with conservative principles on all other abstract policy issues. Aggregative conceptions of justice and the de-emphasis of citizen participation are also positively and often significantly related to conservative principles. However, the weakness of these relationships also suggests that principles regarding economic growth, justice, and democratic process are only loosely linked to urban ideologies.

47. Walzer, *Spheres of Justice*, 6.

48. See, for example, Schattschneider, *The Semisovereign People*, 60–75; and Riker, *The Art of Political Manipulation*.

## CHAPTER 5. CHALLENGING EXISTING INSTITUTIONS AND LEADERSHIP

1. Although Lawrence calls its legislative body a "commission" and its members "commissioners," it does not have a typical commission form of government; its commissioners do not serve as heads of particular administrative departments.

2. Challenges against reformed institutions in other communities are described in Adrian and Sullivan, "The Urban Appointed City Executive, Past and Future," and in Browning, Marshall, and Tabb, *Protest Is Not Enough*, 201.

3. The quotes in this section and elsewhere were derived from the 239 interviews conducted for this study or from public documents and newspaper accounts. When quotes are not attributed to particular people, they were derived from interviews in which anonymity was promised.

4. Occasionally, participants in the wards issue argued that the policy orientations of local government might be different if there were a change in governmental structure. For example, an official with the chamber of commerce argued that economic growth might be hindered by the passage of the wards proposal because "prospective employers will not move into a community without the professionalism in government that a city manager provides." Also, some activists thought that creating wards would significantly enhance their access to decision makers, increasing their chances of protecting neighborhoods from intrusive developments. However, neither participants nor citizens significantly related their economic-growth or neighborhood-protection principles to their preferences on the wards issue. By downplaying the relevance of such policy principles, participants implicitly acknowledged the growing consensus among urbanists in political science that differences in governmental structures have only minimal policy effects (see Morgan and Pelissero, "Urban Policy: Does Political Structure Matter?").

5. *Lawrence Journal-World (LJW),* 24 March 1977, 1.

6. *LJW,* 1 April 1977, 7.

7. See Table 2.2 for definitions of these opposing interests. Although a fuller description of the winning and losing segments of the community is necessary for the subsequent analysis of complex equality in Chapter 13, some winners and losers are identified here and on subsequent issues for purposes of illustration.

8. It should not be concluded that pro-growth principles are irrelevant to this issue. These principles may fail to be significantly related to positions on the mayor issue in the multivariate regression model because the small number of cases make unstable the estimates of the effects of these principles. The methodological criteria employed here simply do not permit the conclusion that these principles are relevant to the mayor issue.

9. Although it is possible to indicate how policy outcomes contribute to simple inequality by providing yet another victory for those interests who usually win on

issues (and yet another loss for those interests who usually lose on issues), such inequalities do not necessarily imply a failure to achieve complex equality. Whether or not complex equality is achieved, despite the existence of simple inequalities, can only be indicated for a larger sample of issues, as shown in Chapter 13.

10. Ironically, the commission's action failed to prevent Marci Francisco from assuming the mayoral office, as she was twice elected to the post by newly elected liberals Shontz and Gleason. Nevertheless, the new method of selecting the mayor did prevent other persons who threatened the interests of the Growth Machine (particularly Nancy Shontz) from simply rotating into the office of the mayor.

11. By the methodological criteria employed here, only aggregative principles are relevant to the manager issue, as there is no direct relationship between support for economic criteria and support for Watson.

## CHAPTER 6. DEVELOPING THE LOCAL ECONOMY

1. Foster and Berger, *Public-Private Partnership in American Cities.*
2. Subsequent chapters will consider neighborhood and downtown redevelopment issues which also involved economic-growth principles.
3. *Lawrence Journal-World (LJW)*, 14 May 1983, 2.
4. *LJW*, 25 June 1980, 1.
5. Personal interview, 4 June 1984.
6. *LJW*, 21 September 1982, 1.
7. *LJW*, 15 January 1983, 4.
8. Because neighborhoods were not threatened by the RAIL proposal, the lack of significant relationships between NEIGHborhood-protection principles and preferences regarding the industrial park (as shown in Table A) is not surprising. However, the relevance of restrictive land-use principles is suggested by analysis of people's responses to the question of whether they gave higher priority to economic growth or to "effective land-use planning." The more participants gave priority to land-use planning over growth, the more they opposed the RAIL proposal ($r_p = .40$).
9. *LJW*, 1 February 1983, 1.
10. Although the Eastern Hills issue has not been systematically studied, casual observation suggests that there has been little opposition to it. Thus, the larger issue of developing an appropriate industrial park has apparently been resolved without any significant interests suffering a defeat.
11. This study uncovered the names of only seven people who actively opposed the research park. Because many proponents of the research park held neighborhood-protection principles, there was only a weak and statistically insignificant relationship between holding neighborhood-protection principles and opposing the research park ($r_p = -.23$).
12. Personal interview, 29 June 1984.
13. The taxpayers of a city have not been at risk when their government issues IRBs because it holds title to land or buildings purchased with the principal and merely "acts as a banker" in the transaction.
14. Usually the commission granted the ten-year tax exemption but required businesses to pay a fee for essential city services (like police and fire protection) in lieu of taxes.

The federal tax advantages of IRBs was phased out between 1986 and 1990. In order to retain the capacity of local government to make certain inducements to industry, Kansas voters approved a property-tax abatement amendment in August 1986. The amendment allows ten-year local property tax-exemptions for new job-creating facilities. Within six months, the Lawrence City Commission had granted its first tax exemption under the law.

15. Peterson, *City Limits.*

## CHAPTER 7. PROTECTING THE NEIGHBORHOODS

1. In *The Logic of Collective Action*, Olson describes the obstacles to mobilization. That such obstacles can be overcome is suggested by Henig, *Neighborhood Mobilization: Redevelopment and Response,* and Thomas, *Between Citizen and City.*

2. In June 1987, the U.S. Supreme Court ruled in *First English Evangelical Church* that property owners are entitled to compensation from local governments when new regulations deprive them of reasonable use of their land. This ruling encouraged opponents of the second Oread downzoning proposal to threaten to sue the city to recover the difference between the value of their property before and after downzoning.

3. In this respect, the resolution of the Bluffs issue may illustrate hyperpluralist politics — a perverted form of pluralism where groups are too strong and representatives are too weak. For discussions of hyperpluralism, see Jones, *Governing Urban America*, 190–92, and Waste, "Community Power and Pluralist Theory."

4. *LJW*, 3 February 1984, 10.

5. *LJW*, 15 February 1985, 4.

## CHAPTER 8. RESTRICTING INDIVIDUAL CHOICES

1. One recurrent theme in discussions of the enrivonmental code was that the liberties at stake went beyond property rights, as there is the widespread perception that the code is selectively enforced against those community activists who complain about the policy directions and management of the city.

2. *LJW*, 24 August 1986, 1.

3. Twelve percent of the respondents in the 1984 and 1986 citizen surveys indicated that they were neutral about these two principles.

4. *LJW*, 25 June 1980, 1.

5. *The* TRIBES *Value Clarification Program* was developed in 1978 by the Center for Human Development in Walnut Creek, Calif.

6. It is appropriate for community power studies to include the resolution of issues by such quasi-governmental bodies as the board of trustees of public hospitals. Despite being largely independent of local governments, LMH is, according to state law, a city hospital and its policies affect the health care available to Lawrence citizens.

7. *LJW*, 20 May 1983, 4.

## CHAPTER 9. PROVIDING PUBLIC SERVICES AND WELFARE

1. Additional controversies involving the provision of communal services and welfare include: (a) privatization (whether publicly financed goods and services are most effectively and efficiently delivered by governmental agencies or by private businesses), and (b) equity (whether public services are available to citizens on some

sort of equal or equitable basis). Such controversies were not apparent in the Lawrence sample.

2. *LJW*, 29 April 1981, 1.

3. *LJW*, 28 July 1986, 4.

4. Because 60 percent of the public supported school closings, the board also had to choose between responding to citizen preferences or the preferences of issue-specific activists.

5. Parents argued that having neighborhood schools was their legal right because the legislation creating statewide school district consolidation and bringing the rural schools into the Lawrence School District provided that their schools could not be closed without their consent; however, the Kansas attorney general rejected this claim. Still, the parents could argue that neighborhood schools were a "right in usage" if not a right in law; see Weber, *On Law in Economy and Society.*

6. *LJW*, 2 February 1982, 1.

7. Although most gas utilities in Kansas are regulated by the Kansas Corporation Commission, the gas utility in Lawrence — Kansas Public Service (KPS) — was regulated by the city commission at the time of the lifeline issue because it served only Lawrence.

8. *LJW*, 22 January 1983, 1.

9. *LJW*, 28 December 1982, 1.

10. *LJW*, 4 January 1983, 4.

11. Henig, *Public Policy and Federalism*, 119–120.

12. Rawls, *A Theory of Justice.*

13. Although the data in Chapter 4 show little support for distributive principles generally, the survey questions used in that analysis did not measure support for specifically Rawlsian distributive principles.

14. Hochschild, *What's Fair?* 65.

15. *LJW*, 31 July 1981, 1.

16. *LJW*, 20 August 1985, 1.

17. Supporters and opponents of social services have expressed several kinds of discontent. For example, supporters expressed concern that "new and innovative" agencies often have difficulty acquiring any funding, that some agencies have been terminated under controversial circumstances, and that the city staff controls much of the input into revenue sharing and CDBG allocations. Opponents of social-service allocations have been concerned that the availability of extensive social services attracts the wandering poor and repels upper-income taxpayers, that there is adequate oversight of social-service agencies, and that governmental funding creates agency dependence on the city.

18. Bureaucrats thought that the intangibles tax was superior to property taxes in one respect. Receipts from the intangibles tax increased with inflation, helping local governments meet the increasing costs of municipal services without increasing tax rates. In contrast, receipts from property taxes do not rise as a result of inflation unless real estate is continuously reappraised.

19. *LJW*, 2 August 1980, 1.

20. Personal interview, 13 July 1984.

21. Brunker and McGovern, "How Fair is the Property Tax System in Lawrence?" and *LJW*, 31 October 1977, 1.

22. Two main explanations have been offered for such local inaction. First, the county appraiser argued that the problem was more apparent than real because reappraisal did occur when improvements were made on property; however, such reappraisals were not based on the market value of property but rather on a formula for

determining "replacement value," which included a depreciation factor that lowered the assessed value of older homes. Second, local officials feared that local action on reappraisal could stimulate a tax revolt, since people had become accustomed to prevailing practices. Though these practices overtaxed utilities and perhaps other businesses, the "hidden taxes" in the form of higher costs to consumers were not apparent to taxpayers. Although older homes might be undertaxed, such tax breaks were generally acceptable because they served to encourage the revitalization of older neighborhoods.

23. Peterson, *City Limits*, 74-75.

## CHAPTER 10. SAVING THE DOWNTOWN

1. No significant relationships were found between the preferences of various actors regarding the Cornfield Mall and their economic-GROWth and NEIGHborhood-protection principles as measured for Table 4.1. However, these measures of growth and land-use principles do not adequately capture the principles involved in the Cornfield Mall proposal. The GROW measure asks about beliefs that government should or should not subsidize growth, but the Cornfield Mall was attractive to some people precisely because it promised growth without the need for governmental subsidies. The NEIGH question asks whether neighborhoods should be protected from unrestricted uses of private property, but there was no residential neighborhood at the proposed site of the Cornfield Mall. Thus, for the Cornfield Mall issue only, alternative measures of abstract principles were employed. Participants and citizens were asked to indicate their priority among several governmental functions including: (a) promoting economic growth and (b) providing effective land-use planning. From these data, ordinal scales of support for growth and protection were developed.

2. Surveys commissioned by the city commission in 1980 and 1987 found high levels of citizen satisfaction with and attachment to the existing downtown, especially its aesthetic and historic qualities.

3. At least this was true until April 1987, when 76 percent of Lawrence voters indicated that they opposed public financing of a shopping mall downtown. However, the interpretation of this result is unclear as a subsequent survey suggested that citizens' votes on the public-funding question were not explained by their spending-and-taxation principles. See Schumaker and Maynard-Moody, *Downtown Redevelopment and Public Opinion*.

4. When the parking lot was first approved, it was thought that the project would serve as a partial inducement for Maupintour, a large national travel agency, to build its new main office in the 600 block of Massachusetts. However, Maupintour decided to build its office near the Alvamar Country Club in western Lawrence.

5. Personal interview, 29 June 1984.

6. Tom Gleason did not seek reelection. Marci Francisco initially intended to step down from the commission but changed her mind after the filing deadline; her bid as a write-in candidate was unsuccessful. Don Binns lost. Barkley Clark resigned from the commission shortly after the election, and Howard Hill was appointed as his replacement. None of the new commissioners campaigned against the project.

7. *LJW*, 11 June 1983, 1.

8. A survey of DLA members revealed strong support for developing a special-benefit district to help finance public improvements required for the Sizeler mall.

9. The rest of the funding was projected to come from a federal UDAG grant, revenue-producing utility bonds, a special-benefit district, and tax-increment financing (TIFs). TIFs permits local governments to apply increased sales and property-tax

revenues derived from redevelopment in a blighted area toward repayment of TIF bonds; under Kansas State Law, TIFs must be approved by public referendum.

10.  The first question asked whether "Massachusetts Street and Vermont Street shall be closed or vacated from Sixth Street to Eleventh Street." Although the Towncenter proposal would have required that only one block of these streets be vacated, such wording may have heightened perceptions that the project would have been highly disruptive to the downtown. The second question asked whether *or not* the city should spend funds for the purpose of assisting in the development of an enclosed mall in the central business district. The third question asked whether or not the city should permit vacating any street in the CBD for purposes of constructing an enclosed mall.

11.  Land use principles (NEIGH) may have been even more relevant to the resolution of the issue than suggested by Table A (as the data on land-use principles and Town-center preferences were collected prior to the enlargement of the mall's footprint). Initially, Towncenter did not seem to encroach on residential neighborhoods, but the site plan submitted in October 1986, moved the mall to within a block of Old West Lawrence (OWL), where neighborhood-protection and historic-preservation values are strong. As a consequence, members of the OWL Association became highly visible opponents of the mall, and they appealed to the neighborhood-protection values of others in the community.

12.  *LJW,* 16 March 1986, 1.

13.  In March 1989, a U.S. district court judge dismissed a suit filed by JVJ against the city and thus upheld the right of the city commission to plan commercial development through zoning policies.

In 1988 a riverfront plaza, a smaller development adjacent to downtown, was approved. Mall opponents and supporters continue to debate whether this project will solve local shopping needs.

## CHAPTER 11. POLITICAL CULTURE: PRINCIPLES, PREFERENCES, AND POLICIES

1.  See Knoke, "Urban Political Cultures," and the studies cited there.

2.  The analysis in this chapter seeks to be both evaluative and explanatory. When the term "principle-policy congruence" is employed, the concern is primarily evaluative, as descriptions are provided of the extent to which a democratic ideal is realized. When the term "cultural perspective" is employed, the concern is primarily explanatory, as analysis focuses on the extent to which policy outcomes are explained by dominant cultural principles. In general, the analyses presented in Chapters 11 through 13 seek to show that explanations of policy outcomes can provide evaluations of these outcomes when the relationships between policy outcomes and explanatory variables concern democratic ideals.

3.  Baskin, *American Pluralist Democracy,* 91–93. The relationships between preferences and policy outcomes (and the power that is indicated by such relationships) are addressed in Chapters 12 and 13 below.

4.  Some dominant principles might be directly related to policies in the sense that they cause outcomes irrespective of people's preferences. Perhaps the notion that there are economic imperatives that require decision makers to emphasize economic growth illustrates such a direct relationship.

5.  In "Diversity and Complexity in American Public Opinion," Kinder summarizes the literature dealing with the orthodox pluralist contention that people (especially the mass public) are "ideologically innocent"—that their policy preferences are not

connected to larger overarching principles. An important challenge to the theory of ideological innocence was provided recently by Peffley and Hurwitz. In "A Hierarchical Model of Attitude Constraint," Peffley and Hurwitz note that research confirming the ideological innocence of people is based on the weakness of horizontal interrelationships among policy preferences. They argue that an examination of the vertical interrelationships between ideology, principles, and policy preferences reveals more sophisticated political thinking than suggested by the idea of ideological innocence.

6. The incompatibility of economic-GROWTH principles and liberal public-WELFARE principles, which are both dominant in Lawrence, has been argued by Peterson in *City Limits*, 167-71. However, the two issues in the sample that most clearly involved welfare principles—the LIFELINE proposal and the funding of SOCIAL services—were not especially opposed by those with pro-growth principles. Only on the issue of retaining the city MANAGER did these principles compete, probably because such officials help set priorities between pursuing economic growth and providing more public welfare. This suggests that there may be little overt competition between economic growth and public welfare; conflict is avoided by banishing redistributive issues from local agendas.

7. See, for example, Elazar, *American Federalism*, 96-99.

8. The relevance of a principle to an issue was measured by adding the absolute values of the beta weights linking principles to preferences for both participants and citizens (which are reported in Table A). Thus, the cultural support score, modified for the relevance of principles, for the WARDS issue (shown in Table 5.1) was .20 because creating wards would have been inconsistent with emphasizing ECONOMIC criteria (which had a weight of .35 reflecting the degree to which participants linked this principle to their position on WARDS) while it would have been consistent with enhancing citizen participation (which had a weight of .55 reflecting the degree to which support for WARDS was linked to the citizen-participation principles (DEMO) of participants (.39) and citizens (.16).

9. The degree of public support for a principle is simply the sum of the mean scores for participants and citizens, shown graphically in Table 4.1. Thus, the cultural support score, modified for the degree of support for relevant principles, for the WARDS issue was −.14, reflecting divided community support for the principle of citizen participation (.65 for citizens but −.18 for participants, yielding a net support score of .47 on DEMO) and more consistent opposition for emphasizing political criteria (−.33 for participants and −.28 for citizens, yielding a net support score of −.61 on ECON).

10. A more demanding test of the idea that the potency of principles depends on their degree of dominance in the culture involves a case-by-case examination of the issues listed in Tables 5.1 through 10.1. In most cases, instances of principle-policy incongruence are accounted for by the relevance to the issue of another more consensually held principle. For example, on the WARDS issue, citizen-participation principles (which are strongly held by citizens but not participants) were trumped by the concerns about the priority of economic criteria (which were shared by both most citizens and participants).

11. Stone, "The Study of the Politics of Urban Development," 1.

12. Peterson, *City Limits*.

13. The index of economic imperatives is also based on the analyses reported in Chapters 5 through 10. For each issue, the number of relevant principles supporting change that were inconsistent with Peterson's economic imperatives were subtracted from the principles that were consistent. For example, the proposal to create WARDS had an economic imperative score of "−2" because it was inconsistent with emphasizing economic criteria and with minimizing public participation. The TOWNCENTER pro-

posal had a score of "2" because it was consistent with subsidizing growth and minimizing public participation.

14. Peterson, *City Limits*, 27.

15. Banfield and Wilson, *City Politics*, 138–50.

16. Peterson, *City Limits*, 37–38.

17. Ibid., 71–77.

18. Ibid., 150–66.

19. Analyses within the pluralist framework are often criticized for their inability to appreciate systemic power; see, for example, Friedland, "Commentary: The Politics of Economic Growth." In this chapter, I have attempted to show that pluralist analyses can contribute to an understanding of the importance and limitations of systemic power, and systemic power can help to explain some of the conservative biases within pluralist politics.

20. Alford and Friedland, *Powers of Theory*, 84.

CHAPTER 12. POLITICAL POWER:
PARTICIPANTS, CITIZENS, AND DEMOCRACY

1. Representatives and citizens also had different dominant preferences regarding SOCIAL services; such differences are more easily compromised on expenditure issues (since allocations can be provided midway between the preferences of opposing actors) than on, for example, land-use issues (where developments either are or are not permitted).

On the VIDEO tax issue the public was split; the preferences of representatives and citizens did not collide. In interviews, representatives indicated little concern about public preferences but noted the persuasive lobbying effort of opponents of the tax. Thus, the issue has been classified as a case of minority persuasiveness (Level 7 of responsible representation), but because dominant citizen preferences were not violated, a higher score could be assigned to the issue.

2. Lineberry and Fowler, "Reformism and Public Policies in American Cities."

3. Stone, Whelan, and Murin, *Urban Policy and Politics in a Bureaucratic Age*, 117.

4. Morlock, "Business Interests, Countervailing Groups, and the Balance of Influence in 91 Cities."

5. Northrop and Dutton, "Municipal Reform and Group Influence."

6. Research in a larger sample of cities is needed to establish the effects of different forms of government on responsible representation. In *Urban Reform and Its Consequences*, Welch and Bledsoe suggest that the deleterious effects of reformism may be overestimated, but their study does not attempt to assess responsible representation directly.

7. Wider variances in responsible representation than the limited range discovered here would facilitate explorations into the factors that impede and facilitate this aspect of democratic performance.

8. The zero-order correlation between the level of responsible representation and whether the issues were resolved by the 1981–83 commission is .30, which is significant at the .10 level.

9. Hunter, *Community Power Structure*, 228–61. Nachmias and Rosenbloom, *Bureaucratic Government USA*, 235–52.

10. Huntington, "The Democratic Distemper."

11. The number of participants on each issue was determined by procedures described under Data Collection in Chapter 3.

12. The levels of citizen awareness on each issue were measured in the citizen surveys

by asking respondents whether they were familiar with the issues in the sample (prior to seeking their preferences on these issues).

13. Verba and Nie, *Participation in America*, 327-28.

14. Stone, *Economic Growth and Neighborhood Discontent*, 204-14.

15. The index of economic imperatives was first discussed in note 13 of Chapter 11.

16. The REAPPRAISAL issue is omitted from this analysis because of the widespread perception that it was a state-level issue and because proponents of reappraisal suffered many losses before finally succeeding in 1986.

17. Because the sample of issues is not random, significance levels cannot reveal the probability that our results are valid for a universe of community issues. Significance levels are reported only as benchmarks of the importance of relationships.

18. Nagel, *The Descriptive Analysis of Power*, 23-34. Two caveats accompany this conception of power. First, power has other dimensions than the "first face" that is revealed in an analysis of who influences policy outcomes; see Lukes, *Power: A Radical View*. Second, the first face of power can only be estimated over a broad sample of issues; the analysis of this face of power cannot determine who *caused* a specific outcome. Recall the city MANAGER case, where the outcome was consistent with the dominant preferences of representatives, bureaucrats, notables, mobilizers, activists, and citizens. Although the outcome was responsive to each of these categories, it is only possible to speculate about which, if any, of them influenced the outcome. Before concluding that citizen preferences, for example, were the determining factor — and thus that citizens wield power — one must look at other issues in which most citizens preferred one outcome and most participants preferred a different one. If citizen preferences still prevailed on such issues, the inference that citizens determine outcomes would be more valid.

19. The results presented in Table 12.2 are based on ordinary least-squares regression procedures. Other regression procedures produce somewhat different coefficients but generally support the major theoretical finding that direct power resides largely in the hands of representatives.

20. Theoretical specification of the causal relationships among the preferences of various kinds of actors is needed to employ regression analysis to distinguish indirect power (i.e., when certain types of people influence the preferences of other types of people, who in turn influence outcomes) from spurious relationships (i.e., when certain types of people get what they want simply because their preferences coincide with the preferences of those who exercise direct influence). Previous theory and research do not provide a clear basis for specifying such interrelationships, and the number of cases at hand is insufficient to examine adequately alternative theoretical possibilities. Thus, contextual information about the Lawrence cases — derived primarily from interviews with representatives — is used to interpret whether indirect power has been applied or whether spuriousness or noncausal responsiveness has occurred.

21. The formal introduction of ordinances and resolutions onto the governmental agenda is probably not an important dimension of power, as officeholders with these formal powers often introduce bills at the urging of others. What is important is the initiation of issues — the formulation and incubation of proposals for policy changes. Such agenda-setting power is part of the second face of power. Of course, focusing on who has initiated the issues in the Lawrence sample fails to estimate the power that actors have exercised in keeping other issues off the agenda. See Bachrach and Baratz, *Power and Poverty*, 3-16.

22. The data on the roles of representatives were derived from interviews. During a series of questions about each issue, Lawrence commissioners were asked whether they viewed their involvement as: (a) initiators, (b) strong supporters or opponents,

(c) weak supporters or opponents, or (d) neutral referees. They were also asked to name those people who played important roles in initiating each issue.

23. In *Protest Is Not Enough*, Browning, Marshall, and Tabb note that the power of individual (minority) commissioners depends on whether they are incorporated into a dominant coalition. The Lawrence data replicate this finding. Because Ed Carter and Bob Schumm were part of the pro-growth coalition that dominated the commission between 1979 and 1981, the positions that they supported prevailed on almost every issue. In contrast, Marci Francisco and Nancy Shontz won on only about 40 percent of the issues in which they participated as commissioners, and Tom Gleason won only 50 percent of the time. These commissioners were much less successful because they formed a fragile liberal coalition between 1981 and 1983. If one of these representatives defected from the coalition on a specific issue, the other members of the coalition suffered defeats.

24. When commissioners were referees on issues, they usually articulated substantive reasons for their ultimate positions. In such cases, their preferences are interpreted as independent judgments. About 3 percent of the time, commissioners expressed a clear preference for outcomes different from that indicated by their votes; in such cases, commissioners usually indicated that they responded to citizen-based pressures.

25. Personal interview, 17 July 1984.

26. Watson said he was involved in all issues in the sample resolved by the city commission, except for the less important DRUG paraphernalia and VIDEO tax issues; however, on some issues — such as the various mall proposals — that involvement was restrained.

27. This section is coauthored by John Bolland.

28. The method used to identify community notables is briefly described under Data Collection in Chapter 3.

29. Bolland, "The Limits to Pluralism."

30. Six notables participated in the STORMwater fee controversy, with four opposing the fee. Thus, most notables won, and most representatives lost. This issue was decided by public referendum, however, and it is difficult to see how it can be construed as a case of elite domination.

31. Schattschneider, *The Semisovereign People*, 35.

32. Browning, Marshall, and Tabb, *Protest Is Not Enough*, 243.

33. Evans, "Women and Politics: A Reappraisal."

34. Groups were identified by methods described under Data Collection in Chapter 3.

35. The media are important in all communities, and they have unique qualities that make them different from other political groups. The *Lawrence Journal-World* has not been included in the analysis of groups below because its positions on issues seem to reflect primarily the views of its publisher, Dolph Simons, Jr., whose views are included among those of other notables.

36. For a discussion of this measure of dominant group pressure, see the subsection on "Group Leader Preferences" in Chapter 3.

37. The measures of most group characteristics listed in Table 12.6 were derived from interviews with group leaders and members. Respondents were asked to estimate the percentage of members of the upper class (those having incomes in the top quartile of the community), women, and minorities in their group. They were also asked to estimate, on five-point scales, the length of time that their group had been in existence (longevity); the extent to which group leaders and members organized group meetings, signed petitions, and engaged in various kinds of protest (mobilization); the number of members in the group (size); the number of group members who were

active participants on a given issue; the amount of agreement among group members regarding the issue (cohesion); the extent to which group leaders and members contacted representatives and bureaucrats and spoke at commission meetings (persuasive participation); and the amount of time that group leaders expended on the issue. The estimates of various respondents were averaged to attain the measures of group characteristics used in the analysis reported in Table 12.6.

38. In a similar analysis of unequal responsiveness to various groups in fifty-one American communities during the early 1970s, some bias against minorities could not be explained; see Schumaker and Billeaux, "Group Representation in Local Bureaucracies."

39. The policy goals of various groups were coded on a five-point scale. Groups seeking benefits that would be available only to specific people – such as LIFELINE gas rates – were scored as "5," and groups seeking benefits that would be available to everyone – such as the elimination of the STORMwater fee on water bills – were scored as "1". The judgments of two coders on these subjective scales were averaged.

40. Schattschneider, *The Semisovereign People*, 22–35. Olson, *The Logic of Collective Action*.

41. Drawing on Peterson's arguments in *City Limits*, groups pursuing allocation policies were ranked at the neutral midpoint (3) on this five-point scale of growth orientation. Groups pursuing developmental policies were ranked as advantaged (4), because they contribute to the economic interest of the city. The goals of the chamber of commerce were ranked higher (5) than other pro-growth groups because of the chamber's leading role in pro-growth coalitions. Groups protesting developmental policies were ranked as relatively disadvantaged (2), because satisfying their goals can reduce the gains sought through developmental policies. Groups seeking redistributive policies were ranked as most disadvantaged (1), because satisfying their goals can have a negative effect on the local economy.

42. Stone, "Systemic Power in Community Decision Making."

43. The measures of net support used in Table 12.6 were obtained by adding the group weights (described under Group Leader Preferences in Chapter 3) for each group ally and subtracting the group weights for each group opponent.

44. Lipsky, *Protest in City Politics*; Schumaker, "Policy Responsiveness to Protest Group Demands."

45. Lowi, *The End of Liberalism*.

46. Yates, *The Ungovernable City*.

47. Truman, *The Governmental Process*.

48. Walker, "The Origins and Maintenance of Interest Groups."

49. Between 56 and 61 percent of all people who were active on the Lawrence issues were classified as individual activists. The low estimate is based on only those people who were interviewed. The high estimate is based on both those who were interviewed and those who were attributed participation by others. People who were attributed participation were coded as individual activists unless data about their elite status or group involvements were available. The latter procedure may overestimate the extensiveness of involvement by individual activists since available information may not have allowed the identification of all group members.

50. Many pluralists argue that democracy requires only opportunities for participation and citizen belief in such opportunities; low levels of actual participation are necessary for stability. See Alford and Friedland, *Powers of Theory*, 59–111.

51. The representation ratios for individual activists are reported under Nongroup Members in Table 12.5.

52. Only with respect to DEMOcratic-involvement principles do citizens and individual

activists differ significantly. Although the finding that activists are less committed to "public involvement" than are citizens seems paradoxical, one must recall that this principle deals with the appropriateness of resolving issues through referenda. Though the normally inactive public strongly endorses referenda as a means of ensuring greater responsiveness to their preferences, individual activists may understand that referenda tend to equalize the power of activists and citizens generally. Activists may believe that their participation will be more effective when it is targeted at representatives rather than voters who may be less attentive to their concerns.

53. Almond and Verba, *The Civic Culture*, 168–85.

54. The Pearson correlation coefficients between the preferences of individual activists and those of representatives and citizens are .56 and .62, respectively.

55. Olson, *The Rise and Decline of Nations*, 17–35.

56. A more stringent definition of the attentive public is found in Devine, *The Attentive Public: Polyarchical Democracy*.

57. Converse, "Attitudes and Non-attitudes."

58. The extensive literature on mechanisms of linking citizen preferences and public policy is summarized by Luttbeg, *Public Opinion and Public Policy*, and Weissberg, *Public Opinion and Popular Government*, 169–243.

59. See Table 5.2 in Chapter 5.

60. Clubb and Traugott, "National Patterns of Referenda Voting."

61. Weissberg, *Public Opinion and Popular Government*, 171.

62. Nie, Verba, and Petrocik, *The Changing American Voter*, 156–64.

63. Pomper, *Elections in America*.

64. Verba and Nie, *Participation in America*.

65. Luttbeg, *Public Opinion and Public Policy*, 7.

66. Weissberg, *Public Opinion and Popular Government*, 208–13.

67. If policy choices are binary (pro or con), there are four possible distributions of dominant citizen and representative preferences: (1) citizen support and representative support, (2) citizen support and representative opposition, (3) citizen opposition and representative support, and (4) citizen opposition and representative opposition. Without any mechanism for linking citizen and representative preferences, the first and last possibilities will each occur randomly one-fourth of the time.

68. In *Public Opinion and Popular Government* (222–42), Weissberg uses the term "manipulation" to describe this process because it points to actions by governmental officials to generate support for their goals. Nevertheless, the argument will be developed that the term is a bit too dramatic.

69. Edelman, *Politics as Symbolic Action*.

70. Wahlke, "Policy Demands and System Support: The Role of the Represented."

71. The concern here is not to justify unresponsive policies on these issues. It can be argued that the tendency to "localize" issues is fundamentally undemocratic. By considering only the immediate interests involved, representatives ignore not only broader public preferences on the issue (however limited and indecisive they may be) but also the broader principles that predominate in the public. Thus, while few citizens may have been aware of the issue, the tendency of citizens to oppose rezoning the BLUFFS and to support OREAD downzoning reflected widespread citizen concerns about neighborhood protection throughout the community.

72. The data in Table 4.1 on DEMOcratic-process principles suggest the prevalence of trustee role orientations in Lawrence. For a more general discussion of trusteeship in local politics, see Eulau and Prewitt, *Labyrinths of Democracy*, 407–23.

73. Kuklinski, "Representativeness and Elections."

CHAPTER 13. POLITICAL JUSTICE:
DIVISIONS, STANDINGS, AND COMPLEX EQUALITY

1. In *Spheres of Justice* (304), Walzer argues that simple inequalities of power become complex equalities of power if such inequalities are based on persuasiveness and independent of the possession of other social resources (e.g., wealth or social status). In the present analysis, simple inequalities of success on policy issues become complex equalities of power if these inequalities have any of a variety of legitimate explanations.

2. See, for example, Karnig and Welch, *Black Representation and Urban Policy*.

3. Table 2.2 defines the teams that compete in each of these thirteen divisions. The operational definitions used to sort persons among competing interests are provided in Chapter 3, pp. 46–47.

4. During the interviews, persons were prompted about each of the cleavages listed in Table 13.1 except for those involving gender, age, sector of employment, and length of residency in the community.

5. One reason why the total number of victories does not always equal the total number of losses within a division is because of such alliances.

6. Because the samples of citizens are much larger than those of participants and because cleavages are defined on the basis of statistical differences (which are much easier to discover in larger samples), methodological considerations would lead to finding more cleavages in the citizen samples than in the participant samples.

7. Miller, "Pluralism and Social Choice."

8. In an earlier collaboration with Nancy Burns ("Gender Cleavages and the Resolution of Local Policy Issues"), we reported more significant gender biases against women participants. Such findings were based on the political standings in Lawrence at the end of 1984. Subsequently, more stringent enforcement of the SIGNS ordinance transformed a tie into a narrow victory for women. More importantly, the public referendum in 1987 that doomed TOWNCENTER also transformed what had been judged a loss for women into a victory. These changes make clear that political standings are continuously subject to revision, and they suggest the growing effectiveness of women in community politics.

9. The concern here is with cleavages as descriptive phenomena at the aggregate level, not with the independent causal effect of class, gender, age, and so forth on policy preferences among individuals. For example, gender cleavages may be explained by the differences between men and women in their attitudes, but this would not make gender theoretically or politically insignificant. If men tend to be Market Providers and members of the Growth Machine, and women tend to be Public Providers and Preservationists, victories by Market Providers and the Growth Machine will be victories for men over women.

10. The factor scores reported here were derived by varimax rotation. The measures of the extent of various cleavages on each issue were based on a simple scale using the measures of participant cleavages, citizen cleavages, and official perceptions of cleavage. For each of these measures, a "0" was assigned to an issue if a particular cleavage was absent. A "1" was assigned if there was a weak cleavage or a significant difference, and a "2" was assigned if there was a strong cleavage ("−1" or "−2" were assigned if such cleavages were resolved in favor of the least potent teams in each division). These scores for participant cleavages, citizen cleavages, and perceived cleavages were then summed to form an index of the degree of conflict in each division on each issue.

11. Schumaker and Getter, "Responsiveness Bias in 51 American Communities."

12. Using the twenty-nine issues as units of analysis, the following simple regression model was analyzed:

$PP = B_1 LC + B_2 MC + B_3 UC + e$, where

$PP$ is policy outcomes (the extent of public policy changes)

$LC$ is percentage of lower-class participants supporting change

$MC$ is percentage of middle-class participants supporting change

$UC$ is percentage of upper-class participants supporting change

13. The procedures used to determine the class of citizens is described under The Preferences of Competing Interests, Chapter 3, pp. 46–47. In order to permit comparisons between participants and citizens, the same scores used as quartile cutpoints to define the classes in the citizen sample were used to determine class membership in the participant sample.

14. Interviewed participants were asked to estimate on five-point rating scales the number of times they contacted representatives, contacted bureaucrats, and addressed officials at public meetings. The scores reported on Table 13.5 are the averages over all twenty-nine issues of these scores for each class. Scores of 2.0 in the table indicate that the lower-class participants reported averaging two to three such actions per issue.

15. Interviewed participants were also asked to estimate on five-point rating scales the number of times they mobilized others into groups, circulated petitions, publicized issues in the media, and engaged in demonstrations and boycotts. The scores reported in Table 13.5 are the averages over all issues of these scores for each class.

16. Net participation is simply the *number* of persons (of a particular class or group) supporting policy change minus the number of such persons opposing policy change. Although the analyses in the second and third rows of Table 13.4 relate policy changes to the *percentage* of lower-class, middle-class, and upper-class participants who support such changes, the analyses in the fourth through ninth rows relate policy changes to the net participation of persons of various classes. This is an important difference because percentage support is a measure independent of the number of persons involved, and net participation is a function both of the number of persons involved and their policy preferences.

Although conceptually distinct, measures of percent support and net participation are strongly correlated empirically across the twenty-nine issues. Because of problems of multicollinearity, measures of percent support and net participation cannot be analyzed simultaneously. In the multivariate analyses reported herein, measures of net participation are employed because they include measures of participation. The alternative "net support" measures ignore class differences in participation.

17. The data in the fifth through ninth rows of Table 13.4 are based on the following regression model.

$PP = B_1 NETLC + B_2 NETMC + B_3 NETUC + B_4 CONT_i + e$, where:

$PP$ is the policy outcome (extent of policy change);

$NETLC$ is the number of lower-class proponents minus the number of lower-class opponents

$NETMC$ is the number of middle-class proponents minus the number of middle-class opponents

$NETUC$ is the number of upper-class proponents minus the number of upper-class opponents

$CONT_i$ are various control variables (the extent of middle-class representation, public support for policy changes, etc.) introduced in the sixth through ninth rows of Table 13.3.

If $B_1 = B_2 = B_3$ (where $B_i$ are standardized regression coefficients, or Beta-weights, estimating the independent effect on policy changes of the net number of lower-class, middle-class, and upper-class participants), then policy changes are equally responsive to increases in the number of persons of various classes who support or oppose policy changes. Significant inequalities in the $B_i$'s indicate that the participation of various classes is unequally effective.

18. The representation-citizenship ratios reported in Table 13.5 (and subsequently in Tables 13.8, 13.11, and 13.14) are the percent of representatives divided by the percent of citizens of each class (or other categories of citizens). The representation-participation ratios reported in these tables are the percent of representatives divided by the percent of participants of each class.

19. The measure of middle-class representation is simply the percent of representatives involved in each issue who are members of the middle class.

20. The index of cultural support is the modified index described in note 9 of Chapter 11.

21. The index of economic imperatives is described in note 13 of Chapter 11.

22. The analyses in the last two rows of Table 13.4 require splitting the sample into issues having class conflict among participants (N=9) and issues without such conflict (N=20). The small number of cases here precludes multivariate analysis.

23. The procedures for measuring the extensiveness of various cleavages (including the class and neighborhood cleavages correlated here) were discussed in note 10.

Although Cellar Dwellers are often members of the lower class, many participants from neighborhoods having lower property values were highly educated professionals whose socioeconomic status placed them in the middle and upper classes. Although Country Clubbers are usually members of the upper class, many participants from neighborhoods having higher property values were businessmen whose modest educational attainments and occupational status placed them in the middle class.

24. The sixth row of Table 13.7 shows that variations in Cellar Dweller representation do not affect the gap between the effectiveness of participation by Cellar Dwellers and Split Levellers. Even when Cellar Dwellers were more highly represented on issues, they lacked a dominant coalition that could control issue outcomes.

25. In "Politics and Older Americans," Cigler and Swanson provide a comprehensive review of the literature on age differences regarding political preferences and participation. Though the literature shows that "older American seem to be somewhat more culturally and morally conservative than younger Americans," Cigler and Swanson argue that there is "little age cleavage" in America.

26. This analysis, reported in the sixth row of Table 13.7, is based on a model similar to that described in note 17 above except that the net participation of Rookies, Veterans, and Seniors on each issue was calculated after the participation of each person was weighted by the index of persuasive participation described in note 14.

27. Marci Francisco — the youngest commissioner in Lawrence — turned thirty before resolving any of the issues in the sample.

28. In a noteworthy exception, Jeffrey Henig, in *Public Policy and Federalism*, describes state and local issues from neoconservative, liberal, and radical perspectives.

29. Wilson and Banfield, "Political Ethos Revisited."

30. In *Urban Policies and Politics in a Bureaucratic Age* (110), Stone, Whelan, and Murin describe the core Managerial beliefs: "There is an overriding public interest that is superior to particular interests," which can be discovered through cooperation and technical problem solving. "Politics is therefore to be minimized." In contrast, Politicos doubt that a single definition of the public interest exists and that there is one best solution to community problems; they challenge the neutrality of experts and seek political representation of their alternative views.

31. Molotch, "The City as a Growth Machine"; Kann, *Middle Class Radicalism in Santa Monica.*

32. This conflict corresponds roughly to that between fiscal conservatives and fiscal liberals described by Clark and Ferguson in *City Money.*

33. Citizens surveyed in public opinion polls and interviewed participants were asked to indicate their priorities among four governmental roles. Respondents were designated as Market Providers if they said that their highest priority for local governments was "keeping taxes to a minimum" and as Public Providers if they said that their highest priority was "providing higher levels of governmental and social services." Those indicating that "promoting economic growth" was their highest priority were regarded as members of the Growth Machine, and those indicating that "providing careful land-use planning" was their highest priority were regarded as Preservationists. Market Providers and Public Providers comprise only 54 percent of all citizens and participants; others indicated their allegiance to the values of the Growth Machine or to Preservationists.

34. In *Protest Is Not Enough*, Browning, Marshall, and Tabb develop the argument that relatively powerless interests must be not only represented but "incorporated" (or represented in coalitions that dominate governing bodies) in order to enhance their influence in policymaking.

35. Schattschneider, *Semisovereign People*, 69.

## CHAPTER 14. CRITICAL PLURALISM AND THE RULES OF THE GAME

1. Barber, *Strong Democracy*, 129.

2. Everson, *Public Opinion and Interest Groups*, 30.

3. Wolff, "Beyond Tolerance"; Connolly, *The Bias of Pluralism.*

4. Dahl and Lindblom, *Politics, Economics, and Welfare*, 277.

5. Issue voting occurs when voters choose candidates whose policy positions mirror their own policy positions. For a more precise definition and analysis of issue voting, see Nie, Verba, and Petrocik, *The Changing American Voter*, 156–73.

6. Epstein, "The Scholarly Commitment to Parties," 129.

7. Because polyarchical rules provide an inadequate basis for understanding both the distribution of power and the regulation of quests for power within communities, Arthur Bentley (in *The Process of Government*) introduced the concept of "the habit background" to refer to the prevailing cultural, social, and political norms that define the limit beyond which players seldom go in seeking victories on political issues. In *The Governmenal Process*, Truman referred to such norms as "the rules of the game" and argued that such rules were enforced by "potential groups"—groups that are normally latent but emerge to bring counterforce to bear on the bullies who do not play by the rules of moderation and tolerance.

8. The comparative-issues method is not sufficient, however, to answer every question about complex equality. At least as developed for this study, this method does not probe into the inequalities that are explained by differences in representation, participation, and public support. Perhaps such differences are rooted in illegitimate factors, and perhaps these factors can be uncovered by complementary political research. For example, in *Urban Reform and Its Consequences*, Welch and Bledsoe have shown how unequal representation of different classes is brought about by electoral arrangements. In *Participation in America*, Verba and Nie show how voluntary organizations promote inequalities in participation. In *Power and Powerlessness,*

Gaventa shows how absentee corporate interests affect citizen receptivity to various policy initiatives.

9. In Lawrence, owners adjacent to land that is proposed for zoning changes to permit higher-density developments may sign protest petitions against the rezoning. If a valid petition is submitted, the rezoning can occur only by approval of an extraordinary majority of the commission (i.e., by a 4–1 vote).

10. Lowi, *The End of Liberalism*, 92–126.

11. This does imply that principle-policy congruence, responsible representation, and complex equality are complementary criteria that can be simultaneously achieved. They are distinct and, at least for the twenty-nine Lawrence issues, they are empirically independent. The empirical relationships concerning the achievement of three goals have been assessed, using the modified index of cultural support (described in note 9 of Chapter 11), the scale of responsible representation (provided in Table 2.1), and a measure of the extent to which each outcome was consistent with the preferences of relatively powerful interests. To obtain this index of (in)equality of treatment, the indices of degree of conflict within each division on each issue (described in note 10 of Chapter 13) were summed for each issue. Thus, an issue had a high positive inequality of treatment score if the most successful teams prevailed. An issue had a high negative inequality of treatment score if the least successful teams prevailed. Inequality of treatment scores approached zero for those issues without cleavages in any of the divisions or with outcomes favoring relatively weak teams in some divisions and relatively strong teams in others. The Pearson correlation coefficients between these measures of policy-principle congruence, responsible representation, and inequality of treatment are as follows:

Inequality of treatment and responsible representation                .12
Inequality of treatment and policy-principle congruence               .08
Responsible Representation and policy-principle congruence            − .06

The independence of these three criteria suggest that reforms to achieve higher performances on one criterion are unlikely to achieve higher performances on other criteria.

12. Research on how political settings affect the distribution of power is summarized in Clark, *Community Power and Policy Outputs*, and Trounstine and Christensen, *Movers and Shakers*, 40–46.

13. In *American Federalism* (96–107), Elazar defines moralistic and individualistic political cultures and provides maps suggesting the distribution of these cultures throughout the United States.

APPENDIX. DETERMINING THE PRINCIPLES AT STAKE ON CONCRETE ISSUES

1. In Chapter 4 (and Table 4.1), measures of support for alternative principles were coded such that higher scores indicated support for conservative principles. Because liberal NEIGHborhood protection, public-SERVice, public-WELFare, social-LIBerty, and public-involvement (DEMO) principles are dominant in Lawrence's political culture, the measures of these abstract issues have been reverse coded to attain the results presented in Table A.

2. In this study all correlations involving unarticulated principles were found spurious in the multiple regression analyses. However, significant relationships between principles and preferences could persist in the multiple-regression analyses even

if related alternative principles were not articulated by participants on both sides of those issues as relevant to the controversy. Thus, relating principles to preferences may be a useful method for uncovering the hidden (unarticulated but nevertheless relevant) interests that are at work on policy issues.

3. A .10 level of statistical significance was employed in the multiple-regression analyses for participants because — even if relationships were strong — it was sometimes difficult to obtain the .05 level of significance when there were several independent variables and $N_p$ was small.

# References

Adrian, Charles R., and James F. Sullivan. 1979. "The Urban Appointed Chief Executive, Past and Future." *Urban Interest* 1: 3-9.

Aiken, Michael. 1970. "The Distribution of Community Power: Structural Bases and Social Consequences." In Michael Aiken and Paul E. Mott, eds., *The Structure of Community Power*. New York: Random House.

Alford, Robert, and Roger Friedland. 1985. *Powers of Theory: Capitalism, the State, and Democracy*. Cambridge: Cambridge University Press.

Almond, Gabriel, and Sidney Verba. 1963. *The Civic Culture*. Boston: Little, Brown.

Arkes, Hadley. 1981. *The Philosopher in the City*. Princeton, N.J.: Princeton University Press.

Bachrach, Peter, and Morton S. Baratz. 1970. *Power and Poverty*. New York: Oxford University Press.

Ball, Terrance. 1976. "From Paradigms to Research Programs: Toward a Post-Kuhnian Political Science." *American Journal of Political Science* 20: 151-77.

Banfield, Edward C., and James Q. Wilson. 1963. *City Politics*. New York: Vintage.

Barber, Benjamin. 1984. *Strong Democracy: Participatory Politics for a New Age*. Berkeley: University of California Press.

Barry, Brian. 1973. *The Liberal Theory of Justice*. London: Oxford University Press.

Baskin, Darryl. 1971. *American Pluralist Democracy: A Critique*. New York: Van Nostrand Reinhold.

Bentley, Arthur. 1967. *The Process of Government*. Peter H. Odegard, ed. Cambridge, Mass.: Belknap.

Bolland, John. 1984. "The Limits to Pluralism: Power and Leadership in a Nonparticipatory Society." *Power and Elites* 1: 69-88.

Brand, Donald. 1985. "Three Generations of Pluralism." *Political Science Reviewer* 15: 109-43.

Browning, Rufus, Dale Rogers Marshall, and David Tabb. 1984. *Protest Is Not Enough*. Berkeley: University of California Press.

Brunker, Cindy, and Jeffrey McGovern. 1977. "How Fair is the Property Tax System in Lawrence?" Unpublished paper. Department of Political Science, University of Kansas.

Burke, Edmund. 1791. "Appeal to the Old Whigs from the New." In Russell Kirk, ed., *The Portable Conservative Reader*. New York: Penguin.

Caro, Robert. 1975. *The Power Broker: Robert Moses and the Fall of New York*. New York: Vintage.

Castells, Manuel. 1983. *City and the Grassroots*. Berkeley: University of California Press.

Cigler, Allan, and Cheryl Swanson. 1981. "Politics and Older Americans." In Forrest J. Berghorn and Donna Shafer, eds., *The Dynamics of Aging*. Boulder, Colo.: Westview.

Clark, Terry N. 1968. "Community Structure, Decision-Making, Budget Expenditures, and Urban Renewal in 51 American Communities." *American Sociological Review* 33: 576–93.

———. 1973. *Community Power and Policy Outputs*. Beverly Hills, Calif.: Sage.

Clark, Terry N., and Lorna Ferguson. 1983. *City Money*. New York: Columbia University Press.

Clubb, John, and Michael W. Traugott. 1972. "National Patterns of Referenda Voting." In Harlan Hahn, ed., *People and Politics in Urban Society*. Beverly Hills, Calif.: Sage.

Connolly, William. 1969. *The Bias of Pluralism*. Chicago: Aldine, Atherton.

Converse, Phillip E. 1970. "Attitudes and Non-attitudes: Continuation of a Dialogue." In Edward R. Tufte, ed., *Quantitative Analysis of Social Problems*. Reading, Mass.: Addison-Wesley.

Crenson, Matthew. 1971. *The Un-Politics of Air Pollution: A Study of Non-Decision-making in Cities*. Baltimore: Johns Hopkins University Press.

Crick, Bernard. 1982. *In Defense of Politics*, 2d ed. New York: Penguin.

Dahl, Robert A. 1956. *A Preface to Democratic Theory*. Chicago: University of Chicago Press.

———. 1961. *Who Governs?* New Haven, Conn.: Yale University Press.

———. 1982. *Dilemmas of Pluralist Democracy*. New Haven, Conn.: Yale University Press.

———. 1958. "A Critique of the Ruling Elite Model," *American Political Science Review* 52: 463–69.

Dahl, Robert A., and Charles Lindblom. 1976. *Politics, Economics and Welfare*. Chicago: University of Chicago Press.

Devine, Donald. 1970. *The Attentive Public: Polyarchial Democracy*. Chicago: Rand McNally.

Durbin, Evan. 1940. *The Politics of Democratic Socialism*. London: Routledge & Kegan Paul.

Dye, Thomas R. 1986. *Who's Running America? The Conservative Years*. Englewoods Cliffs, N.J.: Prentice-Hall.

Eckstein, Harry. 1975. "Case Study and Theory in Political Science." In Fred I. Greenstein and Nelson Polsby, eds., *Handbook of Political Science*, Vol. 7. Reading, Mass.: Addison-Wesley.

Edelman, Murray. 1971. *Politics as Symbolic Action*. Chicago: Markham Publishing Co.

Elazar, Daniel. 1972. *American Federalism: A View from the States*, 2nd ed. New York: Thomas Y. Crowell.

Elkin, Stephen. 1987. *City and Regime in the American Republic*. Chicago: University of Chicago Press.

Epstein, Leon. 1983. "The Scholarly Commitment to Parties." In Ada Finifter, ed., *Political Science: The State of the Discipline*. Washington D.C.: American Political Science Association.

Eulau, Heinz, and Kenneth Prewitt. 1973. *Labyrinths of Democracy: Adaptations, Linkages, Representation, and Policies in Urban Politics*. Indianapolis: Bobbs-Merrill.

Eulau, Heinz, and Paul D. Karps. 1978. "The Puzzle of Representation: Specifying Components of Responsiveness." In Heinz Eulau and John Wahlke, eds., *The Politics of Representation*. Beverly Hills, Calif: Sage.

Evans, Judith. 1980. "Women and Politics: A Reappraisal." *Political Studies* 28: 210–21.

Everson, David. 1982. *Public Opinion and Interest Groups in American Politics*. New York: Franklin Watts.

Foster, R. Scott, and Renee Berger. 1982. *Public-Private Partnership in American Cities*. Lexington, Mass.: Lexington.

Friedland, Roger. 1986. "Commentary: The Politics of Urban Growth." In Terry N. Clark, ed., *Research on Urban Policy*, Vol. 2A. Greenwich, Conn.: JAI Press.

Gaventa, John. 1980. *Power and Powerlessness: Quiescence and Rebellion in an Appalachian Valley*. Urbana: University of Illinois Press.

Hawley, Willis D. 1973. *Nonpartisan Elections and the Case for Party Politics*. New York: John Wiley.

Hawley, Willis D., and James H. Svara. 1972. *The Study of Community Power: A Bibliographic Review*. Santa Barbara, Calif.: ABC-CLIO.

Held, Virginia. 1970. *The Public Interest and Private Interests*. New York: Basic Books.

Henig, Jeffrey R. 1982. *Neighborhood Mobilization: Redevelopment and Response*. New Brunswick, N.J.: Rutgers University Press.

———. 1985. *Public Policy and Federalism: Issues in State and Local Politics*. New York: St. Martin's Press.

Hochschild, Jennifer. 1981. *What's Fair: American Beliefs about Distributive Justice*. Cambridge, Mass.: Harvard University Press.

Hunter, Floyd. 1953. *Community Power Structure: A Study of Decision-Makers*. Chapel Hill: University of North Carolina Press.

Huntington, Samuel P. 1975. "The Democratic Distemper." *Public Interest* 41: 10–38.

Jones, Bryan D. 1983. *Governing Urban America: A Policy Focus*. Boston: Little, Brown.

Kann, Mark E. 1986. *Middle Class Radicalism in Santa Monica*. Philadelphia: Temple University Press.

Karnig, Albert, and Susan Welch. 1980. *Black Representation and Urban Policy*. Chicago: University of Chicago Press.

Kelso, William Alton. 1978. *American Democratic Theory: Pluralism and Its Critics*. Westport, Conn.: Greenwood.

Kinder, Donald. 1983. "Diversity and Complexity in American Public Opinion." In Ada Finifter, ed., *Political Science: The State of the Discipline*. Washington, D.C.: American Political Science Association.

Kirk, Russell. 1962. *A Program for Conservatives*. Chicago: Henry Regnery.

Knoke, David. 1981. "Urban Political Cultures." In Terry N. Clark, ed., *Urban Policy Analysis: Directions for Future Research*. Beverly Hills, Calif.: Sage.

Kuklinski, James H. 1978. "Representativeness and Elections: A Policy Analysis." *American Political Science Review* 72: 165–77.

Lane, Robert E. 1986. "Market Justice, Political Justice." *American Political Science Review* 80: 383–402.

Levy, Frank S., Arnold J. Meltsner, and Aaron B. Wildavsky. 1974. *Urban Outcomes*. Berkeley: University of California Press.

Lindblom, Charles E. 1959. "The Science of 'Muddling Through.'" *Public Administration Review* 19: 79–88.

———. 1977. *Politics and Markets: The World's Political-Economic System*. New York: Basic Books.

Lineberry, Robert L. 1977. *Equality and Urban Policy: The Distribution of Municipal Public Services.* Beverly Hills, Calif.: Sage.

Lineberry, Robert L., and Edmund P. Fowler. 1967. "Reformism and Public Policies in American Cities." *American Political Science Review* 61: 701–17.

Lineberry, Robert. L., and Ira Sharkansky. 1978. *Urban Politics and Public Policy,* 3d ed. New York: Harper and Row.

Lipsky, Michael. 1970. *Protest in City Politics.* Chicago: Rand McNally.

Lowi, Theodore J. 1979. *The End of Liberalism* 2d ed. New York: W. W. Norton.

Lukes, Steven. 1974. *Power: A Radical View.* London: Macmillan.

Luttbeg, Norman. 1974. *Public Opinion and Public Policy,* Rev. ed. Homewood, Ill.: Dorsey.

Macridis, Roy. 1988. *Contemporary Political Ideologies,* 4th ed. Boston: Little, Brown.

Manley, John. 1983. Neopluralism: A Class Analysis of Pluralism I and Pluralism II. *American Political Science Review* 77: 368–89.

Mill, John Stuart. 1861. *Considerations on Representative Government.* London: Parker, Son, and Bourn.

Miller, Nicholas. 1983. "Pluralism and Social Choice." *American Political Science Review* 77: 734–47.

Molotch, Harvey. 1976. "The City as a Growth Machine: Toward a Political Economy of Place." *American Journal of Sociology* 82: 309–32.

Morgan, David, and John P. Pelissero. 1980. "Urban Policy: Does Political Structure Matter?" *American Political Science Review* 74: 999–1005.

Morlock, Laura L. 1974. "Business Interests, Countervailing Groups, and the Balance of Influence in 91 Cities." In Willis A. Hawley and Frederick M. Wirt, eds., *Search for Community Power,* 2d ed. Englewood Cliffs, N.J.: Prentice-Hall.

Nachmias, David, and David H. Rosenbloom. 1980. *Bureaucratic Government USA.* New York: St. Martin's Press.

Nagel, Jack. 1975. *The Descriptive Analysis of Power.* New Haven, Conn.: Yale University Press.

Newton, Kenneth. 1976. "Feeble Governments and Private Power: Urban Politics and Policies in the United States." In Louis H. Masotti and Robert L. Lineberry, eds., *The New Urban Politics.* Cambridge, Mass.: Ballinger.

Nie, Norman, Sidney Verba, and John Petrocik. 1976. *The Changing American Voter.* Cambridge, Mass.: Harvard University Press.

Nisbet, Robert. 1975. *Twilight of Authority.* New York: Oxford.

———. 1975. "Public Opinion versus Popular Opinion." *Public Interest* 41: 166–92.

Nivola, Pietros, and David H. Rosenbloom. 1986. *Classic Readings in American Politics.* New York: St. Martin's Press.

Northrop, Alana, and William H. Dutton. 1978. "Municipal Reform and Group Influence." *American Journal of Political Science* 22: 691–711.

Nozick, Robert. 1974. *Anarchy, State and Utopia.* New York: Basic Books.

Olson, Mancur, Jr. 1965. *The Logic of Collective Action.* New York: Schocken Books.

———. 1982. *The Rise and Decline of Nations.* New Haven, Conn.: Yale University Press.

Page, Benjamin I., and Robert Y. Shapiro. 1983. "Effects of Public Opinion on Policy." *American Political Science Review* 77: 175–90.

Peffley, Mark A., and Jon Hurwitz. 1985. "A Hierarchical Model of Attitude Constraint." *American Journal of Political Science* 29: 871–90.

Peterson, Paul E. 1979. "A Unitary Model of Local Taxation and Expenditure Policies." In Dale R. Marshall, ed., *Urban Policy Making.* Beverly Hills, Calif.: Sage.

——. 1981. *City Limits*. Chicago: University of Chicago Press.

Pitkin, Hannah F. 1972. *The Concept of Representation*. Berkeley: University of California Press.

Polsby, Nelson. 1980. *Community Power and Political Theory*, 2d ed. New Haven, Conn.: Yale University Press.

Pomper, Gerald M. 1971. *Elections in America: Control and Influence in Democratic Politics*. New York: Dodd, Mead.

Prothro, James W., and Charles W. Grigg. 1960. "Fundamental Principles of Democracy: Bases of Agreement and Disagreement." *Journal of Politics* 22: 276–86.

Rae, Douglas, et al. 1981. *Equalities*. Cambridge, Mass.: Harvard University Press.

Rawls, John. 1971. *A Theory of Justice*. Cambridge, Mass.: Harvard University Press.

Ricci, David. 1980. "Receiving Ideas in Political Analysis: The Case of Community Power Studies, 1950–1970." *Western Political Quarterly* 33: 451–75.

——. 1984. *The Tragedy of Political Science*. New Haven, Conn.: Yale University Press.

Riker, William H. 1982. *Liberalism against Populism: A Confrontation between the Theory of Democracy and the Theory of Social Choice*. San Francisco: W. H. Freeman.

——. 1986. *The Art of Political Manipulation*. New Haven, Conn.: Yale University Press.

Schattschneider, E. E. 1960. *The Semisovereign People*. Hinsdale, Ill.: Dryden Press.

Schumaker, Paul. 1975. "Policy Responsiveness to Protest Group Demands." *Journal of Politics* 37: 488–521.

Schumaker, Paul, and Russell W. Getter. 1977. "Responsiveness Bias in 51 American Cities." *American Journal of Political Science* 21: 247–81.

Schumaker, Paul, and David Billeaux. 1978. "Group Representation in Local Bureaucracies." *Administration and Society* 10: 285–316.

Schumaker, Paul, and Nancy E. Burns. 1988. "Gender Cleavages and the Resolution of Local Policy Issues," *American Journal of Political Science* 32: 1070–95.

Schumaker, Paul, and Steven Maynard-Moody. 1988. "Downtown Redevelopment and Public Opinion: A Survey of Citizen Attitudes for the Downtown Improvement Committee." Report No. 135, Institute for Public Policy and Business Research, University of Kansas.

Sombart. Werner. 1976. *Why There Is No Socialism in America*. Armonk, N.Y.: M. E. Sharpe.

Stone, Clarence N. 1976. *Economic Growth and Neighborhood Discontent: System Bias in the Urban Renewal Program in Atlanta*. Chapel Hill: University of North Carolina Press.

——. 1980. "Systemic Power in Community Decision Making: A Restatement of Stratification Theory." *American Political Science Review* 74: 978–90.

——. 1987. "The Study of the Politics of Urban Development." In Clarence Stone and Heywood T. Sanders, eds., *The Politics of Urban Development*. Lawrence: University Press of Kansas.

——. 1987. "Elite Theory and Democracy: A Populist Perspective." In Thomas Dye and Harmon Ziegler, *The Irony of Democracy*, 7th ed. Monterey, Calif.: Brooks Cole.

——. 1989. "Paradigms, Power, and Urban Leadership." In Bryan Jones, ed., *Leadership and Politics: New Perspectives in Political Science*. Lawrence: University Press of Kansas.

——. 1989. *Regime Politics: Governing Atlanta, 1946–1988*. Lawrence: University Press of Kansas.

Stone, Clarence N., Robert K. Whelan, and William J. Murin. 1986. *Urban Policy and Politics in a Bureaucratic Age*. Englewood Cliffs, N.J.: Prentice-Hall.

Sullivan, John, et al. 1981. "The Sources of Political Tolerance: A Multivariate Analysis." *American Political Science Review* 75: 92–106.

Swanstrom, Todd. 1988. "Semisovereign Cities: The Politics of Urban Development." *Polity* 21: 83–110.

Taylor, D. Garth. 1986. *Public Opinion and Collective Action: The Boston School Desegregation Conflict*. Chicago: University of Chicago Press.

Thomas, John Clayton. 1986. *Between Citizen and City: Neighborhood Organizations and Urban Politics in Cincinnati*. Lawrence: University Press of Kansas.

Trounstine, Philip J., and Terry Christensen. 1982. *Movers and Shakers: The Study of Community Power*. New York: St. Martin's Press.

Truman, David. 1970. *The Governmental Process*, 2d ed. New York: Knopf.

Verba, Sidney, and Norman H. Nie. 1972. *Participation in America: Political Democracy and Social Equality*. New York: Harper and Row.

Wahlke, John C. 1978. "Policy Demands and System Support: The Role of the Represented." In Heinz Eulau and John Wahlke, eds., *The Politics of Representation*. Beverly Hills, Calif.: Sage.

Walker, Jack. 1966. "A Critique of the Elitist Theory of Democracy." *American Political Science Review* 60: 285–95.

———. 1983. "The Origins and Maintenance of Interest Groups in America." *American Political Science Review* 77: 390–406.

Walzer, Michael. 1983. *Spheres of Justice: A Defense of Pluralism and Equality*. New York: Basic Books.

Waste, Robert J. 1986. *Power and Pluralism in American Cities: Research in the Urban Laboratory*. Westport, Conn.: Greenwood.

———. 1986. "Community Power and Pluralist Theory." In Robert J. Waste, ed., *Community Power: Directions for Future Research*. Beverly Hills, Calif.: Sage.

Weber, Max. 1967. *On Law in Economy and Society*. M. Rheinstein, ed. New York: Simon and Schuster.

Weissberg, Robert. 1976. *Public Opinion and Popular Government*. Englewoods Cliffs, N.J.: Prentice-Hall.

Welch, Susan, and Timothy Bledsoe. 1988. *Urban Reform and Its Consequences*. Chicago: University of Chicago Press.

Will, George F. 1983. *Statecraft as Soulcraft*. New York: Simon and Schuster.

Williams, Oliver P., and Charles R. Adrian. 1963. *Four Cities*. Philadelphia: University of Pennsylvania Press.

Wilson, James Q., and Edward C. Banfield. 1971. "Political Ethos Revisited." *American Political Science Review* 65: 1048–62.

Wirt, Frederick. 1974. *Power in the City: Decision Making in San Francisco*. Berkeley: University of California Press.

Wolff, Robert P. 1965. "Beyond Tolerance." In Robert P. Wolff, Barrington Moore, Jr., and Herbert Marcuse, *A Critique of Pure Tolerance*. Boston: Beacon Press.

Wolfinger, Raymond E. 1960. "Reputation and Reality in the Study of Community Power." *American Sociological Review* 25: 636–44.

Yates, Douglas. 1977. *The Ungovernable City*. Cambridge, Mass.: MIT Press.

# Index